Theory of Public Finance in a Federal State

The last few decades have seen a substantial increase in the mobility of capital and population between the individual jurisdictions of long-established federal states (such as Canada, Germany, and the United States) and among the formerly independent member countries of the European Union. This book examines the consequences of this development for government policy. Its central question is whether the assignment of government functions to the individual jurisdictions in a federal state can ensure an optimal allocation of resources and a fair distribution of income. The analysis thereby gives a new answer to the old question about the optimal degree of fiscal decentralization in a federal state. It shows that fiscal decentralization is a viable method to disclose the preferences of currently living and future generations for local public goods, to limit the size of government, and to avoid excessive public debt finance. The allocative branch of the government benefits from this decentralization, although it is difficult to obtain an income distribution much different from that induced by the market.

Dietmar Wellisch is Professor of Economics at the Technical University of Dresden, Germany. He has also taught or held visiting positions at Indiana University and the University of Dortmund. Professor Wellisch is the author of *Intertemporale und internationale Aspekte staatlicher Budgetdefizite* (1991) and *Dezentrale Finanzpolitik bei hoher Mobilität* (1995), both published by Mohr [Siebeck]. His articles have appeared in the *Journal of Public Economics, European Economic Review, Journal of Urban Economics, Regional Science and Urban Economics, International Tax and Public Finance, Environmental and Resource Economics,* and *European Journal of Political Economics,* among other English-language journals.

Theory of Public Finance in a Federal State

DIETMAR WELLISCH
Technical University of Dresden

CAMBRIDGE
UNIVERSITY PRESS

CAMBRIDGE UNIVERSITY PRESS
Cambridge, New York, Melbourne, Madrid, Cape Town, Singapore, São Paulo

Cambridge University Press
The Edinburgh Building, Cambridge CB2 2RU, UK

Published in the United States of America by Cambridge University Press, New York

www.cambridge.org
Information on this title: www.cambridge.org/9780521630351

First published 2000
This digitally printed first paperback version 2006

A catalogue record for this publication is available from the British Library

Library of Congress Cataloguing in Publication data
Wellisch, Dietmar.
Theory of public finance in a federal state / Dietmar Wellisch.
p.   cm.
Includes bibliographical references and index.
ISBN 0-521-63035-5 (hb)
1. Intergovernmental fiscal relations.   2. Finance. Public.
3. Decentralization in government.   4. Federal government.
I. Title.
HJ197.W454   1999
336 – dc21   99-22729
                                                            CIP

ISBN-13 978-0-521-63035-1 hardback
ISBN-10 0-521-63035-5 hardback

ISBN-13 978-0-521-02687-1 paperback
ISBN-10 0-521-02687-3 paperback

Contents

v

Acknowledgments

In preparing this study, I have received support from many individuals. First, I thank Scott V. Parris, the Economics Editor of Cambridge University Press, for pleasant and fruitful cooperation, and also three anonymous readers of an earlier version of the manuscript for encouraging me to present a more updated study on several recent developments in the area of local public finance. Next, I benefitted greatly from discussing many topics presented in this book over several years with my various coauthors Wolfram F. Richter, Uwe Walz, and in particular David E. Wildasin. Indeed, it was Dave Wildasin who stimulated my interest in issues of local public finance. Without his support, I would never have written this book.

In addition, I thank Jan K. Brueckner, Helmuth Cremer, Michael Keen, Maurice Marchand, Gordon M. Myers, Wallace E. Oates, Pierre Pestieau, David Pines, Robert M. Schwab, Hans-Werner Sinn, and John D. Wilson for bringing my attention (or providing access) to important published and unpublished work as well as for their comments during the preparation of this book. I also discussed the contents of this study several times with Elke Baumann, Ulrich Hange, Jörg Hülshorst, and Jörg Kroschel, who read the entire manuscript more than once. I thank them for their patience and hope that they forgive me my pedantry. Of course, none of them bears any responsibility for remaining errors and omissions, and it is not their fault if the text lacks the elegance of a native English writer.

Finally, and most importantly, I am grateful to Dorothee for her endless patience and for releasing me from many problems of daily work over a long period of time without giving up her own career.

My thanks to all.

CHAPTER 1

Fiscal Decentralization: Benefits and Problems

Active tax competition, in short, tends to produce either a generally low level of state–local tax effort or a state–local tax structure with strong regressive features.
George Break (1967)

The mobility of individual economic units among different localities places fairly narrow limits on the capacity for local income redistribution.
Wallace Oates (1977)

Policies that promote residential mobility and increase the knowledge of the consumer–voter will improve the allocation of government expenditures in the same sense that mobility among jobs and knowledge relevant to the location of industry and labor improve the allocation of private resources.
Charles Tiebout (1956)

If jurisdictions compete with each other and taxpayers/consumers are able to vote with their feet, there may be fairly strong pressures for subnational governments to respond to the wishes of the electorate.
Charles McLure, Jr. (1986)

1.1 Assignment of Government Functions and Mobility

1.1.1 Assignment of Government Functions

Issues of public finance appear in a new light when an economy is divided into several regions. If a state consists of many jurisdictions, the question arises of how to assign the various government activities to different governmental levels. The general functions of the government – to support an efficient allocation of scarce resources (where the private sector fails to do so) and to guarantee a fair income distribution – must first be divided into several components. Once a fundamental line of government policy is chosen, these functions must be assigned to the jurisdictions. However, such an assignment cannot be made once and for all; it critically depends on the economic environment that characterizes the federal state.

A substantial increase in interregional mobility, which we can observe today in many federal states, changes the economic environment in an important way. For the problem of decentralizing government activities, mobility across regions is a critical factor. This can be illustrated by considering the use of a head tax. In a unitary state, the head tax does not distort economic decisions and is therefore, leaving distributional problems aside, an ideal instrument for financing government expenditures from an efficiency viewpoint. If, however, households are mobile across the regions of a federal state then any uncoordinated use of head taxes by regional governments causes pure fiscal incentives to relocate, leading to migration distortions.

The question of an optimal assignment of government functions to several governmental levels does not arise only in long-established federal states. It is also relevant when independent states grow together. For example, the member states of the European Union (EU) want to appropriate the benefits of the international division of labor. They committed themselves to abolish any borders among them on January 1, 1993, and to guarantee the *four fundamental economic liberties:* goods, services, capital, and labor can now move freely among all member countries without any legal obstacles.[1] Although this right reflects a de jure rather than a de facto freedom of movement in Europe, the European countries grow more and more together and will form an economic unit. Today and in the immediate future, the EU member countries must decide which government activities they will assign to the EU itself and hence to a supranational European institution. In other words, how much Europe is necessary for an economic unification?

The Maastricht Treaty of 1991 (Treaty on the European Union) seems to decide in favor of a strong decentralization of government functions. In order to calm down such Euro-skeptics as Denmark, Germany, and Great Britain, the "subsidiarity" principle of decisions was introduced into the treaty. This principle means that only those functions should be assigned to the EU center that cannot satisfactorily be fulfilled by the member states. However, taking a closer look, the meaning of the subsidiarity principle is rather empty. Its main purpose is to delegate the burden of proof to those member states that want to have a stronger centralization (see Sinn 1994). Aside from this, there is no operational criterion that can be used to decide which government activities should be assigned to the center and which tasks can still be placed in the hands of the individual member countries.

Contrary to the situation in long-established national federal states with rather rigid institutional structures, an optimal or less demanding – an economically reasonable – assignment of governmental functions could be realized in the EU.[2] The division of government tasks is still an open question after Maastricht and offers a real chance to Europe. It is therefore rather surprising that

---

[1] Padoa-Schioppa (1987) provides a comprehensive overview of the benefits of free trade in goods and services and an unconstrained migration of labor and capital.

[2] The German unification provides an example of how difficult it is to overcome a given assignment of government functions in long-established national federal states. The division of functions

the political discussion of how much Europe is necessary is lacking a foundation in terms of economic theory. Many contributions discussing that problem consist of long philosophical debates about normative legal principles and of rather artificial analogies between the competition of firms and regions. The purpose of the present book is to establish such an economic foundation.

1.1.2   Mobility and Taxation: Empirical Facts

In enhancing the mobility of goods, capital, and people, economic integration leads to an increased international mobility of tax bases. As many economists expect, this will imply a downward pressure on national tax rates and welfare benefits. Our objective in this section is to investigate if an increasing degree of mobility as well as lower taxes on mobile bases can actually be observed in existing federations.

For this purpose, we consider the development within two federations: the EU as a still-growing union of national states; and the United States as an existing, rather homogeneous federal state. Let us first turn to the EU. An interesting observation is that per-capita gross domestic product (GDP) levels have been converging among the twelve EU members since 1960, as Table 1.1 shows. This convergence cannot be explained by a single factor. However, besides the reduction of real income disparities due to EU transfer programs (such as the European Regional Development Fund and the European Social Fund), convergence can be taken as evidence that free trade in goods, capital, and labor in the EU – guaranteed by the Treaty of Rome – has had an effect.

Because subsequent chapters concentrate on the mobility of factors and its implications for tax policy, it is of particular importance to see how capital and labor mobility have changed over time. Table 1.2 indeed demonstrates that there is an increasing degree of capital mobility in the EU. A comparison of the growth of direct investments within the EU (intra) with the growth of those coming from (extra inward) or going outside (extra outward) the EU shows that capital mobility among member states has increased to a much larger extent than capital mobility between the EU and the rest of the world.

Most current data indicate that the level of intra-EU capital mobility rose further compared with extra-EU capital mobility. Owing to the increased attractiveness of the EU to other countries for direct investments, the ratio of intra- to extra-EU direct investments almost reached unity in 1995. This could be interpreted as the achievement of equal importance of direct investments from within and from outside the EU (Eurostat 1997a).

between the federal government and the old state governments has simply been extended to the relation between the federal government and the *Neue Länder,* although this unique historical event would have provided a chance to think about the division of tasks in more systematic terms and to establish a greater revenue autonomy for the state governments, which is an old yet unsolved problem in Germany.

Table 1.1. *Divergence of GDP per capita among the EU:*
GDP per capita relative to the EU average

	1960	1970	1980	1990	1993
Belgium	97.5	101.1	106.4	104.9	106.2
Denmark	115.2	112.2	105.0	105.8	107.5
France	107.7	112.7	113.9	110.0	111.9
Germany	124.3	118.6	119.1	117.6	116.4
Greece	34.8	46.4	52.3	47.5	47.8
Ireland	57.2	56.1	60.2	69.0	71.6
Italy	86.6	95.5	102.5	102.8	104.0
Luxembourg	155.3	138.4	115.6	127.2	129.8
Netherlands	116.8	114.1	109.2	102.4	102.6
Portugal	37.2	46.9	52.7	53.7	58.1
Spain	58.3	72.2	71.7	75.4	77.2
United Kingdom	122.6	103.5	96.4	100.5	96.2
EU 12	100.0	100.0	100.0	100.0	100.0
Standard deviation	36.6	29.1	24.4	24.3	23.8

Notes: Per-capita GDP is given at current market prices per head of national population
and in purchasing power parities. Figures for 1993 are estimated; figures for Germany
refer to the former Western part.
Source: Commission of the European Communities (1993).

Table 1.2. *Growth in intra- and extra-EU direct investments*

	Average annual growth rate		Total growth
Investment	1984–89	1984–91	1984–91
Extra inward	35.3%	19.3%	344%
Extra outward	13.8%	6.0%	54%
Intra	51.6%	32.7%	724%

Sources and definition of investment: Eurostat (1991, 1994); see also Lejour (1995).

Considering tax policy during that time, Table 1.3 indicates that governments have lowered statutory overall corporate tax rates. Although there is no
clear-cut interpretation of these developments, international tax competition
might have been a driving force.

As far as labor mobility is concerned, individuals seem to be considerably
less mobile than capital across EU member states. According to our own calculations (based on Eurostat 1993, 1995a, 1996),[3] annual mobility rates in 1991,

[3] As registrations of migratory flows within the EU are still not harmonized among the member
states, data concerning this subject are very rough and hence subject to severe measurement

Table 1.3. *Statutory overall (national and local) corporate tax rates in the EU*

	1980	1985	1991	1992
Austria	61.5/38.3	61.5/38.3	39.0	39.0
Belgium	48.0	45.0	39.0	39.0
Denmark	37.0	50.0	38.0	38.0
France	50.0	50.0	34.0/42.0	34.0
Germany	61.7/44.3	61.7/44.3	56.5/44.3	58.6/46.0
Greece		49.0	46.0	46.0
Ireland	45.0	50.0	43.0	46.0
Italy	36.3	47.8/36.0	47.8/36.0	47.8/36.0
Luxembourg	45.5	45.5	39.4	39.4
Netherlands	46.0	42.0	35.0	35.0
Portugal	51.2/44.0	51.2/44.0	39.6	39.6
Spain	33.0	33.0	35.0	35.0
Sweden	40.0	52.0	30.0	30.0
United Kingdom	52.0	40.0	34.0	33.0
EU average	45.8	47.3	40.8	41.1
Standard deviation	8.6	7.3	7.1	7.8

Notes: Where two tax rates are given, the former reflects the tax rate on retentions, the latter the tax rate on distributions. Average and standard deviation are calculated on the basis of retained profits, excluding the new member states Austria and Sweden. No data available for Finland.
Sources: OECD (1992a) and author's calculations; see also Owens (1993).

1992, and 1994 (i.e., EU citizens moving into EU member states) are about 0.2% in terms of total EU population and thus one tenth to one fifteenth of the respective mobility rates in the United States (reported in Table 1.7).[4] It seems that returns of citizens to their home country and immigration into EU countries from outside the EU are more important than intra-EU mobility. About 50% of immigrants to Denmark, Greece, Spain, Ireland and the United Kingdom are of the respective country's own nationality. The number of Germans immigrating into Germany is also very high, though it is outnumbered by the even larger share of *Aussiedler* (native Germans) coming from Eastern Europe (Eurostat 1995c).

errors. Some countries provide no data on migration at all or only on foreigners or the labor force. This should be kept in mind when interpreting the calculated figure.

[4] When comparing the figures of the United States and the EU, please note the following. The EU mobility rate refers to the citizenship – that is, EU migrants into an EU member state do not have to come from another EU-member state but can also be EU nationals coming from abroad. In contrast, the U.S. figure indicates the mobility of the U.S. population independent of their nationality. Thus, the rates are truly comparable only if we assume that the largest share of U.S. movers are Americans and that most EU movers come from another member state.

Table 1.4. *Current expenditures on social security in EU member states as percentage of GDP*

	1970	1980	1990	1991	1992	1993	1994
Austria					28.2		30.2
Belgium	18.7	28.0	27.0	27.4	27.0	27.6	27.0
Denmark	19.6	28.7	29.8	31.0	32.0	33.2	33.7
Finland					35.4		34.8
France	18.9	25.4	27.7	28.4	29.2	30.9	30.5
Germany	21.5	28.8	26.9	28.8	30.1	31.0	30.8
Greece	7.6	9.7	16.1	15.7	16.3	16.3	16.0
Ireland	13.7	20.6	19.5	20.6	21.3	21.4	21.1
Italy	14.4	19.4	24.1	24.6	25.7	25.8	25.3
Luxembourg	15.6	26.5	22.1	23.3	23.5	24.9	24.9
Netherlands	19.6	30.1	32.2	32.4	33.0	33.6	32.3
Portugal	9.1	12.9	15.0	17.1	17.8	18.3	19.5
Spain	10.0	18.2	20.6	21.7	22.9	24.0	23.6
Sweden					40.0		
United Kingdom	14.3	21.5	22.7	25.3	27.0	27.8	28.1
EU average	17.4	24.5	25.4	26.6	27.8	28.4	28.2

Note: Figures for Austria, Finland and Sweden not included in calculating EU average.
Sources: Statistisches Bundesamt (1994, 1996), World Bank (1994), Eurostat (1995b, 1997b), author's calculations.

Straubhaar and Zimmermann (1993) report that a stock of about 13.4 million foreigners lived in the EU countries in 1989, which is a share of 4%. However, of these 13.4 million, 8.2 million came from outside of the EU (see also Zimmermann 1995). This could be attributed to income disparities, which are much higher between EU countries and neighboring nonmember states – in Eastern and South Eastern Europe as well as in North Africa – than among member states (see Table 1.1 and Wellisch and Wildasin 1996a). Take, for example, Turkey as a typical source country of labor migration and Germany as the basic host country of Turkish workers in the EU. For both countries, per-capita GDP at current market prices (in U.S. dollars) differ significantly from each other. In 1970, per-capita GDP was $274 in Turkey and $3.103 in Germany. Corresponding figures for 1990 are $2.679 in Turkey and $24.477 in Germany (United Nations 1976, 1995).

Table 1.4 demonstrates that expenditures on social security did not decrease in the EU between 1970 and 1994 but rather increased. This might be explained by the fact that EU member countries are not forced by mobility of individuals to drop social benefits. Because of low intra-EU mobility, no country fears becoming a welfare magnet. This observation points in the same direction as

Table 1.5. *Top central government marginal personal tax rates on earnings*

	1980	1986	1990	1991	1992
Austria	62	62	50	50	50
Belgium	72	72	55	55	55
Denmark	36.6	45	40	40	40
France	60	65	56.8	56.8	56.8
Germany	56	56	53	54	55
Greece	63	63	50	50	50
Ireland	60	60	53	52	52
Italy	72	62	50	50	50
Luxembourg	57	57	56	51.25	51.25
Netherlands	72	72	60	60	60
Portugal	84.4	61	40	40	40
Spain	56.5	66	56	56	56
Sweden	50	50	20	20	25
United Kingdom	60	60	60	40	40
EU average	62.5	61.6	52.5	50.4	50.5
Standard deviation	11.9	7.3	6.7	6.9	7.0

Notes: Data for the new EU member countries Austria and Sweden are not included in the EU-average and standard deviation calculations but are listed for informational purposes. No data available for Finland.
Sources: OECD (1992b) and author's calculations; see also Owens (1993).

the empirical study of Kirchgässner and Pommerehne (1996). This study shows that even the higher mobility of individuals among the *Kantone* in Switzerland – a country with a regional structure similar to that of the EU and with a population consisting of four different native-speaking groups (German, Italian, French, Raetho-Romanic) – does *not* induce regional governments to decrease the degree of interpersonal redistribution, a basic theoretical result derived in the literature.

Although these figures seem to suggest that mobility of individuals does not play a major role in the EU, there are some reasons to expect that migration will become (and even has already become) an important phenomenon in Europe. *First,* the Treaty on the European Union (Article 48) provides a legal basis for unrestricted migration of EU citizens among member countries. *Second,* different languages in the EU countries are more of an impediment to migration of low-skilled individuals than of high-skilled professionals. This might be why EU countries have reduced marginal personal tax rates on earnings at the top of the income scale, as Table 1.5 documents. The EU average decreased by more than ten percentage points from 1980 to 1992. The standard deviation

Table 1.6. *Divergence of real per-capita income in U.S. regions: Real regional per-capita income relative to U.S. average*

	1900	1990
New England	133.6	120.8
Mideast	138.6	115.8
Great Lakes	106.5	98.3
Plains	97.2	94.2
Southeast	47.9	85.6
Southwest	68.2	87.5
Rocky Mountain	145.2	89.8
Far West	163.3	109.0
United States (total)	100.0	100.0
Standard deviation	42.2	13.2

Notes: Real per-capita income is given in U.S. dollars at the 1982–84 base. Regional classifications according to the Bureau of Economic Analysis.
Sources: Barro and Sala-i-Martin (1995); author's calculations.

also dropped from 1980 through 1990, indicating that top marginal tax rates on earnings moved closer together during these years. From 1990 on, the standard deviation moved around 7, increasing only slightly.

Third, whereas the applications for EU membership by Finland, Sweden, and Austria were accepted rather quickly, that of Turkey has been delayed more or less indefinitely. Of course, many factors are important for decisions about EU membership. However, one fear expressed by existing members is that a full membership for Turkey would induce an uncontrolled influx of low-skilled workers from Turkey, such that countries like Germany would become welfare magnets (cf. the per-capita GDP disparity between these countries discussed previously). This fear might be why – besides its high preference for autonomy – Switzerland has refused to become an EU member state. A similar explanation applies to the Norwegian refusal of a full membership. Both countries, Switzerland and Norway, are at the top of the income scale among European countries and have extended systems of social welfare. *Fourth,* the United States is seen by some economists (Inman and Rubinfeld 1992) as a federal state, which describes the situation of a future fully integrated Europe. It would therefore be fruitful to look at the degree of convergence and mobility among the individual states in the United States.

As in the EU case, but to a far more pronounced extent, real income differences have vanished during the last decades. According to Table 1.6, real

Table 1.7. *Annual geographical mobility
rates among the U.S. states for selected
periods: Movers within the same state
and from a different state as percentage
of total population*

Mobility period	Same state	Different state
1949–50	3.0	2.6
1959–60	3.3	3.2
1969–70	3.1	3.6
1980–81	3.4	2.8
1990–91	3.2	2.9
1993–94	3.2	2.6

Source: U.S. Bureau of the Census (1995).

per-capita income in the Southeast was about 48% of the U.S. average in 1900, while incomes in the Far West and New England/Mideast exceeded the national average by more than 60% and 30%, respectively. Although there are still some income differences among states, Table 1.6 shows that these per-capita disparities have almost disappeared during the last 90 years, as can be seen by the enormous decline in the standard deviation.

Because there are no limits to interstate trade in goods or mobility of capital and people, it is not surprising that flows in capital and goods have diminished per-capita income differentials among U.S. states. However, and remarkably, migration seems to contribute far more than in Europe to an equalization of incomes across different regions in the United States. This can be seen by Table 1.7, showing significant annual migration rates among U.S. states. Mobility rates are of approximately the same size for movers within the same state as from a different state. If the development in the United States is taken as some herald of the situation in a more integrated Europe in the next century, migration will be important. Hence, the results derived in the following chapters, which hinge on a high degree of population mobility among regions, become empirically relevant for the EU, too.

1.2   Purpose, Justification, and Limits of the Study

1.2.1   Purpose of the Book

Within a uniform theoretical framework, this book aims to study the economic consequences of fiscal decentralization when the regions of a federal state are connected by a high degree of mobility. However, the study does not intend to consider all areas of government activities. Following Musgrave's (1959) division of government functions into three parts, the following analysis concentrates on the allocative and distributive branch of the government and leaves the stabilization function out of consideration.[5] The exclusion of the stabilization function in this book is not made because stabilization is unimportant. The idea is rather to appropriate the gains of a scientific division of labor by specializing on the first two functions. Furthermore, the analysis concentrates on problems of direct taxation. Problems of indirect taxation in a federal state (taxation of consumption, like the harmonization of VAT systems in the EU) are discussed very broadly in the literature and will be ignored in the following.[6] The basic question of the present study thus becomes:

> *Provided that regions are linked by high mobility of individuals and firms, is it possible to rely on a regional responsibility for the allocative and the redistributive branch of the government in order to achieve an efficient allocation of resources and the desired (optimal) distribution of income between poor and rich households?*

Of course, a number of contributions have already studied elements of this question.[7] Hence, a further analysis of these problems must be defended, and it will be justified by the following arguments.

1.2.2   Justification of the Study

First, the present study takes a closer look at the many different and often inconsistent views about the benefits and problems of decentralizing government activities, and it derives the conditions under which they are true.

Advocates of a stronger decentralization argue that the degree of interregional household mobility is a decreasing function of the size of the regions. Because they can emigrate, individuals can force self-serving regional politicians to take their preferences into account (McLure 1986). A high degree of

---

[5] In doing so, the present study follows the recent textbook literature on public economics. See e.g. Atkinson and Stiglitz (1980), Tresch (1981), Boadway and Wildasin (1984), Stiglitz (1986), Starrett (1988), Richter and Wiegard (1993), and Myles (1995). Oates (1972) analyzes in great detail the question of how to divide the stabilization task among governmental levels. More recent contributions on this problem are von Hagen (1992) and Eichengreen (1993).

[6] See e.g. Wiegard (1980), Berglas (1981), Keen (1983), Mintz and Tulkens (1986), Keen (1987, 1989), Crombrugghe and Tulkens (1990), Sinn (1990), Haufler (1993), Lockwood (1993), Smith (1993), Keen and Lahiri (1994), Lockwood, de Meza, and Myles (1994a,b), Keen and Smith (1996), and Richter (1999).

[7] An important monograph studying this problem is Oates (1972); Wildasin (1986) provides a comprehensive survey on many of the issues involved. Further interesting surveys can be found in McLure (1986), Rubinfeld (1987), Wildasin (1987), and Sinn (1994).

interregional mobility can improve efficiency in the governmental sector in the same way as the mobility of labor and capital improves the resource allocation in the private sector of the economy.

In contrast to that view, authors like Musgrave (1971), Buchanan and Goetz (1972), Oates (1977), Gordon (1983), Wildasin (1991), Inman and Rubinfeld (1992), and Sinn (1994), among many others, derive various distortions of decentralized government decisions. They argue that, in many cases, decentralization of government activities leads to an inefficient allocation and to a suboptimal income distribution. Regional governments neglect the well-being of individuals living in other regions and thus cause interregional externalities.

These different views can partly be explained by their reliance on equally different perceptions of how policy making works; also, some assertions are derived from a theoretical framework while other claims are based on rather vague analogies between the competition of firms and of regions (McLure 1986, p. 344; Tiebout 1956, p. 423).[8] Even for those claims derived from theoretical models, it is often not clear whether they apply only to situations with perfect competition for mobile factors among small regions, or if they apply also to larger regions like the EU member countries. In order to compare the benefits and problems of fiscal decentralization, it is necessary to derive all conclusions from a consistent theoretical framework.

The second, more important justification of this analysis is to derive some novel results and to present selected topics of recent research. Of course, this selection reflects a personal view of influential areas and includes the following routes of research.

(1) This book analyzes the policies of local governments in great detail. Since the taxation of mobile individuals and firms causes locational distortions that are specific to the local level, it is worth deriving a second-best taxation theory for local governments. Following Wellisch and Hülshorst (1999), among others, this study thereby extends optimal taxation results to the local level.

(2) The problem of interregional tax competition for a mobile tax base like capital has attracted great attention by the contributions of Wilson (1986) and Zodrow and Mieszkowski (1986a). Edwards and Keen (1996) have extended this analysis to study whether interregional tax competition is a method to put the Leviathan in his place.

(3) The determination of the optimal territorial structure of a federal state has regained interest by the study of Hochman, Pines, and Thisse (1995). They argue that the famous principle of *fiscal equivalence* developed by Olson (1969) – having one layer of government for each public good – neglects one basic

---

[8] The rather intuitively derived assertion made by Tiebout (1956) that the local supply of public goods ensures an efficient allocation has been rigorously examined by many authors in the last decades, including McGuire (1974), Berglas (1976), Bewley (1981), Stahl and Varaiya (1983), and Scotchmer and Wooders (1987).

condition of an efficient allocation. Local governments must have the correct incentives to choose an efficient allocation in their own interest. With high mobility of individuals among jurisdictions, only metropolitan governments supplying all necessary local public goods to their citizens have the correct incentives.

(4) Myers (1990b), Krelove (1992), Henderson (1994), and Wellisch (1994, 1995a) have derived that perfect interregional household mobility takes away all incentives of (large) regions to behave strategically with regard to neighboring regions. This might call into question some widely accepted views about the failure of decentralized government activities, summarized by Gordon (1983).

(5) Wildasin (1991, 1992) has analyzed the redistribution policies of regional governments in great detail and has derived a central government intervention that ensures an optimal income distribution among individuals and additionally avoids migration distortions.

(6) Another widely held view in the literature (see e.g. Gandenberger 1981) is that a decentralization of government activities does not properly take into account the interests of future generations compared to a central solution. Children and parents usually live in the same country but need not live in the same state, province, or community. Hence, parents cannot influence the well-being of their children by participating in the regional political process. Contrary to this opinion, Wellisch and Richter (1995) and Oates and Schwab (1996) show that high interregional household mobility provides an incentive mechanism to take the preferences of generations living in future periods in the region into account, since migration decisions affect the rents to local property. A regionalization of government activities may therefore better protect the interests of future generations.

(7) Although the informational advantage of decentralized decision making has always been one of the central arguments in favor of fiscal decentralization (Oates 1972), the literature has only recently developed analytical frameworks that encompass issues of asymmetric information between regions and the central government. This literature borrows from contributions on adverse selection and efficient income taxation (e.g. Stiglitz 1982) and from the literature on incentive problems (Laffont and Tirole 1993). Raff and Wilson (1997), Baumann and Wellisch (1998), and Bucovetsky, Marchand, and Pestieau (1998), among others, show that a central government intervention facing such informational constraints cannot achieve an optimal allocation when regional decisions fail to do so.

In summary, the basic justification of this book is to update the discussion on fiscal decentralization and to derive the conditions under which these insights – which are sometimes inconsistent with the traditional view – hold.

1.2.3   Limits of the Study

In trying to give an answer to the central question of this book (displayed in Section 1.2.1), this study concentrates on theoretical contributions to the literature – mainly on research areas of the author and the related literature. It should be mentioned, however, that there are further important fields of ongoing research in local public finance which this book cannot consider in detail. It has already been emphasized that issues of stabilization policy and of indirect taxation will be excluded from the main text. Moreover, a voluminous research field in local public finance concerns the problem of how to model public choice mechanisms at the local level. We shall solve this problem in a rather simple way in order to concentrate on incentive problems caused by fiscal decentralization. What is not considered in detail in this book are voting models (see Rubinfeld 1987; Wildasin 1986, 1987). Finally, this book excludes empirical issues. However, it is important to note that it is just the large number of jurisdictions in federal states that has provided a broad data basis for cross-sectional analysis and has thus formed the basis of intensive and ongoing empirical research in this area.[9]

Given the central question of this book – to find out whether a decentralization of taxation and spending decisions can achieve an efficient allocation and a fair income distribution – these omissions seem to be innocuous on the following grounds. First, the government's stabilization branch is excluded in order to concentrate on efficiency and distributional issues. Second, as many texts explain (see e.g. Boadway and Wildasin 1984; Rosen 1995), voting models predict that governments choose an inefficient provision of public goods even in a closed economy. Hence, all the more can an efficient supply of public services not be expected when jurisdictions are connected by mobile individuals. Therefore, in order to not exclude the possibility that regions choose an efficient allocation right at the beginning, this book relies on very simple population structures and omits difficult public choice problems. This allows us to trace distortions of decentralized decisions back to regional incentive problems, which a central government does not have. Finally, this study intends to provide a theoretical and not an empirical analysis of the economic consequences of fiscal decentralization.

It is also important to say that this theoretical analysis abstracts from country-specific institutional aspects. Although European integration and German unification have been important developments for this study, it tries to be a general

---

[9] Oates (1969), Bergstrom and Goodman (1973), and Oates (1985) are three path-breaking contributions to important areas of empirical research: tests of the Tiebout hypothesis, estimates of the demand for local public goods, and tests of the Leviathan hypothesis of governments.

one that can be applied to all federal states.[10] The subsequent analysis often uses the rather general term *region*. However, its interpretation depends on the model used and the specific problem which is examined. If the study concentrates on small regions, then the model can be applied to the local level and questions of local government behavior are studied. If the analysis considers larger regions where some kind of strategic behavior is possible, then regions can be interpreted as *Bundesländer* in Germany, as states in the United States, or as member countries of the EU. The meaning of the expression *central* or *national government* also depends on the intended application. If the model refers to a national federal state then it stands for the federal government, while in the EU case it denotes some supranational institution like the EU commission. Models with perfect household mobility are appropriate depictions of homogeneous national federal states like Germany or the United States, whereas setups that model attachment of households to home as some kind of imperfect mobility describe the situation of the member states in the EU or the provinces in Canada.

Before we provide an overview of the study, it is instructive to compare the basic benefits and problems of decentralized fiscal policy at a more systematic level than we have done so far.

## 1.3	Benefits of Fiscal Decentralization

### 1.3.1	Sensitivity to Diverse Regional Preferences

In the eyes of many economists, the benefits of decentralizing government activities dominate.[11] Probably the best-known advantage is that regional governments, being closer to the people, may better reflect individual preferences. Any governing independent of the citizens' tastes should be avoided, and central government decisions often suffer from a lack of sensitivity to diverse regional preferences. The problem is that the provision of public goods almost always requires compromises. Some citizens prefer expanded and high quality programs of public goods, while others would like to have smaller public budgets and less taxation. Such a compromise is unavoidable for truly national public goods, like national defense, which are consumed by all citizens of a federal state. However, there are many local public goods that can only be consumed in the region where they are offered, and the preferences for these public goods may differ interregionally. In this case, there is at least a partial solution to the

---

[10] Padoa-Schioppa (1987) for the European integration and Sinn and Sinn (1992) for the German unification are interesting studies that also take institutional problems into account.

[11] Oates (1972), McLure (1986), and Siebert (1991), among others, discuss various advantages of decentralizing public expenditure and taxation decisions.

problem when regional governments provide such public goods. A revelation of preferences for local public goods is more likely when regional residents themselves vote for the supply of public goods they consume. In contrast to this, a provision of local public goods by the center tends to offer all regions the same amount and the same quality of public goods (see e.g. Oates 1972; Boadway and Wildasin 1984). This causes efficiency losses.

1.3.2 Preference Revelation by Household Mobility

A further important benefit of decentralized government decisions is based on the high interregional mobility of households. Similar to the closeness of regional governments to their citizens, the mobility of households helps to reveal the preferences of regional residents for local public amenities. Governments face a fundamental problem when deciding on the provision of public goods. Assuming they are interested in the welfare of their citizens, how can they disclose their preferences for different tax–expenditure bundles? Consumers are not interested in revealing their true willingness to pay and so may take on a "free rider" position, since they cannot be excluded from the consumption of public goods. Tiebout (1956) offered an ingenious idea as a solution to this fundamental question: he argued that the problem can be solved by a local provision of public goods. Mobile households vote with their feet and choose their region of residence where the combination of local public goods and taxes best reflects their preferences. Such spatial arbitrage behavior of households results in some kind of market solution for an efficient supply of local public goods. This preference revelation process can be thought of as follows. A higher provision of local public goods in a region attracts mobile households, who compete for jobs and housing in the region. This reduces regional wages and increases regional housing rents until the reservation utility of mobile households has been reached once again in that region. The changes in regional wages and housing rents therefore reveal the preferences of mobile households for the higher supply of local public goods and cause an increase in the value of such regional property as land, buildings, or firms. When regional governments take into account the effects of their decisions on local property values, they (are forced to) internalize the willingness to pay of mobile residents.

1.3.3 Protecting the Interests of Future Generations

It is widely unrecognized that this mechanism may also induce regional governments to take into account the interests of future generations living in the region. Let us consider, for example, the emissions of long-lived local pollutants like toxic waste, which are controlled by a local environmental agency.

Any increase in today's emissions worsens the environmental situation in future periods. This causes emigration of residents, who would otherwise live in future periods in the region, until the remaining local residents can again receive their reservation utility level due to a reduction in housing rents or an increase in wages. The changes in housing rents and wages reflect the marginal willingness to pay of future generations to avoid current emissions. By capitalization, the future drop in the return to local property causes a fall in the current value of local property. Any such decrease reveals the preferences of future generations for a clean environment. If the local environmental agency takes into account the changes in the value of local property, it is forced to internalize any long-lasting effects of current emissions generated in the region. Hence, even in the absence of altruistic motives, the interests of future generations are protected by internalizing their marginal willingness to pay for a decrease in today's emissions. Tiebout's hypothesis that migration responses reveal the preferences of mobile households for local amenities is also true in an intergenerational context. This revelation of preferences does not work at the central level since its driving force is the mobility of households across regions, and the degree of household mobility decreases with the size of the jurisdiction. It is therefore possible that a decentralization of (some) government activities not only facilitates the revelation of preferences for public goods today but also better protects the interests of future generations than a more centralized system.

By the same line of argument, decentralization might also be a way to prevent excessive public debt finance of current government expenditures at the expense of future generations. Any shift in the tax burden to future generations living in a region due to debt finance will be answered by emigration of these households. This response will lower the rents of local property in future periods and therefore the current value of local property as well. This capitalization at least takes away the incentives for excessive debt finance and for other forms of intergenerational redistribution like public pension payments on a pay-as-you-go base.

1.3.4   Restraining the Leviathan

The benefits listed so far have considered a world with benevolent governments seeking to maximize the welfare of their constituents. There exists, however, also a radically different perception of how policy making works. According to this view, governments (whether local or national) are intrinsically untrustworthy revenue maximizers, and tax competition between jurisdictions serves a valuable purpose. Investors choose to invest their capital in low-tax jurisdictions, decreasing the tax base when Leviathan-type governments try to maximize revenues by choosing inefficiently high tax rates. Since capital is more mobile among smaller jurisdictions in a federal state than among countries, any decentralization of government functions serves to restrict the taxing power of governments that are unconcerned with the welfare of residents. Hence, decentralization and competition may be institutionally efficient and can be seen as objectives in their own right. As with decentralization and competition in the private sector of the economy, competition among governmental units forces self-interested governments to take the utility of their constituents into account and thereby improve the conditions for socially efficient public taxation and expenditure decisions (Brennan and Buchanan 1980; McLure 1986). This perception of how policy measures are chosen has become increasingly influential during the last decade. Several European government administrations – most notably, the British government – opposed an EU coordination of taxes since a single European market would cause downward pressure on tax rates, and this helps to restrict built-in pressures for increased public expenditure and taxation (U.K. Treasury 1988).

1.4   Problems of Fiscal Decentralization

First, it is important to note that regional governments in principle face the same problems that a central government must solve. Public goods affect the interests of many persons, and public decision makers must reveal the preferences of their citizens. Since regional governments are closer to the people and households can vote with their feet among several regions, this problem could be better solved by a decentralized system. Moreover, in order to finance public services and to design their redistribution programs, governments must collect taxes that should leave private economic decisions as undistorted as possible. This is true on the regional level as well as on the central level. However, an analysis that aims to consider issues of decentralized fiscal policy should emphasize such problems that are specific to regional decisions aside from these more general problems. In particular, additional problems for regional decision making arise because regions are open with respect to other regions.

1.4.1   Inefficient Interregional Resource Allocation

One aspect of this openness is that households, firms, and capital are mobile among the individual regions of a federal state. However, their interregional allocation cannot be arbitrary if an efficient allocation is to be achieved. The locational pattern must meet conditions that characterize an efficient allocation across regions. Since locational choices of private households and firms are influenced by the provision of public services and by the collection of taxes, a first important problem arises. Do regional governments have incentives to choose their taxes and their expenditures on public goods and transfers in such a way that these instruments do not distort the interregional allocation?

1.4.2   Destructive Tax Competition for Mobile Factors

The second problem is closely related to the first one. Regions compete for mobile households and mobile firms by providing public services with the objective to increase the welfare of their residents. It is often feared that regions therefore provide local public goods and factors strategically in order to gain locational advantages over their neighbors. For example, a regional government might underprovide local public goods in order to restrict immigration of households if new residents would increase the costs of providing a certain level of public services. Or it might overprovide local public infrastructure in order to increase local wages and tax revenues by attracting mobile firms. Here, the following question arises: Under what conditions do regions supply public services in a socially efficient way when they follow region-specific objectives and take locational responses of mobile households and firms to their own actions into account? Have regions any incentives to distort the provision of public services in order to gain locational advantages?

The problem of an *interregional tax competition* for a scarce mobile factor is widely discussed in the literature, and it can directly be traced back to the problem just described.[12] In order to explain the essence of the problem, let us suppose that the provision of local public goods must be financed by a tax on a highly mobile factor like capital. When providing public goods, a single region must take into account two cost factors. The first one is the normal income loss for private households, a consequence of the redistribution of resources from the private sector to the government. However, if capital is taxed too much then it will leave the region, and this decreases local wages and tax revenues. This is the second cost component from the viewpoint of a single region. Each region will therefore try to avoid the capital flight by choosing rather low capital tax rates, thus leading to an inefficiently low supply of public goods.

The problem of interregional tax competition can also be explained by standard externality theory. If a region levies a tax on a mobile factor such as capital, this tax base leaves the region and increases the tax base elsewhere. Thus, the taxing region causes a positive *fiscal externality* to other regions and consequently chooses an inefficiently low level of the externality-producing activity – that is, too low tax rates and thus inefficiently low levels of local public goods. This fiscal externality arises even in small regions lacking any power in the interregional capital market; larger regions cause an additional external effect when taxing capital. Since they can influence the interregional interest rate by choosing their capital tax rate, larger regions behave strategically in order to

---

[12] The basic feature of the problem has already been described by Oates (1972, pp. 142–3). A more formal treatment of the problem of interregional tax competition can be found in Wilson (1986) and Zodrow and Mieszkowski (1986a).

increase the regional income. A net capital exporter, for example, will tax capital at low rates in order to increase the demand for capital and thereby drive the interest rate up. This causes a negative *pecuniary externality* on regions that are net capital importers, since their interest liabilities increase. Consequently, the supplied amount of local public goods is further biased downward.

1.4.3   Tax Export and Spillover Effects

Aside from the interregional competition for a scarce mobile tax base, there are two other well-known sources of an inefficient provision of public goods by regions: the interregional export of taxes and interregional public good spillover effects. These phenomena also arise because regions are open.

In the case of an interregional tax export, regions can partly shift taxes to nonresidents. While the benefits of supplying local public goods are internalized by the residents of a region, the costs are partly borne by residents of other regions. As a consequence, an inefficiently high supply of local public goods must be expected. Well-known examples are (a) the source-based taxation of land rents when land is partly owned by nonresidents, and (b) origin-based consumption taxes that increase the consumer price of regional products that are also bought by nonresidents. An example of an international tax export is the origin-based taxation of internationally traded goods, such as the future VAT system in the EU. Tax revenues are collected by the country where goods are produced, yet the tax burden is shifted to residents of countries where goods are consumed. Typical exporting countries shift their tax burden to consumers living in typical importing countries and have incentives to overexpand activities financed by these taxes.

If nonresidents cannot be excluded from the consumption of public goods provided by a region, then a spillover problem arises. In contrast to an interregional export of taxes, here the costs of providing public goods are internalized by a region while the benefits (partly) flow out. Examples are sewage treatment by an upstream city (reducing the need for purification by downstream cities) and the benefits from education provided by one jurisdiction that may be enjoyed by households elsewhere if educated individuals decide to relocate. As a consequence, the provision of public goods will be too low from a social point of view. This problem also arises with reversed signs, as when nonresidents suffer from regional pollution.

1.4.4   Suboptimal Income Distribution within Regions

In addition to supplying public goods, the government also has the function of redistributing income between rich and poor households in order to achieve a fair income and wealth distribution. The basic problem of decentralized redistribution policy is that a region must take into account the migration responses to a transfer program. To make the problem intuitively transparent, let us suppose that a single region increases its transfer payments to all low-income households living within its boundaries, and that the region finances this program by collecting higher taxes from its high-income residents. From the viewpoint of the single region, the costs of this redistribution program are rather high, since poor households from neighboring regions are attracted to – and rich residents are repelled from – the region. In other words, the regional redistribution program leads to some kind of adverse selection. One can therefore expect that the assignment of the redistribution branch to regions would result in a suboptimally low degree of income redistribution.[13] However, a suboptimally low level of redistribution between rich and poor households is not the only problem. Moreover, regions will levy different taxes on mobile high-income residents and provide different transfer payments to low-income households. This causes pure fiscal incentives to relocate, resulting in migration distortions.[14] If the redistribution function is assigned to the central government, then neither problem arises. Migration responses are much lower at the national level, and migration distortions can be avoided by choosing identical tax rates and transfer levels across all regions of the federal state.

If, however, intergenerational redistribution (e.g., excessive public debt finance) is seen as undesirable because future generations must bear the tax burden without being asked to do so, fiscal decentralization of the redistribution branch can also be beneficial.

1.4.5   Suboptimal Income Distribution across Regions

It seems to be obvious that regional governments who are interested in the welfare of their own residents have hardly any incentives to redistribute income toward other regions, since this would imply a decrease in consumption for their constituents. As intuitive as this argument might be, it resists a rigorous analysis only if individuals are unable to move across regions. However, individuals are typically free to move in a federal state. For instance, the citizens of any one region in the EU have access to the labor market of – and receive the same fiscal treatment in – any other region; this is legally guaranteed in Article 48 of the EU treaty. Therefore, even a rationally acting government that considers the welfare of only its own constituency must take migration responses to its policy into account. This may imply voluntary interregional transfers to poorer regions in order to restrict immigration and thus to avoid a drop in per-capita income of

---

[13] This expectation is the prevailing view. It is advocated by Musgrave (1971), Oates (1972, 1977), Brown and Oates (1987), Wildasin (1991), and Sinn (1994). See Cremer et al. (1995) for an overview on various redistribution studies.

[14] This problem is underlined by Musgrave (1971), Wildasin (1991), Burbidge and Myers (1994a), and Wellisch (1996).

residents due to immigration. However, as long as there exist migration costs – immobility of individuals is an extreme case of such costs – migration does not succeed in equating net incomes of individuals across regions. If the central government wants or is obliged (e.g., by Article 106 in combination with Article 72 of the German Constitution) to smooth interregional income disparities, then it must redistribute further. Without any central intervention, per-capita income differentials across regions continue to exist unless migration costs are significantly reduced for all types of individuals. However, if the central government decides to redistribute among regions, incentive problems on behalf of regional governments may result. Regions might reduce their own efforts to achieve a high income level by cutting investments in public infrastructure.

1.4.6   Suboptimal Stabilization Policy

Besides the tasks of providing public goods and redistributing income, the government also has the function of cushioning economic shocks in order to stabilize the economy. However, the fact that regions are open causes problems for regional stabilization policies. These problems are only touched here without going into detail in the main text. There are, in principle, two ways that a government can perform macroeconomic policies. It can stabilize the economy in the presence of shocks either by changing the supply of money – monetary policy – or by employing expenditure–tax programs – deficit spending (see Oates 1972).

There is some doubt whether monetary policy can indeed stimulate the economy when it is rationally anticipated by private agents, employers and labor unions alike. Given such anticipation, attempts of regional policy makers to stimulate the regional economy by using the money press would result in a higher inflation rate without any significant reduction in regional unemployment. If there is a single currency in a federal state with monetary policy performed by a central institution, then regional policy makers are lacking the monetary policy instrument to cushion region-specific economic shocks. A central authority does not try to cushion region-specific unemployment, and the inflation rate will be lower. In addition, if individuals are mobile across regions then region-specific shocks will be answered by migration into high-employment areas, which helps to smooth the unemployment rates across regions at lower levels.

The effectiveness of regional expenditure–tax programs to stimulate regional economic activity is rather limited, too. The Keynesian expenditure and tax multipliers are low because each region imports a lot. A decrease in regional taxes, for example, does little to increase economic growth, since a huge fraction of the additional disposable income in the hands of regional residents goes to foreign production and services.

1.4.7   Optimal Degree of Fiscal Decentralization

In discussing the benefits and problems of fiscal decentralization so far, we have assumed politically predetermined jurisdictional boundaries. This might be an appropriate assumption in the short run. However, at least in the long run, one must also decide about the optimal governmental structure in a federal state. As long as the welfare of citizens can be increased by a restructuring of jurisdictional boundaries, there is scope for a Pareto improvement. Hence, the question arises about the optimal population size of the individual jurisdictions. The optimal governmental structure is a difficult problem to analyze, since the benefits and problems considered so far must be balanced in order to determine the optimal size of jurisdictions. One objective is to avoid any interregional externality caused by decentralized government decisions. This points in the direction of rather large governmental entities. Another important objective is to ensure that governments are concerned with the wishes of their constituents and do not behave strategically with respect to neighboring regions. This argument tends in the direction of smaller governmental units. The optimal degree of fiscal decentralization is a compromise between these opposing forces. Olson's (1969) *principle of fiscal equivalence* and the *correspondence principle* developed by Oates (1972) are two early theories on how to determine the optimal degree of fiscal decentralization.

1.5   Outline of the Book

With the basic objective of deriving the benefits and problems of decentralized government decisions, the study is divided into ten further chapters.

Chapter 2
This chapter assumes that the boundaries of the jurisdictions in the federal state are politically fixed. Within this environment, it pursues two objectives. The first one is to derive the necessary conditions of an efficient allocation in a federal state and to explore whether an interregional transfer of resources is needed to sustain efficiency. The efficiency conditions serve as a reference point to evaluate the outcome of decentralized government activities. If the outcome of decentralized tax and expenditure decisions does not meet these conditions, then regional fiscal policies result in an inefficient allocation, and an intervention by a central government or the assignment of some government functions to the central level is required to achieve efficiency. Chapter 2 in particular concentrates on the derivation of the first-order conditions of an *efficient locational pattern*.

The second aim of this chapter is to deduce a complete set of tax instruments at the disposal of regional governments, so that they are able to achieve an efficient interregional allocation of mobile firms and individuals and to finance the efficient level of public services without violating their budget constraint. This chapter does not analyze the behavior of regional governments and therefore it does not examine whether they have incentives to ensure an efficient allocation when they can rely on this set of tax instruments. However, the derivation of a complete set of tax instruments is a necessary condition for avoiding allocative distortions. Without such a complete set of taxes at the regional level, regional governments cannot achieve an efficient allocation, even if they had incentives to do so.

In Chapters 3–10, the behavior of regional governments is studied.

Chapter 3
Chapter 3 assumes that regions are small and that there is perfect competition among regions for mobile firms and mobile households. No single small region can influence such interregional variables as the utility level of mobile households or the profit level of mobile firms. We study whether conditions of perfect interregional competition provide regional governments with the correct incentives to choose an efficient allocation. The analysis differentiates between the case in which regional governments have a complete tax instrument set available and cases in which the tax instrument set is incomplete. The study confirms that interregional competition results in an efficient allocation in the case of a complete tax instrument set, and it derives the resulting distortions if regions face constraints in the availability of taxes.

Chapter 4
Chapter 4 studies in great detail the problem of interregional competition for the scarce (mobile) capital tax base. This, too, is a second-best problem. Regional governments must tax the mobile capital base in order to finance local public goods, since undistortive tax revenue sources are institutionally not feasible, by assumption. The analysis shows that regional governments systematically underprovide local public (consumption) goods and illustrates several ways how this problem can be solved.

However, the conclusions about interregional tax competition are quite different if politicians are partly self-serving and waste some fraction of the tax revenues. Although interregional tax competition still distorts the division of resources between the private and the public sector, it cuts down expenditures that serve only politicians or bureaucrats. Therefore, tax competition may be in the interest of citizens.

A final observation is that the tax on mobile capital can be interpreted as a local property tax on structures – the predominant tax source of local governments in many countries. Therefore, this chapter uses the model of interregional tax competition to review the incidence of property tax, and it closes with some remarks on the effects of land taxation.

Chapter 5

In many federal states, there is an ongoing debate about the restructuring of jurisdictional boundaries in order to save costs in the public sector. Indeed, many American cities have grown by annexation, and in Germany there has been a large restructuring of communities during the 1970s. Although the analysis so far has excluded issues of the optimal structure of jurisdictions in a federal state, these problems will be examined in Chapter 5. An optimal allocation requires more than an efficient supply of local public goods and an efficient distribution of individuals and firms among a fixed number of jurisdictions; in addition, it requires an optimal size of the individual jurisdictions. The number of jurisdictions must be chosen such that the population size is optimal in each jurisdiction.

This chapter considers several models to determine the optimal size of jurisdictions. It starts with a Tiebout model without any fixed factors of production. It next assigns land to the jurisdictions, and it finally considers the case in which local public goods have overlapping market areas. For all these cases, this chapter studies whether the optimal allocation can be decentralized. Most remarkably, the analysis shows that only governments of large metropolitan areas have the correct incentives to choose the optimal allocation.

Chapter 6

Perfect competition among regions is one incentive mechanism for regional governments to choose an efficient allocation in their own interests. However, this result is restricted to small regions and can only be applied to the behavior of local governments. Chapter 6 demonstrates that conditions of perfect interregional household mobility also take away all incentives from large regions to perform a *beggar-my-neighbor policy*. To make this argument as clear as possible, this chapter shows that even the existence of the three classical reasons why decentralized fiscal policy may fail – interregional export of taxes, public good spillover effects, and interregional tax competition – does not cause distortions.

Chapter 7

That household mobility serves as a perfect substitute for Coasian negotiations among large regions may be an ingenious idea from a theoretical viewpoint, but it hinges on very strong assumptions and there is some doubt that these conditions can be found in existing federations. The most critical assumption is that all households are identical and perfectly mobile. If one introduces the realistic assumption that there are migration costs, the strong result that uncoordinated regional activities always result in a cooperative-like outcome must be modified. Chapter 7 proceeds with this issue. Its basic purpose is to study how the outcome of decentralized tax and expenditure decisions depends on the degree of interregional household mobility and, given any degree of mobility, how the results can be altered by the set of tax instruments available to regions.

Chapter 8
Whereas the analysis described so far concentrates on the allocative branch of the government, decentralized redistribution policy is at the core of Chapters 8–10. In Chapter 8, we will assume (a) that regions are connected by a high degree of interregional household mobility and (b) that the government in each region taxes high-income residents and uses the tax revenues to grant transfer payments to low-income individuals living within its boundaries. The analysis shows that the level of redistribution is suboptimally low. In addition, uncoordinated regional redistribution causes migration on pure fiscal reasons and thereby distorts the interregional labor allocation. This chapter also derives a corrective central government intervention that avoids distortions by internalizing all fiscal externalities caused by regional decisions.

Chapter 9
In contrast to the static analysis of the preceding chapters, Chapter 9 uses an overlapping generations model to study whether a decentralization of some government activities may better protect the interests of future generations. Two government fields are at the center of the analysis: the local emission control of long-lived pollutants like toxic waste; and intergenerational redistribution by local public debt policy. Both phenomena have in common that they create intergenerational externalities: by worsening the future local environmental situation, the current emission of toxic waste causes intergenerational technological externalities; and by increasing the tax burden of future generations, issuing local public debt generates fiscal externalities on future generations.

The analysis shows that migration responses in future periods force regional governments to take the welfare of future generations living in this region into account. While this results in a perfect internalization of pollution externalities on future generations, it does not take away all incentives to issue public debt or to run a pay-as-you-go financed pension system.

Chapter 10
Incentive problems caused by asymmetric information between regions and the center are at the core of Chapter 10. The analysis differentiates between problems of adverse selection and moral hazard. The issues are exemplified by one problem that might receive high priority in the EU and has already become important in other federal states owing to an increase in interregional mobility of individuals: the link between a suboptimal income distribution within and

across regions. A central government intervention is needed in order to smooth both interpersonal and interregional income differences. However, to implement its interregional transfer program, the center must induce governments of rich regions not to hide information about per-capita income levels, and it must ensure that they still have incentives to achieve high incomes by investment in public infrastructure. This chapter derives the distortions that result from such incentive constraints.

Chapter 11

Finally, Chapter 11 concludes by giving a comprehensive answer to the central questions of the study. It reviews the conditions under which regional government decisions result in an efficient allocation, reveals the basic reasons why decentralized decisions may fail, and explains why the redistribution branch of the government should be assigned to the central level. Using these general results, some policy applications are drawn to the problem of decentralizing government activities in federal states.

CHAPTER 2

Locational Efficiency and Efficiency-Supporting Tax Systems

Each federal state consists of several regions, which are linked by a high degree of mobility of individuals and firms. The high degree of interregional mobility causes allocative problems that cannot be found in a unitary state. The problem of an efficient allocation in a federal state – for a politically predetermined jurisdictional structure – is mainly a problem of the *efficient locational pattern*. Therefore, the first basic objective of this chapter is to derive the efficient interregional allocation of mobile factors of production, firms, and individuals. Of course, efficiency in a federal state also requires the efficient provision of public goods and factors, but this is achieved in much the same way as in a unitary state. Differences only arise if regions take on the responsibility of supplying some kinds of public goods for which consumption also extends to nonresidents. To achieve the efficient allocation in this case, these spillover effects must be internalized.

The second objective of this chapter is to study whether the efficient allocation can be achieved by decentralized decisions of firms and individuals. The regional tax system is of particular importance. It affects firms' decisions to employ mobile factors of production and is an important determinant of the locational choice of firms, and households make their residential choice dependent on the tax system. A set of tax instruments that allows regions to achieve the efficient locational pattern and simultaneously finance the efficient amount of public services will be called an *efficiency-supporting* or simply a *complete* tax system. It should be noticed that this chapter does not try to answer the question of whether regions actually have incentives to use their tax system in a socially efficient way. This important question will be answered in the following chapters. However, regions without a complete tax system cannot realize the efficient allocation even if they have the correct incentives to do so. Deriving an efficiency-supporting tax system can therefore be regarded as a necessary condition to ensure that local government behavior results in an efficient allocation.

Many researchers have studied the design of a regional tax system that does not distort the locational pattern of individuals. A comprehensive treatment of this problem can be found in Wildasin (1986, 1987). This chapter extends these contributions by introducing firm mobility into the analysis and thereby follows some recent contributions by Richter and Wellisch (1996) and Wellisch and Hülshorst (1999).[1] The discussion about the efficient taxation of mobile individuals can be traced back (at least) to an article by Flatters, Henderson, and Mieszkowski (1974). This study demonstrates that free residential choices of individuals may lead to so-called *fiscal externalities* and are therefore inefficient. If public expenditures must be financed by residence-based taxes and if the per-capita costs of supplying local public services differ among regions, then there are pure fiscal reasons to relocate. Starting from this observation, Flatters et al. (1974) and more recently Boadway and Flatters (1982a,b) have proposed a system of (direct) interregional transfers – from regions with low per-capita expenditures on local public goods to regions with high per-capita expenditures – to equate the per-capita tax burden and thereby avoid the fiscal externalities. As Myers (1990a,b) and Krelove (1992) emphasize, the efficient allocation can also be achieved if (pure) local public goods are financed by land taxes, provided that individuals are equally endowed with land in all regions independently of where they live. In this case, a land tax is an undistortive revenue source for public expenditures and moreover ensures the efficient interregional transfer of resources.

In discussing the problems of locational efficiency, this chapter proceeds as follows. Section 2.1 derives the efficient allocation in a federal state and analyzes whether an interregional transfer of resources is necessary to sustain locational efficiency. In Section 2.2, we study how the locational behavior of firms and individuals is affected by taxation and use this observation to derive efficiency-supporting tax systems.

2.1   Efficient Locational Pattern

2.1.1   The Model

Consider a federal state consisting of I regions. The federal state is inhabited by a large number of N identical mobile individuals, and N_i denotes the number of individuals living in region $i = 1, \ldots, I$. We characterize an individual by its utility function $U^i \equiv U(x_i, z_i)$, where x_i is the consumption level of a private numeraire good and z_i denotes the local public good supply. We assume that there are no spillover effects in the provision of z_i. Each mobile household is endowed with one unit of labor, which is inelastically supplied in the

---

[1] See also Richter and Wellisch (1993), Krumm and Wellisch (1994), Richter (1994), Wellisch (1995b), and Hülshorst and Wellisch (1996).

individual's region of residence. The costs of providing local public goods are given by $C^i(z_i, N_i)$. These costs are expressed in units of the private good and vary with the public good level and with the number of users. The specification is sufficiently flexible to allow for both increasing returns in the provision of z_i, $C_z^i \equiv \partial C^i/\partial z_i < C^i/z_i$, and increasing returns with respect to the number of users, $C_N^i \equiv \partial C^i/\partial N_i < C^i/N_i$. The local public good is said to be *pure* if there is no congestion, $C_N^i = 0$. However, some positive marginal congestion is the empirically more relevant case.[2]

There are M identical mobile firms in the federation; M is exogenous, which excludes the formation of new firms. We thus model only the locational choices of firms and not market entry. We use M_i to denote the number of mobile firms locating in region i. Firms are said to be *identical* if they use the same technology, represented by the production function $F^i \equiv F(l_i, n_i, g_i)$. Production makes use of three factors: l_i is the (immobile) land factor, n_i the (mobile) labor factor, and g_i the local public factor.

Regions are endowed with a fixed amount of land, L_i. We assume that there are no spillover effects in the use of the local public factor. The costs of providing the public factor are given by the function $H^i(g_i, M_i)$. These costs are also expressed in units of the private good and depend on the level of public inputs as well as on the number of firms locating in the region. The special case of pure public inputs, $H_M^i \equiv \partial H^i/\partial M_i = 0$, is included. In general, however, public factors will be impure, $H_M^i > 0$. For simplicity, we treat N_i and M_i as real numbers, expressing the idea that households and firms are small relative to their markets.

Previous studies do not model firm mobility explicitly.[3] This can be justified if production is characterized by linear homogeneity and if public inputs are quasi-private – that is, if average costs H^i/M_i are linear in g_i and constant in M_i. Only with these special assumptions is the locational pattern of firms indeterminate at an efficient allocation, so that it makes no sense to differentiate between firms at the individual level. To be sure, these simplifying assumptions are useful when concentrating on other problems of interregional competition, and we will rely on them in the following chapters. Since, however, locational issues are at the core of the analysis now, we choose the more general model specification where the local number of firms is a nontrivial endogenous variable.

The functions U, F, H^i, and C^i are twice differentiable and satisfy standard assumptions. We indicate derivatives by subindices. First partial derivatives

---

[2] Empirical studies by Borcherding and Deacon (1972) and Bergstrom and Goodman (1973) find strong empirical evidence of congestion. In many cases, costs become nearly proportional to the population once a minimum size of 10–50 thousand inhabitants is reached.

[3] For a comprehensive overview, see Wildasin (1986). However, the contributions by Fischel (1975) and White (1975b) are exceptions that also consider mobility of firms.

have the usual signs. The function F is strictly concave in the private factors l_i and n_i and may be linear-homogeneous in l_i, n_i, and g_i. For the results derived in this study, we need not be more specific about the degree of homogeneity.

In order to achieve efficiency, a central planner would have to

$$\text{maximize} \quad U(x_1, z_1) \tag{2.1}$$

in the vectors (x_i), (z_i), (g_i), (l_i), (M_i), (n_i), (N_i) subject to

$$U(x_1, z_1) = U(x_i, z_i), \quad i = 2, \ldots, I, \tag{2.2}$$

$$N_i - M_i n_i = 0, \quad i = 1, \ldots, I, \tag{2.3}$$

$$L_i - M_i l_i = 0, \quad i = 1, \ldots, I, \tag{2.4}$$

$$(\gamma): \quad N - \sum_i N_i = 0, \tag{2.5}$$

$$(\mu): \quad M - \sum_i M_i = 0, \tag{2.6}$$

$$(\lambda): \quad \sum_i [M_i F(l_i, n_i, g_i) - N_i x_i$$
$$- C^i(z_i, N_i) - H^i(g_i, M_i)] = 0, \tag{2.7}$$

where γ, μ, and λ are Lagrange multipliers. We mention only those that are needed in the following. According to (2.1), the planner maximizes the utility of a representative mobile resident in region 1. Condition (2.2) reflects costless migration of mobile households by ruling out interregional utility differentials that would be incompatible with free locational choices. Of course, if the central planner can directly control migration, the efficient allocation generally differs from the one derived here.[4] According to (2.3), the regional labor supply is equally distributed among local firms; (2.4) requires the same for the fixed regional endowment of land. Conditions (2.5) and (2.6) state that mobile households and firms must locate somewhere in the federation. Finally, (2.7) is the global feasibility condition of the private good. Aggregate production must meet households' consumption and the real costs of providing public goods and factors.

2.1.2   First-Order Conditions

A solution to the planner's problem may involve allocations for which no production takes place in some region. We ignore this well-known problem in

---

[4] Recent studies by Myers and Papageorgiou (1996, 1997a,b) have incorporated immigration quotas or a different fiscal treatment of immigrants and natives into models of population mobility.

regional economics and instead focus exclusively on so-called interior solutions characterized by N_i, $M_i > 0$ for all i. The first-order conditions turn out to be $(i = 1, \ldots, I)$

$$N_i \frac{U_z^i}{U_x^i} = C_z^i, \tag{2.8}$$

$$M_i F_g^i = H_g^i, \tag{2.9}$$

$$F_n^i - x_i - C_N^i = \frac{\gamma}{\lambda}, \tag{2.10}$$

$$F^i - l_i F_l^i - n_i F_n^i - H_M^i = \frac{\mu}{\lambda}. \tag{2.11}$$

Condition (2.8) is the Samuelson rule of the efficient supply of local public goods. Efficiency requires that the marginal willingness to pay of all residents must be equal to marginal costs. Accordingly, condition (2.9) is the corresponding Samuelson rule of the efficient provision of local public factors, and it requires equating the marginal product of local public factors and their marginal costs. The marginal product is obtained by summing over all firms locating in the region. Conditions (2.10) and (2.11) characterize the efficient locational pattern of households and firms, respectively. According to (2.10), the net social benefit of an additional mobile household to a region must be equal in all regions. The benefit of the marginal household is its marginal product F_n^i. The costs consist of its consumption of private goods x_i and of congestion costs C_N^i.

It is important to emphasize that (2.10) does not coincide with the necessary condition of the efficient allocation of a mobile factor of production. To deduce this condition from (2.10), suppose for a moment that individuals live in one particular region but may work in other regions. However, individuals consume public goods only in the region in which they reside. Thus, the migration equilibrium condition (2.2) reduces to $x_1 = x_i$ for all $i \neq 1$, and there are no congestion costs involved with a relocation of workers, $C_N^i = 0$ for all i. Inserting these assumptions into (2.10), we derive that marginal products of the mobile factor labor F_n^i must be equalized across regions if the efficient interregional allocation of labor is to be achieved. This condition extends to other mobile factors such as capital.

Following (2.11), the efficient locational pattern of mobile firms is similarly achieved if the social net benefit of a firm to a region is interregionally equalized. The social net benefit of a firm is measured by its pure profit $F^i - l_i F_l^i - n_i F_n^i$ minus marginal congestion costs H_M^i.

If local public factors are quasi-private and if F is linear-homogeneous in l_i, n_i, and g_i, then the efficient locational pattern of mobile firms turns out to be indeterminate. Consider the case of an efficient allocation (n_i^*, M_i^*, g_i^*).

Then, any allocation (n_i, M_i, g_i) satisfying $n_i M_i = n_i^* M_i^*$, $g_i M_i = g_i^* M_i^*$, and $\sum_i M_i = M$ is equally efficient.

It should be emphasized that (2.8)–(2.11) are necessary conditions. They need not be sufficient for the efficient allocation. The problem of lacking sufficiency is well known from the literature and will be ignored in the sequel (but see e.g. Stiglitz 1977 and Richter 1994). This study will focus only on allocations that satisfy the necessary conditions (2.8)–(2.11).

2.1.3   Efficient Interregional Resource Distribution

A focal question of the literature is whether an interregional transfer of resources is needed to sustain efficiency. Myers (1990b), Hercowitz and Pines (1991), and Krelove (1992), among others, make the remarkable observation that rents must flow out of regions if market equilibria are to be efficient. The assertion is that the equality of local production $M_i F^i$ and local utilization of goods, $y_i \equiv N_i x_i + C^i + H^i$, is in general incompatible with efficiency. To show this, we solve (2.10) for x_i and (2.11) for F_n^i. We use the resulting expressions and substitute them into $y_i = N_i x_i + C^i + H^i$. The equality of local production and local expenditures, $M_i F^i = y_i$, then turns out to be equivalent to

$$\frac{R_i}{N_i} = -\frac{\gamma}{\lambda}, \tag{2.12}$$

where $i = 1, \ldots, I$ and

$$R_i \equiv L_i F_l^i + M_i \frac{\mu}{\lambda} - (C^i - N_i C_N^i) - (H^i - M_i H_M^i)$$

can be interpreted as the net rent generated in region i. Here R_i is equal to the land rent plus the social marginal benefit of local firms minus noncongestion costs of providing local public goods and factors. Equation (2.12) states that per-capita rents must be equalized across regions at the efficient allocation if efficiency is to be achieved without any interregional resource transfer. This is, however, not possible. If the problem is well-behaved then (2.2)–(2.11) include $7I + 2$ conditions that must uniquely determine $7I + 2$ variables at the efficient allocation: the I-dimensional vectors (x_i^*), (z_i^*), (g_i^*), (l_i^*), (M_i^*), (n_i^*), (N_i^*) and the Lagrange multipliers $(\gamma/\lambda)^*$, $(\mu/\lambda)^*$. Of course, these variables do not satisfy (2.12), in general. Hence, we can state

Proposition 2.1.   *If individuals are mobile and migration cannot be controlled (directly), then the efficient allocation is unique and requires an interregional transfer of resources.*

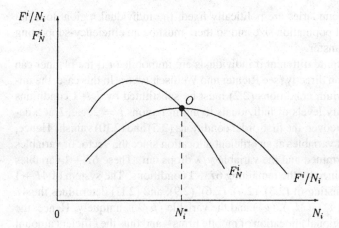

Figure 2.1. Locational efficiency with self-sufficient regions.

The need for an interregional transfer of resources can be explained very instructively if we assume for a moment that there are no public goods and factors and that production in each region takes place by the (classical) production function $F^i \equiv F(L_i, N_i)$. Since there are no local public goods in the economy, the efficient interregional allocation of individuals requires equalizing marginal products of labor across regions, $F_N^i = F_N^j$ for all i, j with $i \neq j$. This follows from condition (2.10) and from the migration equilibrium condition (2.2), implying $x_i = x_j$ for all i, j with $i \neq j$. However, identical marginal labor products across regions are only compatible with self-sufficient regions, $F^i = N_i x_i$, if marginal labor products are equal to average products, $F_N^i = F^i/N_i$. The latter requirement is met if the average product in each region – and thus the consumption of the private numeraire good by a representative resident, $x_i = F^i/N_i$ – is maximized in the number of residents N_i. In other words, if each region has its optimal population size, then no interregional transfer of resources is needed to achieve the efficient locational pattern of individuals across regions. This can be illustrated by Figure 2.1, which depicts average and marginal labor products in some region i. The optimal population size N_i^* is achieved in point O, where average and marginal labor products are identical. By an appropriate assignment of land or people to jurisdictions, point O can be realized in all jurisdictions at the same marginal labor products.

As discussed at length in Chapter 5, this result extends to cases in which local public services are supplied. If each jurisdiction is of optimal size, there must be no interregional transfer of resources to achieve the efficient locational pattern of individuals across regions. However, since we have assumed so far that jurisdictional boundaries are politically fixed, the individual region does not have its optimal population size and so there must be an efficiency-supporting interregional transfer.

Matters are quite different if individuals are immobile or if the planner can control migration directly (see Richter and Wellisch 1996). In this case, the migration equilibrium conditions (2.2) must be substituted by $I - 1$ conditions that fix the utility levels of individuals living in regions $i = 2, \ldots, I$ at a desired level. Moreover, the first-order conditions (2.5) and (2.10) vanish. Hence, there are $6I + 1$ variables at an efficient allocation since the vector of variables (N_i) is predetermined and the variable γ/λ drops out. These $6I + 1$ variables must be determined by the remaining $6I + 1$ conditions. The system of $4I + 1$ conditions consisting of (2.3), (2.4), (2.6), (2.9), and (2.11) determines the $4I$ variables (l_i^*), (n_i^*), (M_i^*), (g_i^*) and the variable $(\mu/\lambda)^*$ uniquely. Hence, the efficient interregional allocation of mobile firms – and thus the efficient amount of production – is still unique at an efficient allocation even if individuals are immobile. DePater and Myers (1994), among others, show that this result extends to an economy with mobile factors of production such as capital. The efficient consumption pattern consisting of the vectors of $2I$ variables (x_i^*) and (z_i^*) is determined by the $I + 1$ conditions (2.7) and (2.8) and by the $I - 1$ conditions (2.2) that now fix utilities at desired levels. However, since the latter conditions depend on the desired interregional welfare distribution, the efficient consumption pattern is not unique. Therefore, the planner can choose the desired utility levels of individuals living in the $i = 2, \ldots, I$ regions to achieve a particular efficient allocation of private and public goods. One possibility is that the planner chooses the desired interregional welfare distribution such that a system of self-sufficient regions, $M_i^* F^{i*} = y_i^*$, achieves the first-best allocation. Any other efficient allocation requires an interregional transfer of resources. Another possibility (discussed in Chapter 4) is that the planner chooses the desired welfare distribution such that a system of *nearly self-sufficient regions*, $M_i^* F^{i*} + \left(N_i \frac{M}{N} - M_i^*\right)(\mu/\lambda)^* = y_i^*$, achieves the first-best allocation. We can interpret $\left(N_i \frac{M}{N} - M_i^*\right)(\mu/\lambda)^*$ as region i's net interregional profit share, with $(\mu/\lambda)^*$ the efficient *profit level* (social marginal benefit) of firms and $E_i^* \equiv \left(N_i \frac{M}{N} - M_i^*\right)$ the efficient *net export of capital* if ownership of firms is equally divided among all individuals living in the federal state.

We can summarize these results in

Proposition 2.2. *If individuals are immobile, then the efficient allocation is not unique and depends on the desired distribution of welfare across regions. A system of (nearly) self-sufficient regions can achieve one particular efficient allocation. If another efficient allocation is to be achieved, an interregional transfer of resources is necessary.*

Proposition 2.2 is reminiscent of the second theorem of welfare economics. According to this result, the efficient allocation in the private sector of the economy is not unique and depends on the desired utility distribution among individuals. Each efficient allocation can be achieved by an appropriate redistribution of resources among individuals that changes their initial endowments. The same holds in a federal state if individuals are immobile. The change in the initial endowments of the regions is obtained by an interregional transfer of resources.

The conclusions stated in Propositions 2.1 and 2.2 are of particular importance to the problem of fiscal decentralization. If individuals are mobile and migration cannot be controlled directly, then an interregional transfer of resources is needed to achieve the efficient allocation. The question arises as to whether regions make this transfer voluntarily. If they do not make the transfer then a central government intervention is in order. However, if individuals are immobile, an efficient allocation can be achieved by regions that face no incentives to make a transfer.

2.2 Efficiency-Supporting Tax Systems

In order to derive an efficiency-supporting tax system, we must study how taxes affect the locational behavior of firms and individuals. Having done this, we analyze whether a tax system is able to support locational efficiency without violating the need to finance the efficient levels of local public services.

2.2.1 Private Behavior

The structure of the model is identical to that described in Section 2.1. All individuals are endowed with one unit of labor, which is inelastically supplied in their region of residence. Hence, as a first income component, they receive a wage rate w_i. Aside from the wage income, individuals additionally receive a nonlabor income component Y that is independent of the region in which they reside; Y consists of profit shares of firms and of land rents. Furthermore, each region collects a direct tax τ_i^N from its residents. The entire net income is used for consuming private goods:

$$x_i = w_i + Y - \tau_i^N. \tag{2.13}$$

Individuals have only one choice problem. They choose a region as their residence if they can attain at least the utility level they get in some other region. Hence, a migration equilibrium is characterized by

$$U(x_i, z_i) = U(x_j, z_j) \quad \forall\, i, j,\ i \neq j. \tag{2.14}$$

Firms have to make two decisions. They must choose their location and they must make production decisions. Although both decisions are made simultaneously, we begin by studying the locational choice. Let π^i denote the after-tax profit of a firm locating in region i. Since firms decide for a location so as to maximize profits, a locational equilibrium is achieved if firms attain the same after-tax profit in all regions, that is,

$$\pi^i = \pi^j \quad \forall\, i, j,\; i \neq j. \tag{2.15}$$

In equilibrium, M_i mobile firms choose region i as their location, and a representative firm locating in i makes the following after-tax profit:

$$\pi^i = F(l_i, n_i, g_i) - \rho_i l_i - w_i n_i - \tau_i^M, \tag{2.16}$$

where ρ_i and w_i are the prevailing factor prices of land and labor in the region, and τ_i^M denotes a location-dependent tax on firms. Let us further suppose that firms are price takers and that they maximize their profits by choosing l_i and n_i. Expressing again partial derivatives by subindices, the use of private production factors follows the rules

$$F_l^i = \rho_i, \tag{2.17}$$

$$F_n^i = w_i. \tag{2.18}$$

Moreover, an equilibrium in the local market for land requires

$$L_i = M_i l_i, \tag{2.19}$$

and the number of mobile workers must be equally divided among firms locating in the region so as to clear the local labor market,

$$N_i = M_i n_i. \tag{2.20}$$

Let us now describe the government sector. The local government must cover the costs of supplying public services by its tax revenues. Aside from levying taxes on mobile households and firms, the local government can collect a proportional tax t_i on local land rents. The budget constraint of the local government reads as

$$N_i \tau_i^N + M_i \tau_i^M + t_i \rho_i L_i = C^i(z_i, N_i) + H^i(g_i, M_i). \tag{2.21}$$

Finally, the material balance sheet of the entire federal state is characterized by the equalization of the nonlabor income of all households and the sum of profits and net land rents in all regions. Let N again stand for the entire number of households in the federal state, M for the entire number of firms, and I for the number of regions. Then

$$NY = \sum_{j=1}^{I} M_j \pi_j + \sum_{j=1}^{I} (1 - t_j) \rho_j L_j. \tag{2.22}$$

2.2.2 Efficient Taxation

The determination of an efficiency-supporting tax system depends crucially on whether there are congestion costs in the provision of local public services and how the number of firms and individuals affects these costs. In order to analyze whether migration decisions sustain the efficient locational pattern of individuals, we must investigate the private budget constraint (2.13). For this purpose, we insert (2.18) for w_i into (2.13) and take into account that individuals receive the same nonlabor income no matter where they live:

$$F_n^i - x_i - \tau_i^N = -Y = F_n^j - x_j - \tau_j^N \quad \forall \ i, j, \ i \neq j. \tag{2.23}$$

Comparing (2.23) with the first-order condition of the efficient locational pattern of individuals (2.10) reveals the necessary condition for the efficient taxation of mobile households:

$$\tau_i^N - C_N^i = \tau_j^N - C_N^j \quad \forall \ i, j, \ i \neq j; \tag{2.24}$$

that is, the difference between location-based taxes and marginal congestion costs must be identical across regions in order to avoid fiscal externalities. As (2.24) makes clear, if each local government chooses the marginal-cost pricing regime $\tau_i^N = C_N^i$, then the efficient allocation of individuals across regions is achieved.

Let us next turn to the efficient taxation of mobile firms. If we insert (2.17) for ρ_i and (2.18) for w_i into (2.16), and then substitute (2.16) into (2.15), we obtain

$$F^i - l_i F_l^i - n_i F_n^i - \tau_i^M = F^j - l_j F_l^j - n_j F_n^j - \tau_j^M \quad \forall \ i, j, \ i \neq j. \tag{2.25}$$

By comparing (2.25) with the first-order condition of the efficient locational pattern of firms (2.11), we can derive the necessary condition for the efficient taxation of firms:

$$\tau_i^M - H_M^i = \tau_j^M - H_M^j \quad \forall \ i, j, \ i \neq j; \tag{2.26}$$

that is, the difference between location-based taxes and marginal congestion costs must be equalized across regions. Again, this condition is satisfied for the benchmark case in which each region chooses the marginal-cost pricing rule $\tau_i^M = H_M^i$.

However, if marginal-cost pricing is used, then the tax revenues generated by the location-based taxes on individuals and firms do not suffice to balance the budget of local governments if average costs of supplying local public goods and factors exceed marginal costs – that is, if $C^i(z_i, N_i) + H^i(g_i, M_i) > N_i C_N^i + M_i H_M^i = N_i \tau_i^N + M_i \tau_i^M$. Even if regions set direct taxes on individuals and firms above marginal congestion costs – yet still satisfying the necessary conditions (2.24) and (2.26) – location-based taxes alone do not allow regions to finance the efficient levels of local public goods and factors. Regions must employ an additional undistortive tax on land in order to finance the efficient amount of local public services without distorting the locational decisions of individuals and firms. Note again that the efficient allocation requires an interregional transfer of resources as derived in Section 2.1. Because individuals own land in all regions, the appropriate choice of taxes on land rents serves as an indirect way of implementing the efficient interregional transfer. Of course, if regions had no land taxes available, then a system of direct interregional transfers would also allow regions to sustain the efficient allocation. However, there is some doubt whether purely self-interested regions would voluntarily choose direct interregional transfers, owing to the associated loss of regional resources. The incentive of regions to perform transfers depends decisively on the possibility of controlling immigration by that measure. We shall return to this problem in Chapters 6 and 7.

The results derived so far can be summarized in

Proposition 2.3. *Suppose that individuals and firms are mobile and cause congestion costs at their location. Then the (unique) efficient allocation can be achieved by a tax system consisting of* (a) *location-based taxes on mobile individuals and firms and* (b) *an undistortive land tax that enables the efficient interregional transfer of resources.*

If there are no congestion costs in the provision of public services, $C_N^i = H_M^i = 0$, then there is no need to collect location-based taxes. The availability of land taxes is sufficient to achieve the efficient allocation since it provides an undistortive tax revenue source and, in addition, provides a method to implement the efficient interregional transfer by an export of land taxes (see also Krelove 1992).

Because mobility of individuals is rather low in some federations like the EU, as emphasized in Section 1.1, it is of equal interest to explore the design of a complete tax instrument set if individuals are immobile. Of course, the direct tax on individuals then becomes a lump-sum tax. In this case, the tax on firms can be used to ensure the efficient allocation of firms across regions satisfying (2.26), and the lump-sum tax can be used to divide the resources between the private and the public sector in each region such that the efficient amount of local public goods and factors can be financed. However, if individuals are immobile then the efficient allocation is not unique. As explained in Section 2.1, although the allocation of firms and the supply of local public factors is unique for the well-behaved problem we consider, the efficient supply of local public goods depends on the desired interregional welfare distribution. The tax system consisting of location-based firm taxes and lump-sum taxes allows us to achieve only one particular efficient allocation. If another efficient allocation is to be achieved with a different interregional distribution of utility levels, then an interregional transfer of resources is necessary. This can be obtained either by a direct transfer instrument like an interregional aid program or by a tax on land. The latter is true if we further assume that all individuals living in the federal state are equally endowed with land in all regions.

We can summarize the results of this discussion in

Proposition 2.4. *If individuals are immobile, then a tax system consisting of a location-based firm tax and an undistortive tax on individuals enables one particular efficient allocation, which consists of the efficient locational pattern of firms, the efficient supply of local public factors, and a particular efficient supply of local public goods. Any other efficient allocation requires an instrument that effects an interregional transfer of resources.*

Let us finally consider the realistic case in which the instrument set of local governments does not include the lump-sum tax on immobile individuals. However, it is quite conceivable that regions are allowed to transfer resources to other regions.[5] Whether regions have any incentive to make such transfers is another matter, which will be studied in subsequent chapters. If regions can collect only a firm tax and can make a transfer (land tax or direct transfer), then it is impossible to choose the level of the private good in one region i independently of the amount of private goods in other regions. As DePater and Myers (1994) have shown, this implies that firm taxes and a transfer instrument are insufficient to support all first-best allocations; only one particular first-best allocation can be achieved for one particular welfare distribution across regions. In general, the constrained efficient allocation without lump-sum taxes does not coincide with the first-best allocation. This conclusion will have important implications if a central government tries to internalize the externalities caused by interregional tax competition, as studied in Section 4.1.

---

[5] Take for example Germany, where interregional transfers among the *Bundesländer* are part of the *Länderfinanzausgleich*.

CHAPTER 3

Perfect Interregional Competition

In Chapter 2 we derived a complete set of tax instruments, one that allows regions to achieve the efficient allocation. However, we have not yet discussed how regions choose their tax instruments and how they supply local public goods and factors. In other words, it is an open question whether decentralized government decisions result in an efficient allocation. To answer this question, the behavior of regional decision makers must be explained. Moreover, in order to derive a corrective central government intervention, it is necessary to know the behavior of regional governments. If decentralized tax and expenditure decisions lead to an inefficient allocation, the center must know the behavior of regional policy makers. Otherwise, the intervention cannot be successful.

By describing the behavior of small regions, this chapter starts with possible explanations of how regional governments choose their policy measures. There is perfect interregional competition for mobile individuals and mobile firms. Such a starting point seems reasonable insofar as no role is played by the strategic behavior of individual regions; policy measures performed by one region cannot affect other regions. This provides a strong parallel to decentralized decisions of households and firms under conditions of perfect competition. Following the first theorem of welfare economics, household and firm decisions result in an efficient allocation under these conditions. Therefore, the question arises as to whether this conclusion can be extended to decentralized government decisions if regions face similar conditions. Perfect competition among private households and firms means that individual decision makers take market prices as given. Similarly, perfect interregional competition means that individual regions cannot noticeably influence the utility level of mobile households and the profit level of mobile firms. From the viewpoint of a single region, these interregional variables are exogenously given.

Within this environment, we intend to pursue three basic analytical objectives. We will first demonstrate that regional governments also have incentives to avoid any allocative distortions, provided that the following conditions are satisfied: (a) regions must have an efficiency-supporting tax instrument set available, including (direct) location-based taxes on mobile households and mobile firms to internalize their crowding costs and an undistortive tax on land (rents) to enable the efficient interregional transfer of resources; and (b) regional governments face the correct incentives to choose the efficient allocation only if they maximize the after-tax rent to immobile local factors like land. Second, we show that conditions of perfect interregional competition take away all incentives of local governments to redistribute income between owners of immobile and mobile factors of production. Third, we derive the distortions caused by regional government decisions when regions face constraints in the tax instrument set. Since these problems of a constrained tax instrument set are at the core of the analysis and offer some new insights, a few further words are in order.[1]

Like Hoyt (1991a), Krelove (1993), and Wilson (1997), we first study the distortions that must be expected if regions cannot tax mobile households upon residence. This is a typical institutional restriction in many federal states at the local level. As a consequence, regions cannot directly internalize the marginal crowding costs associated with their supply of local public goods. Moreover, in this chapter we discuss the distortions that occur when regions cannot tax mobile firms upon location and hence cannot internalize the congestion costs firms create at their location. This restriction, too, is observable in many federal states where local governments are not able to levy a firm tax, with profits of local firms being the single tax base. A similar problem arises if local firms create pollution externalities at their location and local governments are restricted to handling environmental issues with direct controls and so cannot levy emission taxes. This restriction characterizes the environmental policy in many states (see Krumm and Wellisch 1994).

Finally, we assume that regions have no undistortive tax on land available. This last scenario is a typical second-best taxation problem. A complete tax system on the local level requires an unrestricted tax access to land rents. However, like lump-sum taxes to finance public goods in a unitary state, a massive taxation of land rents involves distributional problems. This might be the basic reason why private property like land is legally protected against confiscatory taxation in almost all countries of the EU (as in Germany by its Constitution). As a consequence, local public goods and factors must be financed by distortionary taxes on mobile households and firms. Because the kinds of distortions caused by these location-based taxes are specific to the local level and cannot be found in a unitary state, it is worth developing a second-best theory of local government policy. The resulting behavioral rules for local governments can

---

[1] The study by Arnott and Grieson (1981) can be seen as a predecessor of this analysis since they also derive the conditions for an optimal state or local government policy. However, in contrast to the analysis in the following sections, Arnott and Grieson do not model locational choices of households and firms.

be interpreted as modified Ramsey (1927) taxation rules. They require balancing locational distortions caused by location-based taxes relative to their impact on land rents among these taxes. This rule also applies to the provision of local public factors; it requires balancing the distortion relative to the impact of local public factors on the land rent against the relative distortions caused by location-based taxes. Interestingly, the provision of local public goods is not distorted in such a situation if all individuals are mobile. However, the expression "second-best theory" of local government policy should not be taken too literally. As Krelove (1993) explains, the allocation is in fact a third-best allocation if there are no undistortive land taxes available. A central government that faces the same constraints in the tax instrument set can increase welfare of all individuals.

There exist numerous contributions to the literature analyzing competition among small regions. Many of them concentrate on the mobility of households across regions (see Wildasin 1986 and the references therein). Following Chapter 2, we deviate from this assumption by assuming that individuals as well as firms are mobile (see also Wilson 1995; Braid 1996). This deviation gives local governments access to a second location-based and potentially distorting tax (a firm tax aside from a tax on mobile households) and therefore enables us to derive a second-best taxation structure for the local level.

In order to analyze the efficiency properties of decentralized government decisions, Chapter 3 is organized as follows. Section 3.1 assumes that regions have a complete tax instrument set available to achieve the efficient allocation. It shows that perfect interregional competition provides local governments with the correct incentives to choose the efficient allocation in their own interest. It also makes clear that local governments have no incentive to redistribute income from the owners of mobile factors of production to the owners of immobile factors. Section 3.2 tries to develop a simple second-best theory of local government policy by studying the behavior of local governments when they have only an incomplete tax instrument set available. Finally, the appendix in Section 3.3 contains some important proofs of the results reported in Sections 3.1 and 3.2.

3.1   Fiscal Decentralization with a Complete Tax Instrument Set

Let us again consider a federal state consisting of many small regions, which can be interpreted as communities. It is sufficient to concentrate on a single region i in order to discuss the efficiency properties of local government decisions. The economy and each individual region have the same structure as in Section 2.2. Since local governments must take locational responses into consideration, let us first briefly recall the decisions of private households and firms.

3.1.1 Private Behavior

There is one type of household living in each region. It is composed of N_i identical and perfectly mobile workers. A household is represented by the utility function $U^i \equiv U(x_i, z_i)$, where x_i denotes consumption of the private numeraire good and z_i the local public good jointly consumed by all regional residents.

Each individual receives a wage income w_i in response to the individual's inelastic supply of one unit of labor and a region-independent nonlabor income Y and must pay a residence-based tax τ_i^N, so that the budget constraint becomes

$$x_i = w_i + Y - \tau_i^N. \tag{3.1}$$

Mobile households choose a region as their residence only if they can attain their reservation utility level $\bar{u}$ there. Hence, a migration equilibrium is characterized by

$$U(x_i, z_i) = \bar{u}. \tag{3.2}$$

In the federal state, there is an exogenously given large number of identical mobile firms. All firms produce the private numeraire good with the same production technology $F^i \equiv F(l_i, n_i, g_i)$, where l_i and n_i stand for the amount of the private factors (land and labor) used by a firm locating in i, and g_i denotes the local public factor provided by region i. In equilibrium, M_i mobile firms choose region i as their location, and a representative firm locating in i makes the following after-tax profit:

$$\pi_i = F(l_i, n_i, g_i) - \rho_i l_i - w_i n_i - \tau_i^M, \tag{3.3}$$

where ρ_i and w_i are the prevailing factor prices of land and labor in the region, and τ_i^M denotes a location-dependent tax on firms. A locational equilibrium is achieved if firms attain the same after-tax profit $\bar{\pi}$ in all regions – that is, if

$$\pi_i = \bar{\pi}. \tag{3.4}$$

Firms are price takers and choose the optimal land and labor employment according to the following rules:

$$F_l^i = \rho_i, \tag{3.5}$$

$$F_n^i = w_i. \tag{3.6}$$

An equilibrium in the local market for land and labor requires that

$$L_i = M_i l_i \tag{3.7}$$

and

$$N_i = M_i n_i, \tag{3.8}$$

respectively.

The local government must finance public services by its tax revenues. Aside from levying taxes on mobile households and firms, the local government can collect a proportional tax t_i on local land rents. Its budget constraint thus becomes

$$N_i \tau_i^N + M_i \tau_i^M + t_i \rho_i L_i = C^i(z_i, N_i) + H^i(g_i, M_i). \tag{3.9}$$

Let us assume that marginal-cost pricing of local governments does not suffice to balance the budget; that is, marginal congestion costs of supplying public services are smaller than average costs, $C_N^i < C^i/N_i$, $H_M^i < H^i/M_i$. Finally, the material balance sheet of the entire federal state is expressed by equalizing the nonlabor income of all households and the sum of after-tax profits and net land rents in all regions. Let N again stand for the entire number of households in the federal state, M for the entire number of firms, and I for the number of regions. Then we have

$$NY = M\bar{\pi} + \sum_{j=1}^{I}(1 - t_j)\rho_j L_j. \tag{3.10}$$

Perfect competition among regions is expressed by the fact that regions can influence neither the equilibrium utility level $\bar{u}$ of mobile households nor the equilibrium profit level $\bar{\pi}$ of mobile firms.

Let us, for convenience, reconsider the variables that have been introduced: ρ_i and w_i are endogenous prices; l_i, M_i, n_i, N_i, and x_i are endogenous quantities determined in the respective region. The terms t_i, τ_i^N, τ_i^M, g_i, and z_i are parameters of the local government. The variables L_i, Y, $\bar{u}$, and $\bar{\pi}$ are exogenous from the single region's viewpoint, where Y, $\bar{u}$, and $\bar{\pi}$ take on the same values in all regions.

Locational decisions of mobile households and firms cannot be directly controlled by local governments. However, local governments must take into account the responses of N_i and M_i to changes in government policy variables. It is possible to use the two locational equilibrium conditions (3.2) and (3.4) in order to express N_i and M_i as implicit functions of τ_i^N, τ_i^M, z_i, and g_i:

$$G(N_i, M_i, \tau_i^N, \tau_i^M, z_i, g_i) \equiv U\left[F_n\left(\frac{L_i}{M_i}, \frac{N_i}{M_i}, g_i\right) - \tau_i^N + Y, z_i\right] = \bar{u}, \tag{3.11}$$

$$P(N_i, M_i, \tau_i^N, \tau_i^M, z_i, g_i) \equiv F\left(\frac{L_i}{M_i}, \frac{N_i}{M_i}, g_i\right) - F_l\left(\frac{L_i}{M_i}, \frac{N_i}{M_i}, g_i\right)\frac{L_i}{M_i}$$

$$- F_n\left(\frac{L_i}{M_i}, \frac{N_i}{M_i}, g_i\right)\frac{N_i}{M_i} - \tau_i^M = \bar{\pi}, \tag{3.12}$$

where (3.1), (3.3), and (3.5)–(3.8) have been inserted into (3.2) and (3.4) in order to eliminate the endogenous variables x_i, ρ_i, w_i, l_i, and n_i. Since t_i does not appear in (3.11) and (3.12), it follows that N_i and M_i are independent of t_i.

When deriving the behavior of local governments, it is important to know how the marginal productivity of labor, F_n^i, responds to a change in the parameters of the local government. For a given $\bar{u}$, it follows from (3.11) that

$$\frac{dF_n^i}{dt_i} = \frac{dF_n^i}{d\tau_i^M} = \frac{dF_n^i}{dg_i} = 0,$$

$$\frac{dF_n^i}{d\tau_i^N} = 1, \qquad \frac{dF_n^i}{dz_i} = -\frac{U_z^i}{U_x^i}. \tag{3.13}$$

3.1.2   Local Government Behavior

In order to study how the local government chooses its policy variables, we must make a behavioral assumption on behalf of the government. Since the local government cannot influence the utility of households, let us follow the literature and assume that it maximizes the after-tax land rent (see e.g. Brueckner 1983; Wildasin 1986; Wilson 1987a; Krelove 1993). This can be explained by the enormous interest that land owners have in influencing the policies in the individual regions. Hence, the government of jurisdiction i has to solve the following problem:

$$\text{maximize} \quad R_i \equiv L_i \rho_i (1 - t_i) \tag{3.14}$$

by choosing the policy variables $\tau_i^N, \tau_i^M, z_i, g_i$, where

$$L_i \rho_i (1 - t_i) = M_i \left(F^i - \frac{N_i}{M_i} F_n^i - \bar{\pi} \right)$$

$$- C^i(z_i, N_i) - H^i(g_i, M_i) + N_i \tau_i^N. \tag{3.15}$$

The term t_i no longer appears as a control variable of the government because the budget constraint of the local government (3.9) has been inserted for t_i into (3.14). The derivation of (3.15) has also used (3.12).

The first-order conditions of solving this problem become

$$\frac{dR_i}{d\tau_i^N} = (\tau_i^N - C_N^i)\frac{\partial N_i}{\partial \tau_i^N} + (\tau_i^M - H_M^i)\frac{\partial M_i}{\partial \tau_i^N} = 0, \tag{3.16}$$

$$\frac{dR_i}{d\tau_i^M} = (\tau_i^N - C_N^i)\frac{\partial N_i}{\partial \tau_i^M} + (\tau_i^M - H_M^i)\frac{\partial M_i}{\partial \tau_i^M} = 0, \tag{3.17}$$

$$\frac{dR_i}{dz_i} = (\tau_i^N - C_N^i)\frac{\partial N_i}{\partial z_i} + (\tau_i^M - H_M^i)\frac{\partial M_i}{\partial z_i} + N_i \frac{U_z^i}{U_x^i} - C_z^i = 0, \tag{3.18}$$

$$\frac{dR_i}{dg_i} = (\tau_i^N - C_N^i)\frac{\partial N_i}{\partial g_i} + (\tau_i^M - H_M^i)\frac{\partial M_i}{\partial g_i} + M_i F_g^i - H_g^i = 0 \tag{3.19}$$

(see Section 3.3.1 for a detailed derivation). Conditions (3.16) and (3.17) reveal that local governments have incentives to internalize marginal congestion costs by choosing marginal-cost pricing, $\tau_i^N = C_N^i$ and $\tau_i^M = H_M^i$, provided that the matrix consisting of the elements

$$\frac{\partial N_i}{\partial \tau_i^N}, \quad \frac{\partial M_i}{\partial \tau_i^N}, \quad \frac{\partial N_i}{\partial \tau_i^M}, \quad \text{and} \quad \frac{\partial M_i}{\partial \tau_i^M}$$

has full rank. Inserting this preliminary result into (3.18) yields the efficient provision of local public goods, $N_i(U_z^i/U_x^i) = C_z^i$. Condition (3.19) shows that the provision of local public factors also follows the Samuelson condition, $M_i F_g^i = H_g^i$. Hence, we can summarize this result in

Proposition 3.1. *If regions have a complete tax instrument set, and if local governments behave as net land-rent maximizers, then conditions of perfect interregional competition provide local governments with the correct incentives to choose the efficient allocation.*

Individuals are endowed with land in all regions, so there is an interregional transfer of resources. Moreover, the availability of a tax on land rents enables local governments to collect an undistortive tax and to implement the efficient interregional transfer in their own interests. As emphasized in Section 2.2, a system of direct interregional transfers would perfectly substitute the indirect transfer via the land tax and would also sustain the efficient allocation. However, small regions have no incentive to make a direct transfer because they cannot control immigration by that measure.

Before turning to inefficiencies caused by an incomplete instrument set in the next section, let us finally point to another important observation. If local governments have a land tax available then they will tax mobile individuals at marginal congestion costs; they have no incentive to tax them for redistributive purposes. Any attempt to set the tax rate above this level – in order to use the resulting tax revenues to reduce the tax on the land rent – will be answered by emigration of individuals. This drops the regional land rent by more than the additional tax revenues and hence results in a decline of the net land rent. The incentives of regions to redistribute income among mobile and immobile factors (or individuals) will be explored further in Chapters 8–10.

3.2   Fiscal Decentralization with an Incomplete Tax Instrument Set

Let us now consider the distortions caused by decentralized government activities if the tax instrument set is incomplete. There are three sources of an incomplete tax set in the model. Either regions cannot tax mobile households, they cannot tax mobile firms, or they have no undistortive tax on land rents available. Let us consider these cases and the associated distortions in turn.

3.2.1 A Direct Household Tax Is Not Available

The basic purpose of this section is to derive the distortions that occur if regions cannot tax mobile individuals and to explain why local governments decide to choose an inefficient allocation. The absence of a direct household tax often depicts the situation on the local level in federal states. In Germany, for instance, local governments are unable to tax their own residents because direct taxation of households is entirely delegated to the federal government. Neither are there any zoning arrangements that might substitute for a direct taxation of households.

If jurisdictions have no tax on mobile households at their disposal, $\tau_i^N \equiv 0$, then the first-order conditions of solving the government's problem reduce to (3.17)–(3.19). However, they change slightly to

$$\frac{dR_i}{d\tau_i^M} = -C_N^i \frac{\partial N_i}{\partial \tau_i^M} + (\tau_i^M - H_M^i) \frac{\partial M_i}{\partial \tau_i^M} = 0, \tag{3.20}$$

$$\frac{dR_i}{dz_i} = -C_N^i \frac{\partial N_i}{\partial z_i} + (\tau_i^M - H_M^i) \frac{\partial M_i}{\partial z_i} + N_i \frac{U_z^i}{U_x^i} - C_z^i = 0, \tag{3.21}$$

$$\frac{dR_i}{dg_i} = -C_N^i \frac{\partial N_i}{\partial g_i} + (\tau_i^M - H_M^i) \frac{\partial M_i}{\partial g_i} + M_i F_g^i - H_g^i = 0. \tag{3.22}$$

The migration responses $\partial N_i / \partial *$ and $\partial M_i / \partial *$ ($* \in \{\tau_i^M, z_i, g_i\}$) can be derived from the conditions (3.11) and (3.12) and are stated by (A.3.8)–(A.3.13) in Section 3.3.1. Inserting them into (3.20)–(3.22), the following distortions result:

Proposition 3.2. *Suppose that regions cannot tax mobile households upon location, $\tau_i^N \equiv 0$. Then the competitive equilibrium among regions is characterized by the following conditions:*

(i) $\quad \tau_i^M - H_M^i = -C_N^i \dfrac{M_i}{F_{nn}^i} \dfrac{\partial F_n^i}{\partial M_i} = C_N^i \dfrac{l_i F_{nl}^i + n_i F_{nn}^i}{F_{nn}^i},$

(ii) $\quad N_i \dfrac{U_z^i}{U_x^i} - C_z^i = C_N^i \dfrac{M_i}{F_{nn}^i} \dfrac{dF_n^i}{dz_i} = -C_N^i \dfrac{M_i}{F_{nn}^i} \dfrac{U_z^i}{U_x^i},$

(iii) $\quad M_i F_g^i - H_g^i = -C_N^i \dfrac{M_i}{F_{nn}^i} F_{ng}^i.$

Of course, the competitive equilibrium is characterized by an inefficient allocation, as a comparison of (i)–(iii) and (3.17)–(3.19) shows. Regions cannot directly internalize the marginal crowding costs of supplying local public goods by levying a location-based tax on mobile households. Therefore, they are looking for other ways to restrict the inflow of mobile households indirectly. These efforts of local governments result in an inefficient allocation. According to condition (i), regions choose an inefficiently high tax on mobile firms, provided that the marginal productivity of mobile labor rises with an increasing number of mobile firms locating in the region, $\partial F_n^i / \partial M_i > 0$. In this case, the inflow of mobile households can be restricted by repelling mobile firms out of the region. A more direct way to limit the number of mobile residents is to choose an inefficiently low supply of local public goods; this is stated in condition (ii). By doing so, the attractiveness of a location decreases directly in the eyes of mobile individuals. If, finally, the marginal productivity of labor rises with an increased supply of local public factors, $F_{ng}^i > 0$, then, following (iii), regions undersupply public factors relative to the Samuelson condition. The inflow of mobile households can also be restricted by that measure. Incidentally, since all distortions stated by (i)–(iii) depend on C_N^i, it is clear that there are no distortions if there are no marginal congestion costs that must be internalized.

The results derived in this section are similar to the conclusions drawn by Hoyt (1991a), Krelove (1993), and Wilson (1997). If regions have no direct tax on mobile residents, they use their remaining instruments to charge mobile households indirectly for the crowding costs they cause. These attempts lead to distortions. Whereas this is achieved in Hoyt and Krelove by choosing the distortionary property tax, regions in the present study use the firm tax, local public goods, and local public factors for this purpose.

3.2.2   A Direct Firm Tax Is Not Available

Let us now go one step further by assuming that regions cannot tax mobile firms upon location. To concentrate on this problem, we assume that local governments can tax mobile households. Since $\tau_i^M \equiv 0$, only the first-order conditions (3.16), (3.18), and (3.19) describe the solution of the government's problem. These necessary conditions change to

$$\frac{dR_i}{d\tau_i^N} = (\tau_i^N - C_N^i)\frac{\partial N_i}{\partial \tau_i^N} - H_M^i \frac{\partial M_i}{\partial \tau_i^N} = 0, \tag{3.23}$$

$$\frac{dR_i}{dz_i} = (\tau_i^N - C_N^i)\frac{\partial N_i}{\partial z_i} - H_M^i \frac{\partial M_i}{\partial z_i} + N_i\frac{U_z^i}{U_x^i} - C_z^i = 0, \tag{3.24}$$

$$\frac{dR_i}{dg_i} = (\tau_i^N - C_N^i)\frac{\partial N_i}{\partial g_i} - H_M^i \frac{\partial M_i}{\partial g_i} + M_i F_g^i - H_g^i = 0. \tag{3.25}$$

Inserting the migration responses $\partial N_i/\partial *$ and $\partial M_i/\partial *$ $(* \in \{\tau_i^N, z_i, g_i\})$ – which are given by (A.3.6), (A.3.7), and (A.3.10)–(A.3.13) in Section 3.3.1 – into (3.23)–(3.25) allows us to state

Proposition 3.3.   *Suppose that regions cannot tax mobile firms, $\tau_i^M \equiv 0$. Then the competitive interregional equilibrium is characterized by the following necessary conditions:*

(i) $\tau_i^N - C_N^i = -H_M^i \dfrac{M_i}{\xi} \dfrac{\partial \pi_i}{\partial N_i} = H_M^i \dfrac{l_i F_{nl}^i + n_i F_{nn}^i}{\xi},$

(ii) $N_i \dfrac{U_z^i}{U_x^i} - C_z^i = 0,$

(iii) $M_i F_g^i - H_g^i = -H_M^i \dfrac{M_i}{\xi} \dfrac{\partial \pi_i}{\partial g_i} = -H_M^i \dfrac{M_i(F_g^i - n_i F_{ng}^i - l_i F_{lg}^i)}{\xi},$

where $\xi \equiv l_i^2 F_{ll}^i + n_i^2 F_{nn}^i + 2 l_i n_i F_{ln}^i < 0$ owing to strict concavity of F^i with respect to l_i and n_i.

As could be expected, the competitive equilibrium is once again characterized by an inefficient allocation. Regions cannot directly internalize the marginal crowding costs of providing local public factors by collecting a location-based tax on mobile firms. Therefore, they use the remaining instruments to restrict the location of mobile firms indirectly. These attempts lead to distortions. Following condition (i), local governments tax mobile households too much if the profit of firms decreases with a decreasing number of mobile local workers, $\partial \pi_i/\partial N_i > 0$. The intuition for this behavior is straightforward. Firms avoid locating in a region if the profit they can attain decreases. If this can be achieved indirectly by displacing households, local governments will do so by choosing a high residence-based household tax. According to condition (ii), regions have incentives to provide local public goods in accordance with the Samuelson rule. Regions have no reason to distort the provision of local public goods, since they can achieve their objective entirely by using the household tax τ_i^N. A suboptimally low provision of z_i has the same effects on workers' incentives to locate in the region – and therefore on firms' profits – as an inefficiently high tax on workers. Regions thus rely completely on τ_i^N for influencing firms' incentives to locate in the region.

However, the supply of local public factors is distorted. If the profit of local firms increases with a higher provision of local public factors, $\partial \pi_i/\partial g_i > 0$, then regions restrict the inflow of mobile firms by undersupplying local public factors relative to the Samuelson rule.

A comparison of the results derived in Sections 3.2.1 and 3.2.2 reveals that there is an important difference between the provision of local public goods and factors. If local governments have no direct household tax, they undersupply local public factors in order to restrict the inflow of households. However, if no firm tax is available, then local public goods are provided in line with the Samuelson condition and are not used to limit the inflow of mobile firms. The basic reason for this difference is that local public factors directly influence the marginal product of labor whereas local public goods affect the profit of mobile firms only via their impact on the number of local workers. Hence local public factors can be used directly to limit the inflow of households, whereas local public goods could be used only indirectly for repelling firms out of the region. This task is therefore delegated entirely to the residence-based tax on workers.

3.2.3   An Undistortive Tax Is Not Available

Let us finally suppose that regions have no undistortive tax at their disposal, $t_i \equiv 0$. This situation resembles very much the second-best problem in a closed economy, when public funds cannot be financed by lump-sum taxes. Regions must finance local public goods and factors entirely by taxes on mobile households and firms, taxes that potentially distort locational choices. The local government can choose three instruments freely. Let us assume that it chooses τ_i^N, z_i, and g_i, and that τ_i^M adjusts endogenously for budget-clearing reasons. It can be shown, however, that all results would remain intact if regions chose τ_i^M instead of τ_i^N and that the latter tax would adapt endogenously in order to balance the government's budget.

The local government has to solve the following problem:

$$\text{maximize } R_i \equiv L_i \rho_i \tag{3.26}$$

by choosing τ_i^N, z_i, g_i, where

$$L_i \rho_i = M_i \left(F^i - \frac{N_i}{M_i} F_n^i - \bar{\pi} \right) - C^i(z_i, N_i) - H^i(g_i, M_i) + N_i \tau_i^N. \tag{3.27}$$

The first-order conditions for solving this problem with respect to τ_i^N, z_i, and g_i are once again stated by (3.16), (3.18), and (3.19) as in Section 3.1. However, the locational responses $\partial N_i / \partial *$ and $\partial M_i / \partial *$ ($* \in \{\tau_i^N, z_i, g_i\}$) differ from the responses described in Section 3.1 and used in Sections 3.1 and 3.2, since τ_i^M now adjusts endogenously in order to balance the government's budget. This influences the number of mobile households and firms locating in the region. Hence, the locational responses are now derived from the two locational equilibrium conditions

$$G(N_i, M_i, \tau_i^N, z_i, g_i) \equiv U\left[F_n\left(\frac{L_i}{M_i}, \frac{N_i}{M_i}, g_i\right) - \tau_i^N + Y, z_i\right] = \bar{u}, \qquad (3.28)$$

$$Q(N_i, M_i, \tau_i^N, z_i, g_i) \equiv F\left(\frac{L_i}{M_i}, \frac{N_i}{M_i}, g_i\right) - F_l\left(\frac{L_i}{M_i}, \frac{N_i}{M_i}, g_i\right)\frac{L_i}{M_i}$$

$$- F_n\left(\frac{L_i}{M_i}, \frac{N_i}{M_i}, g_i\right)\frac{N_i}{M_i} - \frac{C^i(N_i, z_i)}{M_i}$$

$$- \frac{H^i(M_i, g_i)}{M_i} + \frac{N_i\tau_i^N}{M_i} = \bar{\pi}. \qquad (3.29)$$

Condition (3.28) simply restates (3.11). Therefore, the responses of the marginal productivity of labor, F_n^i, to changes in τ_i^N, z_i, and g_i are further given by (3.13). Condition (3.29) follows from (3.12) by inserting the government's budget restriction (3.9) (with $t_i \equiv 0$) for τ_i^M. The locational responses derived from (3.28) and (3.29) are stated by (A.3.17)–(A.3.22) in Section 3.3.2. Inserting (A.3.17)–(A.3.22) into the first-order conditions (3.16), (3.18), and (3.19) allows us to state

Proposition 3.4. *Suppose that regions have no undistortive tax available,* $t_i \equiv 0$. *Then the competitive equilibrium is characterized by the following conditions:*

(i) $\dfrac{\tau_i^N - C_N^i}{F_{ln}^i} = \dfrac{\tau_i^M - H_M^i}{-(l_i F_{ll}^i + n_i F_{nl}^i)},$

(ii) $N_i \dfrac{U_z^i}{U_x^i} = C_z^i,$

(iii) $\dfrac{(\tau_i^N - C_N^i)M_i}{F_{ln}^i} = \dfrac{M_i F_g^i - H_g^i}{F_{lg}^i}.$

To interpret the behavioral rules in Proposition 3.4, let us assume that the cross partial derivatives of the production function are positive, $F_{nl}^i > 0$, and that own effects dominate cross effects, $l_i F_{ll}^i + n_i F_{nl}^i < 0$. Because we have assumed that marginal congestion costs of supplying public services are lower than average costs, $C_N^i < C^i/N_i$ and $H_M^i < H^i/M_i$, condition (i) implies that both tax rates must exceed marginal crowding costs in order to balance the government's budget. Interpreting the excess of a tax over marginal crowding costs as its distortionary part, (i) can be regarded as an optimal taxation rule if no land taxes are available. Recall that the local government maximizes the land rent.

The denominator on the left side of (i) reflects the change in the land rent due to a change in the number of mobile households, while the denominator on the right side is the impact on the land rent of a changed number of mobile firms. Since the household tax directly influences the number of mobile residents and the firm tax the number of mobile firms, (i) states that an optimal tax structure is achieved if the distortion caused by a tax relative to its induced impact on the land rent is equalized among taxes. This is a modified Ramsey taxation rule for distortionary taxes on the local level. The ordinary Ramsey rule requires that we equate the distortions caused by taxes relative to their induced change in tax revenues among taxes. On the local level, regions balance the distortions relative to the impact of the taxes on land rents among taxes. Whereas the traditional second-best taxation theory models distortionary effects of taxation on labor supply, saving, and consumption decisions, the present framework explains substitution effects through locational responses of firms and households.

The land rent is influenced not only by the number of households and firms locating in the jurisdiction; it is also directly affected by the provision of local public factors. As a general optimal policy rule, the local government tries to balance the distortions of those instruments that directly affect the land rent relative to the induced impact on the land rent. Therefore, following condition (iii), the distortion caused by an inefficiently low supply of local public factors (relative to the Samuelson rule), measured in terms of the associated change in the land rent as expressed by the denominator on the right side, must be equal to the relative distortion caused by taxes on the left side.

However, according to (ii), local governments have no incentive to distort the provision of local public goods, since such a distortion would influence the local land rent in the same way as the household tax and this tax is already set optimally. Balancing the trade-off between the distortion and the impact on the land rent is entirely delegated to the residence-based tax on individuals. The novel insight that Proposition 3.4 offers is that the decentralizing provision of public goods is able to reveal the preferences of mobile households for public goods (Tiebout 1956) and that local governments internalize them correctly if the tax instrument set is complete (Wildasin 1986). In particular, it states that local governments have incentives to internalize the preferences of mobile households in a socially efficient way even if they must rely on distortionary taxes. This result holds regardless of whether or not local governments provide local public factors. The important condition for this conclusion to hold is that regions must have a second revenue source aside from the residence-based tax on mobile households.

As a final remark, the analysis in this section confirms the result derived by Krelove (1993) that local governments do not achieve a constrained efficient allocation if they are lacking a complete tax instrument set. Take, for example, the case in which there is no undistortive land tax available (as analyzed in this section), and suppose that all regions are identical. Clearly, a first-best allocation can be achieved by a fully informed central government, since uniformly collected location-based taxes do not distort the allocation and can be set such that the efficient supply of local public goods and factors may be financed. However, Proposition 3.4 states that regions undersupply local public factors. Although regions choose the efficient allocation in their own interest if they have a complete tax instrument set, there is scope for an efficiency-enhancing intervention if one tax instrument is not available. For the more general case with different regions, this observation suggests that the optimal behavioral rules stated in Proposition 3.4 are in fact third-best rather than second-best policy rules.

3.3   Appendix

3.3.1   First-Order Conditions and Migration Responses

Let us first derive the necessary conditions (3.16)–(3.19). The optimal choice of τ_i^N will be explained in detail. The remaining first-order conditions (3.17)–(3.19) can be derived analogously. Inserting (3.15) into (3.14) and differentiating with respect to τ_i^N, it follows (with the help of the envelope theorem) as a necessary condition that

$$
\frac{dR_i}{d\tau_i^N} = -C_N^i \frac{\partial N_i}{\partial \tau_i^N} - H_M^i \frac{\partial M_i}{\partial \tau_i^N} + \tau_i^N \frac{\partial N_i}{\partial \tau_i^N} + N_i
$$

$$
+ \frac{\partial M_i}{\partial \tau_i^N} \left(F^i - \frac{N_i}{M_i} F_n^i - \bar{\pi} \right)
$$

$$
- M_i \left(F_l^i \frac{L_i}{M_i^2} \frac{\partial M_i}{\partial \tau_i^N} + \frac{N_i}{M_i} \frac{dF_n^i}{d\tau_i^N} \right) = 0. \tag{A.3.1}
$$

Now, substitute (3.5)–(3.8) into (3.3) and then (3.3) into (3.4). It follows that $F^i - n_i F_n^i - \bar{\pi} = l_i F_l^i + \tau_i^M$. Furthermore, (3.13) yields $dF_n^i/d\tau_i^N = 1$. Inserting both expressions into (A.3.1) and collecting terms yields the necessary condition (3.16).

We now prove that the matrix

$$
\begin{pmatrix}
\dfrac{\partial N_i}{\partial \tau_i^N} & \dfrac{\partial M_i}{\partial \tau_i^N} \\[3mm]
\dfrac{\partial N_i}{\partial \tau_i^M} & \dfrac{\partial M_i}{\partial \tau_i^M}
\end{pmatrix} \tag{A.3.2}
$$

has full rank. The migration responses $\partial N_i/\partial *$ and $\partial M_i/\partial *$ ($* \in \{\tau_i^N, \tau_i^M\}$) can be derived from the conditions (3.11) and (3.12). We also need the migration responses for $* \in \{z_i, g_i\}$, so all responses are calculated. Total differentiation of (3.11) and (3.12) yields, in matrix form,

$$
\begin{pmatrix} G_N & G_M \\ P_N & P_M \end{pmatrix} \begin{pmatrix} dN_i \\ dM_i \end{pmatrix}
$$

$$
= \begin{pmatrix} -G_{\tau N} & -G_{\tau M} & -G_z & -G_g \\ -P_{\tau N} & -P_{\tau M} & -P_z & -P_g \end{pmatrix} \begin{pmatrix} d\tau_i^N \\ d\tau_i^M \\ dz_i \\ dg_i \end{pmatrix}, \tag{A.3.3}
$$

with

$$
G_N = U_x^i \frac{F_{nn}^i}{M_i}, \qquad G_M = -U_x^i \left(\frac{L_i}{M_i^2} F_{ln}^i + \frac{N_i}{M_i^2} F_{nn}^i \right),
$$

$$
P_N = -\frac{L_i}{M_i^2} F_{ln}^i - \frac{N_i}{M_i^2} F_{nn}^i, \qquad P_M = \frac{L_i^2}{M_i^3} F_{ll}^i + 2 \frac{N_i L_i}{M_i^3} F_{ln}^i + \frac{N_i^2}{M_i^3} F_{nn}^i,
$$

$$
G_{\tau N} = -U_x^i, \quad G_{\tau M}^i = 0, \quad G_z = U_z^i, \quad G_g = U_x^i F_{ng}^i,
$$

$$
P_{\tau N} = 0, \quad P_{\tau M} = -1, \quad P_z = 0,
$$

$$
P_g = F_g^i - \frac{L_i}{M_i} F_{lg}^i - \frac{N_i}{M_i} F_{ng}^i. \tag{A.3.4}
$$

With A denoting the 2×2 matrix on the left side of (A.3.3), it follows that

$$
|A| = U_x^i \frac{L_i^2}{M_i^4} [F_{nn}^i F_{ll}^i - (F_{nl}^i)^2]. \tag{A.3.5}
$$

The determinant $|A|$ is positive owing to strict concavity of F^i with respect to l_i and n_i. In the following analysis, we will use the abbreviation

$$
a \equiv \frac{U_x^i}{M_i |A|}.
$$

Solving (A.3.3) with the help of Cramer's rule and making use of (A.3.4) yields

$$
\frac{\partial N_i}{\partial \tau_i^N} = a[l_i^2 F_{ll}^i + 2l_i n_i F_{ln}^i + n_i^2 F_{nn}^i] < 0, \tag{A.3.6}
$$

$$
\frac{\partial M_i}{\partial \tau_i^N} = a[l_i F_{nl}^i + n_i F_{nn}^i], \tag{A.3.7}
$$

$$
\frac{\partial N_i}{\partial \tau_i^M} = a[l_i F_{nl}^i + n_i F_{nn}^i] = \frac{\partial M_i}{\partial \tau_i^N}, \tag{A.3.8}
$$

$$\frac{\partial M_i}{\partial \tau_i^M} = a F_{nn}^i < 0, \tag{A.3.9}$$

$$\frac{\partial N_i}{\partial g_i} = -a l_i F_{ng}^i [l_i F_{ll}^i + n_i F_{ln}^i]$$
$$\qquad\qquad - a[F_g^i - l_i F_{lg}^i][l_i F_{nl}^i + n_i F_{nn}^i], \tag{A.3.10}$$

$$\frac{\partial M_i}{\partial g_i} = -a[F_{nn}^i(F_g^i - l_i F_{lg}^i) + l_i F_{ln}^i F_{ng}^i], \tag{A.3.11}$$

$$\frac{\partial N_i}{\partial z_i} = -\frac{U_z^i}{U_x^i} a[l_i^2 F_{ll}^i + 2n_i l_i F_{ln}^i + n_i^2 F_{nn}^i]$$
$$\qquad = -\frac{U_z^i}{U_x^i} \frac{\partial N_i}{\partial \tau_i^N} > 0, \tag{A.3.12}$$

$$\frac{\partial M_i}{\partial z_i} = -\frac{U_z^i}{U_x^i} a[n_i F_{nn}^i + l_i F_{ln}^i] = -\frac{U_z^i}{U_x^i} \frac{\partial M_i}{\partial \tau_i^N}. \tag{A.3.13}$$

Inserting the migration responses (A.3.6)–(A.3.9) into the matrix (A.3.2) gives

$$\det \begin{pmatrix} \dfrac{\partial N_i}{\partial \tau_i^N} & \dfrac{\partial M_i}{\partial \tau_i^N} \\[2ex] \dfrac{\partial N_i}{\partial \tau_i^M} & \dfrac{\partial M_i}{\partial \tau_i^M} \end{pmatrix} = a M_i > 0. \tag{A.3.14}$$

Therefore, the matrix (A.3.2) has full rank.

3.3.2   Distortionary Taxation

In the absence of a land-rent tax, the migration responses $\partial N_i/\partial *$ and $\partial M_i/\partial *$ ($* \in \{\tau_i^N, z_i, g_i\}$) – set out in the first-order conditions (3.16), (3.18), and (3.19) – can be derived by implicitly differentiating the two-equation system (3.28) and (3.29). Note that τ_i^M is assumed to adapt endogenously for budget-clearing purposes. Since τ_i^M does not appear in (3.28), the derivations G_* ($* \in \{N, M, \tau^N, z, g\}$) set out in (A.3.4) are still valid. Differentiating the modified locational equilibrium conditions of firms (3.29) yields

$$Q_N = -\frac{L_i}{M_i^2} F_{ln}^i - \frac{N_i}{M_i^2} F_{nn}^i - \frac{C_N^i - \tau_i^N}{M_i},$$

$$Q_M = \frac{L_i^2}{M_i^3} F_{ll}^i + 2\frac{N_i L_i}{M_i^3} F_{ln}^i + \frac{N_i^2}{M_i^3} F_{nn}^i - \frac{H_M^i - \tau_i^M}{M_i},$$

$$Q_{\tau^N} = \frac{N_i}{M_i}, \qquad Q_z = -\frac{C_z^i}{M_i},$$

$$Q_g = F_g^i - \frac{L_i}{M_i} F_{lg}^i - \frac{N_i}{M_i} F_{ng}^i - \frac{H_g^i}{M_i}. \tag{A.3.15}$$

Next, substituting Q_* for P_* ($* \in \{N, M, \tau^N, z, g\}$) into (A.3.3) and recalling that the local government has no freedom to choose the firm tax, $d\tau_i^M \equiv 0$, we have

$$\begin{pmatrix} G_N & G_M \\ Q_N & Q_M \end{pmatrix} \begin{pmatrix} dN_i \\ dM_i \end{pmatrix} = \begin{pmatrix} -G_{\tau^N} & -G_z & -G_g \\ -Q_{\tau^N} & -Q_z & -Q_g \end{pmatrix} \begin{pmatrix} d\tau_i^N \\ dz_i \\ dg_i \end{pmatrix}. \tag{A.3.16}$$

Let B denote the 2×2 matrix on the left side of (A.3.16). Solving (A.3.16) with the help of Cramer's rule and using the abbreviation

$$b \equiv \frac{U_x^i}{M_i |B|}$$

yields the following locational responses:

$$\frac{\partial N_i}{\partial \tau_i^N} = b[l_i^2 F_{ll}^i + n_i l_i F_{ln}^i + \tau_i^M - H_M^i], \tag{A.3.17}$$

$$\frac{\partial M_i}{\partial \tau_i^N} = b[l_i F_{nl}^i - \tau_i^N + C_N^i], \tag{A.3.18}$$

$$\frac{\partial N_i}{\partial z_i} = b\left[\frac{C_z^i}{M_i}(l_i F_{ln}^i + n_i F_{nn}^i) \right.$$
$$\left. - \frac{U_z^i}{U_x^i}(l_i^2 F_{ll}^i + 2n_i l_i F_{ln}^i + n_i^2 F_{nn}^i + \tau_i^M - H_M^i) \right], \tag{A.3.19}$$

$$\frac{\partial M_i}{\partial z_i} = b\left[\frac{C_z^i}{M_i} F_{nn}^i - \frac{U_z^i}{U_x^i}(l_i F_{ln}^i + n_i F_{nn}^i - \tau_i^N + C_N^i) \right], \tag{A.3.20}$$

$$\frac{\partial N_i}{\partial g_i} = b\left(\frac{H_g^i}{M_i} - F_g^i + l_i F_{lg}^i \right)(l_i F_{ln}^i + n_i F_{nn}^i)$$
$$- b F_{ng}^i (l_i^2 F_{ll}^i + n_i l_i F_{ln}^i + \tau_i^M - H_M^i), \tag{A.3.21}$$

$$\frac{\partial M_i}{\partial g_i} = b\left[\left(\frac{H_g^i}{M_i} - F_g^i + l_i F_{lg}^i \right) F_{nn}^i - F_{ng}^i (l_i F_{ln}^i - \tau_i^N + C_N^i) \right]. \tag{A.3.22}$$

Inserting (A.3.17) and (A.3.18) into the first-order condition (3.16), it follows that

$$\frac{\tau_i^N - C_N^i}{F_{ln}^i} = -\frac{\tau_i^M - H_M^i}{l_i F_{ll}^i + n_i F_{nl}^i},$$

(A.3.23)

that is, part (i) of Proposition 3.4.

Substituting (A.3.19) and (A.3.20) into the first-order condition (3.18), dividing the entire expression by b, collecting terms, and using (A.3.23), we have

$$N_i \frac{U_z^i}{U_x^i} = C_z^i$$

(A.3.24)

and thus part (ii) of Proposition 3.4. Finally, substituting (A.3.21) and (A.3.22) into (3.19), dividing by b, collecting terms, and using (A.3.23) yields

$$\frac{(\tau_i^N - C_N^i)M_i}{F_{ln}^i} = \frac{M_i F_g^i - H_g^i}{F_{lg}^i},$$

(A.3.25)

which is part (iii) of Proposition 3.4.

CHAPTER 4

Interregional Tax Competition for Mobile Capital

We have derived in Section 3.2 that decentralized tax and expenditure decisions distort the allocation if regions are constrained to finance local public goods by taxes on mobile factors. This case is commonly referred to as *interregional tax competition* for a mobile tax base. The literature (see e.g. Oates 1972; Wilson 1986, 1987b; Zodrow and Mieszkowski 1986a) pays great attention to this issue and emphasizes that regions respond by providing inefficiently low levels of local public goods. A sufficient instrument set to induce regions to choose an efficient allocation would include a nondistorting land tax – which is, however, not available because of institutional restrictions (e.g., it is prohibited by the German Constitution). Although an inefficient interregional tax competition can arise for the taxation of mobile households, firms, and capital, the literature concentrates almost entirely on taxing the mobile factor of production capital. Oates (1972, p. 142) describes the basic problem as follows:

> The result of tax competition may well be a tendency toward less than effi-
> cient levels of output of local public services. In an attempt to keep tax rates
> low to attract business investment, local officials may hold spending below
> those levels for which marginal benefits equal marginal costs, particularly for
> those programs that do not offer direct benefits to local businesses.

The individual regions are in a "prisoner's dilemma" (see Boadway and Wild-asin 1984, p. 504), since each regional government fears that capital leaves the region when it is taxed too much. As a consequence, all regions choose inefficiently low capital tax rates and the interregional capital allocation changes very little. Higher taxes on mobile capital would be beneficial to all regions because the same interregional capital allocation would result, but the division of resources between public and private goods would better reflect individual preferences. However, an efficient taxation of mobile capital cannot be expected by uncoordinated decentralized decisions.

Whether regions indeed undersupply local public services depends critically on the kind of services they offer. Hence, it is important to differentiate between public services as pure consumption goods and as public production factors. If the capital tax is earmarked to finance local public inputs, then the capital productivity increases and so then does the demand for capital by regional firms. Such an earmarked use of capital tax revenues need not result in a capital flight. Therefore, it cannot generally be concluded that regions underprovide public production factors.

An inefficiently low provision of local public (consumption) goods is not the only problem caused by uncoordinated regional taxation decisions. Any uncoordinated tax policy may result in different capital tax rates among regions, leading to an inefficient interregional capital allocation. Moreover, regions may try to manipulate the interregional interest rate by choosing their capital tax rates strategically in order to increase their capital income from abroad. However, in order to concentrate on the problem of interregional tax competition for the scarce factor of capital – and to show as clearly as possible that regions respond by undersupplying local public goods – this chapter largely ignores (with the exception of Section 4.3) these problems by assuming identical regions. In a symmetric equilibrium, identical regions choose the same capital tax rate and have no incentives to manipulate the terms of trade, since they are neither importers nor exporters of capital.

A number of recent studies have confirmed the intuitive conclusions about interregional tax competition made by Oates (1972) and Boadway and Wildasin (1984). Zodrow and Mieszkowski (1986a) and Wilson (1986) show that regions supply inefficiently low levels of local public goods if they must finance these expenditures by capital taxes. Sinn (1997) demonstrates that this result does not extend to the provision of local public factors, provided that the public infrastructure increases the productivity of private capital employed in the region. Wildasin (1989) explains that the phenomenon of tax competition can be traced back to the existence of a positive fiscal externality on other regions that is ignored by a single region when making its decisions. Myers (1990a) and DePater and Myers (1994) emphasize that Wildasin's explanation of an inefficiently low level of local public goods holds without qualification only if regions are identical or without any market power in the national capital market. Otherwise, a pecuniary externality must be taken into account, which – taken for itself – points in the direction of an *over*supply of public goods if a region is a net importer of capital. Hoyt (1991b) shows that the extent to which regions undersupply local public goods increases with the number of competing regions in the federal state because the degree of competition for capital rises. Following Bucovetsky (1991) and Wilson (1991), if regions are of different size then small regions may oppose a coordinated provision of local public goods that satisfies the Samuelson condition; small regions may prefer interregional tax competition over such a situation. Finally, Edwards and Keen (1996) analyze interregional tax competition in a model in which politicians in each governmental administration are partly self-serving. They confirm that interregional tax competition distorts the allocation of resources between the private and the public sector. However, if politicians waste part of the tax revenues then tax competition is not necessarily harmful.

In order to discuss the effects caused by interregional tax competition for mobile capital, this chapter is organized as follows. The basic problem of interregional tax competition is outlined in Section 4.1. Regions must finance local public goods by a source-based tax on mobile capital employed within their boundaries. This section also explains how a central government can overcome the problem of an underprovision of local public goods. The center's method of intervention is to provide matching grants to the regions that reduce the regional costs of taxing mobile capital. Section 4.2 studies cooperation in tax and expenditure policies among several regions, and it shows that cooperation in this field lowers the extent to which regions undersupply local public goods. Section 4.3 illustrates that small regions may have incentives to prefer tax competition over a situation with harmonized tax rates and a provision of local public goods in accordance with the Samuelson condition. In Section 4.4, politicians are partly self-serving and spend some fraction of the tax revenues for own purposes. The analysis shows that, in this case, interregional tax competition can increase the welfare of citizens. A final observation is that the tax on mobile capital can be interpreted as a local property tax on structures. Therefore, the model of interregional tax competition can also be used to summarize the basic views on another important problem – the incidence of property tax. Section 4.5 is devoted to this issue and also makes some remarks on the effects of land taxation. Section 4.6 contains an appendix that proves an important result reported in Section 4.4.

4.1   Underprovision of Local Public Goods

4.1.1   Private Behavior

To describe the problem of interregional tax competition, let us assume that the federal state consists of I identical regions. All households are immobile, and there are L_i identical households in each region i that are endowed with one unit of land each. They inelastically supply this immobile factor to local firms and attain the gross land rent ρ_i in response. We assume that households do not have to pay taxes on land rents. Furthermore, each household living in the federal state is endowed with the same fraction $k = K/\sum_1^I L_i$ of the exogenously given capital stock K of the federal state. Households invest their capital where it attains the highest return. As a consequence, the same interest rate r must prevail in all regions in equilibrium. Households use their income to finance the consumption of the private numeraire good x_i, and the budget constraint of a representative household living in region i reads as

$$x_i = \rho_i + kr. \tag{4.1}$$

Regional production takes place by a linear homogeneous production function. The immobile factor (land) and the mobile factor (capital) are employed to produce the private good. It will prove useful to use per-capita notation in this chapter. Let $f^i(k_i)$ denote the production function in units of land employed and let $k_i \equiv K_i/L_i$ stand for capital used by regional firms, K_i, per unit of land. With this notation, the profit of firms in region i can be written as

$$L_i f^i(k_i) - L_i \rho_i - (r + \tau_i^K) k_i L_i, \tag{4.2}$$

where τ_i^K stands for the source-based tax on capital levied by the government of region i. From the viewpoint of regional firms, the costs of capital are hence composed of the return to capital owners (the interest rate) and of the capital tax. Regional firms maximize their profits and take r, ρ_i, and τ_i^K as parametrically given when they choose the amount of production factors used, K_i and L_i. They behave according to the following rules:

$$(K_i): \quad f_k^i = r + \tau_i^K \equiv \phi_i, \tag{4.3}$$

$$(L_i): \quad f^i - k_i f_k^i = \rho_i, \tag{4.4}$$

with firms' choice variables shown in parentheses. Following (4.3), capital is employed until its marginal productivity, $f_k^i \equiv \partial f^i / \partial k_i$, is equal to the costs of capital ϕ_i. Condition (4.4) shows that the marginal productivity of land, $f^i - k_i f_k^i$, is equal to the land rent.

A capital market equilibrium for the entire federal state is achieved when the demand for capital by all firms is equal to the exogenously given entire capital stock – that is, if

$$\sum_{i=1}^{I} L_i k_i = \sum_{i=1}^{I} L_i k. \tag{4.5}$$

For the following analysis it is useful to derive the regional resource constraint. Insert (4.3) and (4.4) into the budget restriction of a representative household (4.1), which yields

$$x_i = f^i - (r + \tau_i^K) k_i + rk. \tag{4.6}$$

Aside from consuming private goods, a representative household also derives utility from its use of the local public good z_i, and the household's utility function is described by $U^i(x_i, z_i)$. Let us assume that there is complete rivalness in the consumption of the local public good. The costs of providing the public good are given by $L_i z_i$. Hence, from a social point of view, one unit of the private good can be transformed into one unit of the local public good. Interregional tax competition arises because each regional government has only one financing measure available – it must finance its expenditures by taxing mobile capital. The budget constraint of the regional government reads as

$$L_i k_i \tau_i^K = L_i z_i \iff k_i \tau_i^K = z_i. \tag{4.7}$$

As a reference situation, it is useful to recall the conditions of an efficient allocation. Since regions are identical, the first-order condition of the efficient interregional capital allocation,

$$f_k^i = f_k^j \quad \forall \, i, j, \, i \neq j, \tag{4.8}$$

is always satisfied because identical regions choose the same capital tax rate in a symmetric equilibrium. The consumption of local public goods is completely rival, and the Samuelson condition of an efficient provision of z_i is therefore given by

$$\frac{U_z^i}{U_x^i} \equiv MRS_i = 1. \tag{4.9}$$

Before we go on to describe the behavior of regional governments, it is instructive first to analyze how a change in the capital tax rate τ_i^K influences the interregional capital allocation and the interest rate. From (4.3), it follows that $k_i' \equiv dk_i/d\phi_i = 1/f_{kk}^i$ with $f_{kk}^i \equiv \partial^2 f^i/\partial k_i^2$. Using this notation, it follows from the capital market equilibrium (4.5) that a change in τ_i^K implies

$$L_i k_i' + \sum_{j=1}^{I} L_j k_j' \frac{dr}{d\tau_i^K} = 0. \tag{4.10}$$

In the case of identical regions, $k' = k_i' = k_j'$ and $L_i = L_j$ for all i, j, condition (4.10) reduces to

$$\frac{dr}{d\tau_i^K} = -\frac{1}{I} \equiv -l, \tag{4.11}$$

where l is the *market share* of a region. Condition (4.11) shows that the interest rate decreases if one region increases the capital tax rate. Furthermore, from (4.3) and (4.11) it follows that

$$\frac{dk_i}{d\tau_i^K} = (1-l)k' < 0,$$

$$\frac{dk_j}{d\tau_i^K} = -lk' > 0 \quad \forall \, j \neq i. \tag{4.12}$$

Hence, whereas the region that increases its tax rate loses capital, the capital employment in all other regions rises. Because of the increase in the tax rate τ_i^K, capital leaves region i and moves to other regions, reducing the marginal capital productivity there. This explains why the interest rate declines, as derived in (4.11).

4.1.2 Regional Government Behavior

Let us now turn to the behavior of regional governments. We will assume that regional governments do not follow their own interests but instead maximize the utility of a representative resident by choosing τ_i^K. The choice of τ_i^K also determines z_i via the budget constraint (4.7). By choosing τ_i^K, the regional government acts under the Nash assumption that all other regions do not respond by changing their tax rates τ_j^K for all $j \neq i$.[1] Its problem is to

$$\text{maximize } U^i(x_i, z_i) \tag{4.13}$$

by choosing τ_i^K, with x_i as defined by (4.6) and z_i by (4.7) and where r and k_i depend on τ_i^K, as explained by (4.11) and (4.12), respectively. The first-order condition of the optimal choice of τ_i^K becomes

$$\frac{dU^i}{d\tau_i^K} \frac{1}{U_x^i} = -k_i + \frac{\partial r}{\partial \tau_i^K}(k - k_i) + MRS_i\left(k_i + \tau_i^K \frac{\partial k_i}{\partial \tau_i^K}\right) = 0. \tag{4.14}$$

Using the assumption of identical regions, $k_i = k$, and inserting (4.12) into (4.14), the first-order condition of an optimal behavior of the regional government (4.14) can be written as

$$MRS_i = \frac{1}{1 + (1 - l)\varepsilon_i}, \quad \text{with } \varepsilon_i \equiv \frac{k_i'}{k_i}\tau_i^K < 0. \tag{4.15}$$

Condition (4.15) allows us to derive some important results. First, since regions are identical, any terms-of-trade effects can be ignored. This implies that, in equilibrium, no region can improve its income from abroad (its share of the interregional distribution of resources) by manipulating the interest rate. Second,

---

[1] Wildasin (1988) emphasizes the importance of different strategies for the outcome of interregional competition. He differentiates between a game in tax rates (τ_i^K) and in local public good levels (z_i). Only for very small regions (i.e., for perfect interregional competition, $l \to 0$) will both games lead to the same results. For larger regions, the game in local public good levels (z_i) implies a stronger competitive behavior of regions. To understand this, notice that an increase in z_i by region i is accompanied by a capital inflow and therefore by an increase in the tax base in all other regions. For given z_j (all $j \neq i$), other regions can reduce their tax rates and so induce a further acceleration of the capital flight out of region i. On the other hand, if the capital tax rates (τ_j^K) are kept constant in response to an increase in τ_i^K, then this indirect effect – increasing the degree of interregional competition – is absent.

a region provides local public goods in line with the Samuelson condition (4.9) if (and only if) its market share becomes infinitely large, $l = 1 \iff I = 1$, that is, if the federal state consists only of this one region. In all other cases – for $0 \leq l < 1 \iff I > 1$ – the provision of local public goods is inefficiently low, $MRS_i > 1$. If there is perfect competition among regions, $l \to 0$, then condition (4.15) restates the results derived by Wilson (1986) and Zodrow and Mieszkowski (1986a).

This important result can be summarized in

Proposition 4.1. *If identical regions must finance local public goods by a source-based tax on mobile capital employed in the regions (interregional tax competition), then they provide inefficiently low levels of local public goods.*

How can we explain the behavior of regional governments when they must rely solely on capital taxes? If a region provides local public goods, it compares the costs with the benefits from its viewpoint. The benefit is equal to the direct increase in utility that regional residents derive from an expanded consumption of public goods. Costs result from taxation. If mobile capital is the tax base, these costs are composed of two elements. First, an increase in the capital tax rate shifts resources from the private sector of the economy to the public sector, leading to a reduction of private consumption. This cost component is the well-known revenue effect of collecting taxes – a common feature of all taxes, even if they are undistortive. However, in the case of an undistortive tax (the land-rent tax), there are no additional costs. If mobile capital is the tax base, then a single region must additionally take into account that capital leaves the region, causing a reduction in the tax base. This is the second cost component of taxing mobile capital. Yet the induced capital flight is no cost component from the viewpoint of the federal state, since capital remains within its borders. Furthermore, the conjecture of each regional government that capital leaves the region in response to an increase in the capital tax rate is wrong. All (identical) regions choose the same capital tax rate in equilibrium and thus the interregional capital allocation is, in effect, independent of the level of the tax rate. The single region is in a kind of prisoner's dilemma and conjectures too high costs of providing local public goods. In an equilibrium of identical regions, condition (4.15) shows that regions supply inefficiently low levels of local public goods because the social rate of transformation between private and public goods is equal to unity.

With the help of Figure 4.1, these conclusions can be illustrated very instructively. This diagram depicts the situation of a single region. The ordinate measures the consumption of private goods by a representative household living in the region, while the abscissa shows the provision of rival local public

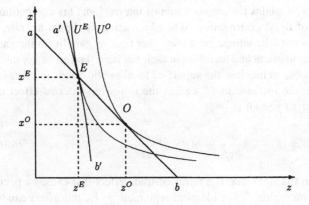

Figure 4.1. Interregional tax competition.

goods. The curve ab is the relevant *production possibility frontier* of the region. All regions are identical and choose the same tax rate in equilibrium, so it follows that the interregional capital allocation is independent of the capital tax rate and that the social rate of transformation between private and local public goods is 1. The curve ab therefore has a constant slope of -1, suggesting that increasing the tax by one unit will generate additional tax revenues of one unit for financing local public goods.

From the viewpoint of a single region, however, the situation is different: the curve $a'b'$ depicts the *consumption possibility frontier* from its point of view. The region conjectures that an increase in its tax rate by one unit generates less than one unit of additional tax revenues because capital leaves the region and so reduces the tax base. Hence, from the viewpoint of a single region, providing an additional unit of the local public good absorbs more than one unit of the private good. This explains the steeper slope of $a'b'$. In a decentralized equilibrium, the indifference curve U^E of a representative household must be tangent to the consumption possibility frontier $a'b'$ that is relevant to the single region. This requirement meets the first-order condition (4.15), and in Figure 4.1 this point of tangency is depicted by E. Since all regions are identical, this point must also be located on the production possibility frontier, for this curve depicts all possible allocations in equilibrium. Therefore, the curve $a'b'$ intersects the transformation curve ab in E. However, the efficient allocation is achieved in point O, where the indifference curve of a representative resident is tangent to the socially relevant production possibility frontier. The corresponding utility level U^O is higher, and more public and fewer private goods have to be provided.

Wildasin (1989) explains the phenomenon of interregional tax competition by the existence of fiscal externalities. When increasing its capital tax rate, a single region does not take into account that other regions gain by an increase in their capital employment and therefore in their tax base. For given tax rates, this makes it possible to increase the supply of local public goods in other regions. Therefore, the increase in τ_i^K causes the following external effect on some other region j ($j \neq i$):

$$\frac{dU^j}{d\tau_i^K} \frac{1}{U_x^j} = (k - k_j)\frac{\partial r}{\partial \tau_i^K} + MRS_j \tau_j^K \frac{\partial k_j}{\partial \tau_i^K}. \tag{4.16}$$

The first effect on the right side is a terms-of-trade effect that causes a pecuniary externality on region j. For identical regions, $k = k_j$, this effect can be ignored. The second effect is clearly positive, since capital moves to region j according to (4.12). Because region i does not take this positive fiscal externality into account when choosing its tax rate, it assesses too high costs of supplying local public goods from a social point of view. Region i's provision of local public goods is therefore inefficiently low.

4.1.3   Central Government Intervention

There are several ways to improve the situation of households living in the individual regions. One possibility is a cooperation among several regions in their tax and expenditure policies; this is studied in Section 4.2. A second possible measure is the central government forcing all regions to increase their tax rates uniformly. Since all regions are identical and must increase their tax rates by the same amount, the interregional capital allocation is unaffected by that measure. The tax increase raises the supply of local public goods at the expense of private goods, where the marginal rate of transformation is equal to unity. In terms of Figure 4.1, each region moves from E along the production possibility frontier ab in the direction of O. This movement clearly increases the welfare of households.

Another possibility for a central government's ensuring an efficient allocation is to provide a system of *matching grants* to the regions in order to avoid any distortion due to uncoordinated capital tax competition. The appropriate design of this corrective intervention lies in the logic of the problem. Since regional governments cause externalities on other regions, the efficiency-supporting grant system must internalize these external effects. Suppose that the central government collects a lump-sum tax T_i from each region i in order to finance a system of matching grants to the regions. For simplicity, we assume that the grant rate S_i to region i is proportional to the capital tax chosen by the region, such that the entire grant becomes $S_i \tau_i^K$.[2] The policy of the central government must satisfy the constraint

$$\sum_{i=1}^{I} S_i \tau_i^K = \sum_{i=1}^{I} T_i. \tag{4.17}$$

Moreover, let s_i and t_i denote the per-capita grant and lump-sum tax rate, respectively. Then the per-capita budget constraint of the regional government changes to

$$k_i \tau_i^K + s_i \tau_i^K = z_i + t_i. \tag{4.18}$$

In order to see how the grant system affects the behavior of regional governments, we have to repeat solving the optimization problem of the regional government (4.13), where z_i must now be replaced by (4.18). The central government acts as a Stackelberg leader with respect to the individual regions. Hence, by choosing τ_i^K, the regional government in i takes not only τ_j^K (for all $j \neq i$) but also s_i and t_i (for all i) as given. The first-order condition for the optimal choice of τ_i^K now becomes

$$\frac{dU^i}{d\tau_i^K} \frac{1}{U_x^i} = -k_i + \frac{\partial r}{\partial \tau_i^K}(k - k_i) + MRS_i\left(k_i + s_i + \tau_i^K \frac{\partial k_i}{\partial \tau_i^K}\right) = 0. \tag{4.19}$$

Thus, the matching grant increases per-capita revenues out of any increase in the capital tax rate, and this stimulates the regional provision of the local public good.

What, though, does the appropriate system of grant rates look like? To answer this question, let us recall that the problem caused by interregional tax competition can be explained by the existence of externalities that a single region imposes on its neighbors when setting its capital tax rate. In the case of a central government intervention, a region choosing its capital tax rate causes two kinds of externalities. The first one is already derived by condition (4.16) and does not change with the simple grant system considered in this section. The second one is new and specific to the central government policy. By increasing its capital tax rate, a region increases the grant it receives from the center. This changes the necessary taxes the center must collect in order to balance its budget, which in the end must be paid by the regions. Since each region takes T_i as given, the acting region therefore causes a second external effect.

---

[2] Wildasin (1989) and DePater and Myers (1994) discuss the more general case where the central government's corrective instrument is a function of the regional tax rate, $S_i(\tau_i^K)$.

Region i affects the central government budget by

$$\frac{d \sum_j T_j}{d\tau_i^K} = S_i,$$ (4.20)

and it causes external effects equal to the sum of (4.16) over all regions $j \neq i$ and (4.20). If the central government's objective is to achieve an efficient allocation, then it must set the grant rates s_i so as to internalize the external effects caused by noncooperative choices of capital tax rates. Thus, the system of efficiency-supporting grant rates (s_i) must satisfy

$$\sum_{j \neq i} L_j \frac{dU^j}{d\tau_i^K} \frac{1}{U_z^j} - \frac{d \sum_j T_j}{d\tau_i^K} = 0 \quad \forall\, i.$$ (4.21)

Note that the necessary change in central government taxes affects the welfare of residents via the induced change in the provision of local public goods. In order to have a common base for both kinds of externalities, we must divide the first expressions on the left side of (4.21) by U_z^j in all regions j. Inserting (4.16) and (4.20) into (4.21) yields, as a matching grant rate for each region i,

$$s_i = \frac{1}{L_i} \sum_{j \neq i} L_j \left[\frac{1}{MRS_j}(k - k_j)\frac{\partial r}{\partial \tau_i^K} + \tau_j^K \frac{\partial k_j}{\partial \tau_i^K} \right].$$ (4.22)

In the general case of different regions, the grant must induce regions to internalize two kinds of externalities. The first one on the right side of (4.22) is a pecuniary externality resulting from a region's objective to increase (decrease) its interest income (liabilities). The second one is the fiscal externality emphasized in Section 4.1.2.

Before we specify the appropriate grant rate for the case of identical regions, one important implication of this intervention scheme for diverse regions should be noticed. The central government's policy provides one additional instrument for achieving an efficient allocation – an interregional transfer. As explained in Section 2.2 (see also DePater and Myers 1994), an instrument set consisting of capital tax rates and an interregional transfer suffices to sustain but one particular first-best efficient allocation for one particular distribution of utilities across regions. The reason is that it is impossible to choose the private good level in one region independently of the amount of private goods in the other regions. Hence, the grant scheme which internalizes all externalities can only achieve the allocation which a central planner could achieve when facing the same constrained set of instruments. In general, this is a constrained efficient allocation, where marginal productivities of capital differ across regions and the supply of local public goods does not satisfy the Samuelson condition. We turn back to this problem at the end of Section 4.3.

These problems do not occur when we return to the environment of identical regions. Here, dropping all indexes, inserting (4.12) into (4.22), and using the definition of the market share l and the elasticity ε yields the efficiency-supporting grant rate

$$s = -(1-l)k\varepsilon. \tag{4.23}$$

Since $\varepsilon < 0$, the efficient grant rate s must be positive for all regional sizes satisfying $0 \le l < 1$. The center must induce regions to choose higher capital tax rates in order to internalize the positive fiscal externality. To verify that this choice of the uniform grant rate results in an efficient provision of the local public good, we must insert (4.23) into the first-order condition (4.19) for the case of identical regions:

$$MRS = \frac{1}{1 + s/k + (1-l)\varepsilon} = 1. \tag{4.24}$$

In summary, we have

Proposition 4.2. *The central government can induce identical regions to choose the efficient supply of local public goods by providing matching grants that reduce the regional price of financing local public goods via capital taxes.*

4.2 Tax Competition and Regional Size

In Section 4.1.3 we discussed two ways in which a central government can overcome the problem of an inefficient provision of local public goods. The center can force regions to undertake a coordinated increase in their capital tax rates, or it can reduce the regional price of supplying local public goods by providing matching grants to the regions. This section shows that cooperation of several regions in their tax and expenditure policies provides another possibility for at least reducing the problem. Regions can decide cooperatively on their supply of local public goods and, consequently, on their capital tax rates. Since each single region within this newly established policy union continues to produce separately and since the use of local public goods is still restricted to the single region's boundaries, it is necessary to assume that a decrease in the number of independent decision units in the federal state is accompanied by a corresponding proportional decrease in the entire capital stock. Alternatively, we could argue that the land endowment increases in each independent decision unit as l becomes larger. Only by making this assumption is it possible to describe the newly established and increased decision unit as a region with the same structure as in Section 4.1. However, the new region consists of several perfectly identical regions. To put it differently, this section studies the behavior of regions when their market share l increases.

Analytically, the integration of several regions to a larger decision unit is modeled by an increase in the market share l (a decrease in I) of a single region. This increase in l will be accompanied by a proportional reduction of K. Consequently, in a symmetric equilibrium of identical regions, this implies

$$\frac{\partial k_i}{\partial l} = 0 \quad \text{and} \quad \frac{\partial k_i}{\partial \tau^K}\frac{d\tau^K}{dl} = 0, \tag{4.25}$$

where $\tau^K \equiv \tau_i^K$ for all i denotes the identical capital tax rate chosen by all regions. Since regions are identical, they will change the capital tax rate uniformly. Following (4.25), an increase in the market share does not affect the interregional allocation of capital per unit of land. Equations (4.25) can also be interpreted by saying that each region within the coalition has the same capital stock available after creating a policy union, because all regions adapt their capital tax rates uniformly. Since the capital employment does not change in any subregion in the new equilibrium, it follows from (4.3), (4.6), and (4.7) that

$$\frac{dr}{d\tau^K} = -1, \quad \frac{dx_i}{d\tau^K} = -k_i, \quad \text{and} \quad \frac{dz_i}{d\tau^K} = k_i. \tag{4.26}$$

Given an unchanged regional capital employment, welfare changes only as a consequence of a change in the capital tax rate. The question then arises of how each single region responds with its capital tax rate to an increase in its market share l – that is, how the coalition changes τ^K. This question can be answered by totally differentiating the first-order condition of choosing τ_i^K, (4.15), with respect to l. Taking into account that all regions are identical, making use of (4.25), and ignoring region-specific indexes, it follows that

$$\frac{dMRS}{d(z/x)}\left[\frac{1}{x}\frac{\partial z}{\partial \tau^K} - \frac{z}{x^2}\frac{\partial x}{\partial \tau^K}\right]\frac{d\tau^K}{dl} = -\frac{1}{A^2}\left(\frac{(1-l)\varepsilon}{\tau^K}\frac{d\tau^K}{dl} - \varepsilon\right), \tag{4.27}$$

with $A \equiv [1 + (1 - l)\varepsilon]$. Using the definition

$$\varepsilon_{zx} \equiv \frac{dMRS}{d(z/x)}\frac{z/x}{MRS} < 0$$

and (4.26), after a few algebraic steps it follows from (4.27) that

$$\frac{d\tau^K}{dl} = \frac{\varepsilon}{A^2\varepsilon_{zx}MRSk(1/z + 1/x) + (1-l)\varepsilon/\tau^K} > 0; \tag{4.28}$$

that is, regions increase their capital tax rate when the decision units become larger (after coalition formation) since $\varepsilon, \varepsilon_{zx} < 0$. Because the number of decentralized decision units in the federal state has decreased, each newly formed single decision unit is now subject to a lower degree of competition for mobile capital. Therefore, a tax increase is now less costly from the viewpoint of a decision unit as it conjectures a lower degree of capital mobility.

The higher capital tax rate increases welfare of all households because the interregional capital allocation does not change in response whereas regions choose higher levels of local public goods, improving the desired composition of public and private goods. Making use of (4.26), the change in utility of a representative household living in a region is equal to

$$\frac{dU}{dl}\frac{1}{U_x} = k(MRS - 1)\frac{d\tau^K}{dl}. \tag{4.29}$$

Condition (4.15) suggests that the initial equilibrium is characterized by an inefficiently low provision of local public goods, $MRS > 1$. Therefore, (4.29) together with (4.28) implies that the formation of a larger decision unit results in a welfare increase of all households.

Proposition 4.3.   *Suppose that all regions are identical. Then an increase in the market share of regions by creating larger decision units reduces the underprovision of local public goods due to interregional tax competition, since the degree of interregional competition for mobile capital decreases.*

The coalition formation corresponds to a movement from point E to O along the production possibility frontier ab set out in Figure 4.1.

4.3   The Advantage of Small Regions

Until now, this chapter has considered only identical regions in order to exclude other motives for strategic behavior and so isolate the problem of interregional tax competition. As a consequence, a symmetric Nash equilibrium among regions is characterized by an inefficiently low provision of local public goods. In contrast, cooperation among regions in tax policy that approaches the Samuelson condition of supplying local public goods increases welfare of all households. This section explains why not all regions agree to a harmonization of capital tax rates at higher levels and local public good levels in accordance with the Samuelson condition when regions differ in size. Small regions may be better off with interregional tax competition, although they experience an underprovision of local public goods relative to the Samuelson rule.

To demonstrate this result, let us assume that the federal state consists of two regions. Both regions differ only with respect to the number of immobile residents and hence (since each household is endowed with one unit of land) in their land endowments. All households living in the federal state have the same utility function $U(x, z)$ and an identical capital endowment k. Furthermore, the production functions per unit of land $f(k)$ do not differ across regions. Let us denote the large region by the index L and the small region by the index S; then, similarly to (4.5), as a capital market equilibrium it follows that

$$\frac{L_L}{L}k_L + \frac{L_S}{L}k_S = k, \tag{4.30}$$

where $L = L_L + L_S$ is the entire population and hence the global land endowment. If region $i = L, S$ increases its capital tax rate, then (4.30) allows us to derive

$$\frac{dr}{d\tau_{i.}^K} = \frac{-\dfrac{L_i}{L}k_i'}{\dfrac{L_S}{L}k_S' + \dfrac{L_L}{L}k_L'}. \tag{4.31}$$

Firms use capital according to the behavioral rule (4.3). Thus we have

$$\frac{dk_i}{d\tau_i^K} = k_i' + k_i'\frac{dr}{d\tau_i^K}. \tag{4.32}$$

In order to make the argument as clear as possible that small regions might prefer tax competition over a situation with identical tax rates and per-capita public expenditures, let us assume that the regional size differs by the maximum possible amount. In this case, the market share L_L/L of the large region approaches 1. Then (4.31) indicates that, from the viewpoint of the large region, a tax increase is accompanied by an equally strong reduction in the interest rate, $dr/d\tau_L^K = -1$, while the change in the interest rate is not important to the small region, $dr/d\tau_S^K = 0$. With the help of (4.32), these results show that large regions can hardly expect any capital flight at all, $dk_L/d\tau_L^K = 0$, while small regions are threatened by an enormous capital outflow, $dk_S/d\tau_S^K = k_S'$. Hence, for the considered huge difference in size between regions, condition (4.15) reveals that the large region provides the local public good in line with the Samuelson condition, $MRS = 1$ for $l = 1$, while the small region provides an inefficiently low level of the local public good, $MRS > 1$ for $l = 0$.

By using the graphical method outlined in Figure 4.1, it is now possible to show that, given the enormous difference in size, the small region is better off in the decentralized Nash equilibrium than with identical tax rates and public good levels satisfying the Samuelson condition. Figure 4.2 depicts the situation in the large and in the small region. The large region chooses point L, where the indifference curve of a representative resident U^L is tangent to the socially relevant production possibility frontier ab. Since the large region does not expect capital flight in response to its own actions, its consumption possibility curve coincides with ab. However, the small region is threatened by an outflow

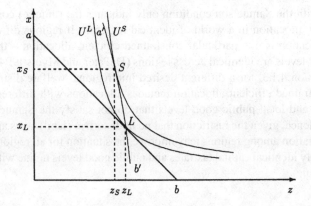

Figure 4.2. The advantage of small regions.

of capital when it chooses a tax on mobile capital and therefore faces the consumption possibility frontier $a'b'$. Of course, the small region could vote for a provision of local public goods in accordance with the Samuelson rule simply by choosing point L. In this case, the capital tax rate and the (per-capita) provision of local public goods are identical across regions. However, in L the indifference curve of a representative household living in the small region is not tangent to the consumption possibility curve $a'b'$ of the small region. The small region therefore chooses point S. Point S must be located on a higher indifference curve U^S, since the solution with identical tax rates would be possible for the small region but, following (4.15) (for $l = 0$), it cannot be optimal.

Notice that the attainable consumption structure in the small region must not be located on ab if it chooses a different capital tax rate. If the capital tax rate is lower, it attracts capital from the large region and can consume a bundle of local public and private goods lying outside of ab. Because of the huge difference in size, this has no noticeable impact on the consumption possibility curve ab of the large region.

We can summarize the results of this section in

Proposition 4.4.   *If differences in regional size are sufficiently large, then small regions may be better off with interregional tax competition than with identical tax rates – even if an underprovision of local public goods results relative to the Samuelson condition.*

Proposition 4.4 does not mean that cooperation among regions is harmful for small regions. Given that regions have no undistortive (land) taxes available, the allocation with identical capital tax rates and levels of local public goods in accordance with the Samuelson condition only indicates the (unique) constrained efficient allocation in a world of identical regions.[3] If regions differ in size, this allocation is one particular constrained efficient allocation – the one where utility levels are identical across regions (DePater and Myers 1994). As noted in Section 4.1.3, for a different desired interregional welfare distribution, the constrained efficient allocation includes allocations with different capital tax rates and local public good levels that do not satisfy the Samuelson condition. Hence, given the restriction that no undistortive (land) taxes are available, cooperation among regions may improve the situation for all regions but need not imply identical capital tax rates and public good levels in line with the Samuelson rule.

4.4   Restraining the Leviathan by Interregional Tax Competition

The analysis so far has neglected the fact that some persons in each governmental administration have strong incentives and the opportunity to use tax revenues for their own purposes. Following Niskanen (1971), these bureaucrats seek to maximize the attainable budget. In such a world, interregional competition for a scarce mobile tax base is a way to limit the taxing power of a Leviathan-type government, as argued by such authors as Brennan and Buchanan (1980) and McLure (1986). This idea has become increasingly influential and has also produced a large amount of empirical literature – most notably Oates (1985). The view is in remarkable contrast to the result that interregional tax competition for a scarce tax base is inefficient. However, taking a closer look, these sharply different views reflect equally different perceptions of government policy making. Whereas previous sections have assumed that local governments are benevolent utility maximizers, the Leviathan government is supposed to be a wholly self-interested revenue maximizer.

In a recent study, Edwards and Keen (1996) try to reconcile these views by assuming that local governments are neither entirely benevolent nor fully self-interested. They conclude that it is an empirical question whether less interregional competition (i.e., less fiscal decentralization) is beneficial or not. The gains derived so far of an increased supply of local public goods must be contrasted with the disadvantage of less competition among self-interested policy makers wasting tax revenues. Using a similar model, this section reveals an important condition of welfare gains from fiscal decentralization. Governments must be constrained to finance local public goods by a tax on a mobile factor like capital. If they have undistortive taxes like a land tax available, there is no welfare gain from fiscal decentralization. If an undistortive land tax is

---

[3] Even if all regions are identical, their allocations may differ; Wilson (1987a) shows this in a Tiebout model with interregional trade in goods.

available, then (identical) jurisdictions would abstain from taxing mobile capital. Hence, there is in fact no tax competition among jurisdictions, and fiscal decentralization no longer means an increase in competition. With benevolent local governments, the condition that governments are able to collect undistortive taxes is necessary to ensure that decentralized decision making results in an efficient allocation. If, on the contrary, politicians are partly self-serving, then the absence of undistortive taxes is a necessary condition for fiscal decentralization to be beneficial. In addition, if the gains of limiting the taxing power dominate the negative effect of underprovision of public goods, then tax competition is in the interest of citizens.

4.4.1   Government Behavior

We assume that the federal state is made up of identical jurisdictions, and that the private sector of the economy is the one described in Section 4.1. In characterizing the behavior of governments, we drop the region-specific index from the notation. In contrast to Section 4.1, governments – potentially including politicians, bureaucrats, and influential lobbies – are assumed to be partly self-interested and to follow an objective that can be expressed by the quasi-concave welfare function $W(c, U)$. Note that W is the objective function of all kinds of governments considered in this section, local or central. This function is defined over the utility of a representative resident $U \equiv U(x, z)$ and over (per-capita) public expenditures c, which benefit only politicians. Of course, the well-being and hence the private and political influence of politicians or bureaucrats increases with higher expenditures. On the other hand, politicians want to be re-elected and hence must bear in mind the utility of residents. Expenditures for the local public good as well as expenditures for purposes of politicians must be financed by collecting the capital tax and a land tax t, if available. For simplicity, the land tax is imposed on each unit of land and not on the land rent. Thus, the private budget constraint (4.6) changes to

$$x = f - (r + \tau^K)k - t + rk. \tag{4.33}$$

The per-capita budget constraint of a government, whether local or central, reads as

$$k\tau^K + t = z + c. \tag{4.34}$$

Recall that the local public good z is assumed to be a publicly provided private good. According to this constraint, a government now has three choice variables. Let us assume that it chooses t, τ^K, and c so as to

$$\text{maximize } W(c, U[x, z]), \tag{4.35}$$

where x and z are as defined by (4.33) and (4.34) and where r and k depend on τ^K, as explained by (4.11) and (4.12), respectively.

Taking into account that there is no terms-of-trade effect in the case of identical regions, the first-order conditions of solving (4.35) become (with choice variables shown in parentheses)

$$(t): \quad \frac{dW}{dt} \frac{1}{W_U U_x} = -1 + MRS = 0 \iff MRS = 1, \tag{4.36}$$

$$(\tau^K): \quad \frac{dW}{d\tau^K} \frac{1}{W_U U_x} = -k + MRS \left(k + \tau^K \frac{\partial k}{\partial \tau^K} \right) = 0$$

$$\iff MRS = \frac{1}{1 + (1-l)\varepsilon}, \tag{4.37}$$

$$(c): \quad \frac{dW}{dc} \frac{1}{W_U} = \frac{W_c}{W_U} - U_z = 0 \iff \frac{W_c}{W_U} = U_z. \tag{4.38}$$

Inserting the first-order condition (4.36) into (4.37), we obtain $\tau^K = 0$. As emphasized in Chapter 3, if governments have an undistortive land tax at their disposal (and if there are no congestion costs with capital employed in the region), then they use only the land tax to finance public goods. This result holds even in an economy with partly self-interested politicians. Condition (4.36) shows that, for a given amount of wasteful expenditures, the resources are divided efficiently between the private and the public sector. This does not mean, however, that governments provide the first-best levels of public goods. The first-order condition (4.38) characterizes how tax revenues are distributed between those government expenditures that benefit only politicians or bureaucrats and outlays on local public goods consumed by residents. The marginal rate of substitution in politicians' preferences for increasing wasteful expenditures in terms of a lower level of a resident's utility, W_c/W_U, must be equal to marginal costs. Marginal costs are given by a decrease in a representative resident's utility level U_z, which negatively affects the chance of being re-elected.

If there are no undistortive taxes available then the government's optimum is composed of the first-order conditions (4.37) and (4.38), where condition (4.37) is the same as in the case of benevolent governments, (4.15). Again, for a given amount of wasteful expenditures, even a partly self-serving government must allocate resources between the private and the public sector efficiently when it is also concerned with the utility of voters. Only the amount of tax revenues spent on the local public good differs from the amount spent by benevolent governments.

4.4.2   Fiscal Decentralization with Undistortive Taxes

The basic characteristic of fiscal decentralization is that tax bases become more mobile among individual jurisdictions. Hence, as in Section 4.2, we depict fiscal decentralization by a decrease in the market share l of each individual jurisdiction. However, since all jurisdictions are identical, the decrease in the market share of each jurisdiction has no impact on the equilibrium amount of (per-capita) capital k employed in each jurisdiction. Thus, if a change in the market share alters the capital tax rate and the (per-capita) level of wasteful expenditures chosen by governments, the induced impacts on the other variables in each jurisdiction are then given by (4.26) and by

$$\frac{dr}{dc} = 0, \quad \frac{dx}{dc} = 0, \quad \frac{dz}{dc} = -1. \tag{4.39}$$

Moreover, the private budget constraint (4.33), the government budget constraint (4.34), and the condition of the optimal capital employment chosen by firms (4.3) make clear that a change in the market share has no direct impact on x, z, or r. It can affect these variables only by changing the optimal choice of τ^K and c. However, if jurisdictions can levy an undistortive land tax, then the first-order condition of choosing the capital tax rate (4.37) is not relevant for the government's optimum. None of the remaining first-order conditions (4.36) and (4.38) depend on the market share directly. Thus, as an important first result we have

Proposition 4.5. *If governments can collect undistortive (land) taxes then they abstain from taxing the mobile source capital. Fiscal decentralization does not affect the behavior of governments; it does not change the incentives of policy makers to waste tax revenues for own purposes.*

If governments have an undistortive tax available, fiscal decentralization is not beneficial if policy makers are partly self-interested. This result is in remarkable contrast to the conclusions drawn so far in this book. One of the basic results has been that the tax instrument set on the regional level must include an undistortive tax if an efficient allocation is to be achieved. If benevolent regional governments cannot affect the interregional terms of trade as assumed in this chapter, they indeed face the correct incentives to choose an efficient allocation. This conclusion turns to its opposite if governments are (at least partly) self-interested. According to Proposition 4.5, the constraint that jurisdictions are unable to use undistortive taxes is a necessary condition to ensure that fiscal decentralization is beneficial.

4.4.3   Fiscal Decentralization with Interregional Tax Competition

As a first step, we must analyze how jurisdictions adapt τ^K and c in response to a decrease in the market share l. This can be derived by totally differentiating the following system of equations, which simply restates the first-order conditions (4.37) and (4.38):

$$G(\tau^K, c, l) \equiv MRS[x(\tau^K, c), z(\tau^K, c)] - \frac{1}{1 + (1 - l)\varepsilon} = 0, \qquad (4.40)$$

$$H(\tau^K, c) \equiv \frac{W_c[c, x(\tau^K, c), z(\tau^K, c)]}{W_U[c, x(\tau^K, c), z(\tau^K, c)]} - U_z[x(\tau^K, c), z(\tau^K, c)] = 0. \qquad (4.41)$$

The appendix in Section 4.6 provides an explicit solution to this problem. Here, we summarize the results in

Proposition 4.6.   *Fiscal decentralization – that is, interregional tax competition – induces regional governments to decrease the capital tax rate, $d\tau^K/dl >$ 0. Governments also cut down wasteful expenditures, $dc/dl > 0$, if x and c are normal goods in the preference functions $U(x, z)$ and $W(c, U)$, respectively.*

The result that regional governments are forced by competition to decrease the capital tax rate is well known from the analysis in Section 4.1. Taken by itself, this points in the direction of less fiscal decentralization, since it causes governments to choose inefficiently low levels of local public goods. On the contrary, increased competition for the mobile capital tax base induces self-interested politicians to decrease the amount of public expenditures used for their own purposes. This is in the interest of citizens.

In order to analyze how the utility of a representative individual is affected by a decrease in the market share of regions, we insert the private budget constraint (4.33) for x and the public budget restriction (4.34) for z into the utility function $U(x, z)$. Taking again into account that k is not affected by a change in l, we obtain

$$\frac{dU}{dl}\frac{1}{U_x} = k(MRS - 1)\frac{d\tau^K}{dl} - MRS\frac{dc}{dl}. \qquad (4.42)$$

If we start from an initial situation with several independent jurisdictions, $l < 1$, (4.42) does not allow us to assess the welfare effect of further fiscal decentralization. According to the first-order condition (4.37), $MRS > 1$ and so the change in welfare can have either sign. This result corresponds to the conclusions drawn by Edwards and Keen (1996). However, if the economy consists of one region, a fundamental argument of standard second-best theory suggests that (at least some degree of) fiscal decentralization is beneficial to all citizens.

If we start from a situation without any fiscal decentralization, there is no competition for capital and the distribution of resources between the private and the public sector is not distorted – even if public goods are financed by a tax on capital. However, since policy makers partly waste tax revenues for own purposes, the use of the resources within the public sector is distorted. Because it is better, in general, to have several small distortions than one huge distortion, welfare may be increased if wasting tax revenues is limited by fiscal decentralization at the expense of an inefficient allocation of resources between the private and the government sectors.

The optimal degree of interregional tax competition is achieved if any further change in the market share of a region leaves the utility of a representative individual unchanged. Inserting (4.37) into (4.42), setting the resulting expression equal to zero, and solving for l yields

$$l^* = 1 + \frac{dc}{dl}\left(\varepsilon k \frac{d\tau^K}{dl}\right)^{-1}.$$ (4.43)

Without any further information on the functional form of the utility and the production function, it is impossible to state the optimal degree of tax competition. However, perfect interregional competition, $l^* \to 0$, is not necessarily optimal owing to the remaining distortions.

4.5   Property Tax Incidence and Land Taxation

The previous sections have analyzed interregional tax competition in a model in which jurisdictions are constrained to finance local public goods by a tax on the mobile factor of capital. This tax can be interpreted as the property tax – the basic local tax source in many federal states. To determine the optimal level of the property tax from the viewpoint of a single jurisdiction, it has been necessary to derive the incidence of the tax. Since all individuals have been assumed identical and thus equally endowed with all sources of income, there are no distributional effects of collecting the tax. If, however, land owners do not coincide with capital owners, benevolent governments must be aware of the distributional consequences of the property tax. The list of the literature on this question is quite long (see e.g. Wildasin 1986, 1987; Mieszkowski and Zodrow 1989), and there are several views about the incidence of the property tax. These hinge on the question of what is taxed – mobile capital (structures) as analyzed so far or residential property – and on the kind of consideration: partial equilibrium analysis within one small jurisdiction, or total equilibrium analysis studying the interaction of all jurisdictions in a federal state. These differences yield three distinct views on the incidence of the property tax: the *traditional view* or classical view, the *new view,* and the *benefit view.* This section illustrates the basic thoughts by using the model of interregional tax competition, and it also touches on the efficiency and incidence considerations of land taxation.

4.5.1   The Traditional View

The traditional view concentrates on the property tax on structures or, more precisely, on mobile capital employed in the jurisdictions' production process. It considers only a single small jurisdiction and argues that, since capital is supplied infinitely elastically to small jurisdictions, the net return to capital is unaffected by a property tax levied in any one jurisdiction. The burden falls on the owners of immobile factors such as land and on consumers of locally produced goods such as housing. Early contributions to the traditional view are Simon (1943) and Netzer (1966). Aaron (1975), Wildasin (1986, p. 103; 1987, p. 1146), and Mieszkowski and Zodrow (1989, p. 1117) survey the studies that can be assigned to this view.

To make the basic insights derived in the literature clear, let us again consider the model outlined in Section 4.1. We further assume that all jurisdictions are identical, $L_i = L_j = L$ and $k_i = k_j = k$ for all i and j, and that jurisdiction i increases its property tax rate. Then, the return to capital changes by (4.11). Moreover, using (4.3) and (4.4), the rent to land in jurisdiction i is affected as follows:

$$L_i \frac{d\rho_i}{d\tau_i^K} = -L_i k_i \frac{dr}{dk_i} - L_i k_i = \left(\frac{1}{I} - 1\right) Lk. \tag{4.44}$$

If jurisdiction i is small, $I \to \infty$, then there is (almost) no change in the net return to capital according to (4.11), $dr/d\tau_i^K \to 0$, and the local land rent falls by $L_i(d\rho_i/d\tau_i^K) = -Lk$. This result seems to support the traditional view that owners of capital completely shift the burden of the property tax on to land owners. Among others, Wildasin (1986, p. 103) and Schneider and Wellisch (1997) have extended the analysis by considering also nontradable goods such as housing in a jurisdiction. Here, the burden of the tax is divided among land owners and consumers of housing, while the net return to capital is not affected as long as capital is supplied perfectly elastically to the jurisdiction.

This analysis suggests that an isolated tax increase in a small jurisdiction leaves other jurisdictions unaffected if the acting jurisdiction does not have any market power in the national capital market. However, Bradford (1978) and Zodrow and Mieszkowski (1986b) have established that this conclusion is incorrect, even for small jurisdictions. To understand this argument, note that the income change to all capital owners in the economy is equal to

$$K \frac{dr}{\tau_i^K} = -\frac{ILk}{I} = -Lk, \tag{4.45}$$

where we have inserted (4.11).

Equation (4.45) implies that capital bears the full burden of an incremental tax increase in a jurisdiction, no matter how small this jurisdiction is. This result is absolutely in line with the result derived in (4.44) that land in the taxing jurisdiction bears the burden of the property tax. The reason is that the induced capital flow raises land rents elsewhere and, on a nationwide basis, the increase in land rents in the other jurisdictions just offsets the reduction in the taxing jurisdiction. To see this, note that the change in land rents in all other jurisdictions becomes

$$\sum_{j \neq i} L_j \frac{d\rho_j}{d\tau_i^K} = -(I - 1)Lk \frac{dr}{d\tau_i^K} = \left(1 - \frac{1}{I}\right)Lk, \tag{4.46}$$

that is, just the opposite to the decrease in the land rent in jurisdiction i as derived in (4.44). Note that we have used (4.3) and (4.4) and have again inserted (4.11) to derive (4.46).

In summary, although the reduction in the net return to capital and changes in land rents in any other jurisdiction may be very small, they are widespread. In the end, capital bears the entire burden.

4.5.2   The New View

The last point just mentioned (i.e., the shifting of the burden of the property tax to the owners of capital) is also the essence of the new view developed by Mieszkowski (1972) and Aaron (1975). However, it is not derived by considering an isolated tax increase in a small jurisdiction. It is rather based on the observation that all jurisdictions use the property tax to finance local public services. Therefore, if the entire capital stock in the economy is given as assumed in this chapter and if all jurisdictions choose the same tax rate, then the net return to capital must fall by the precise amount of the tax rate and is not shifted to other factors or consumers. The traditional view seems flawed because it considers the incidence in a partial equilibrium framework. Contrary to the traditional view, the new view suggests that the property tax is highly progressive.

This conclusion has already been derived in the previous sections of this chapter for the case of identical jurisdictions that choose uniform property tax rates. As a consequence, increasing the tax rate does not change the capital allocation among jurisdictions, and the return to capital decreases by the exact amount of the uniform tax increase in order to satisfy condition (4.3) and the capital market equilibrium (4.5) simultaneously. This also holds for different jurisdictions, as can easily be understood by looking at Figure 4.3. For simplicity, we assume in the figure that the economy is made up of only two jurisdictions. Note again that K_i is the amount of capital used in jurisdiction i and that F_K^i is the marginal productivity of capital at the employment level K_i. The amount of capital employed in jurisdiction 1 is depicted from the left origin to the right, while K_2 is measured from the right origin to the left. If both jurisdictions choose the same property tax rate, $\tau_1^K = \tau_2^K = \tau^K$, the return to capital r falls by an amount equal to the tax rate.

There are, however, at least two objections to the assumptions that generate such clear-cut results. First, although the assumption of a fixed national capital stock is useful in order to highlight the implications of high mobility of capital across jurisdictions, it is certainly no more than a simplifying assumption.

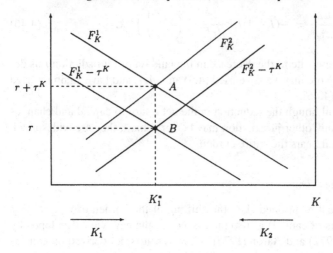

Figure 4.3. The new view for identical property tax rates.

Among others, Kotlikoff (1984) and Sinn (1987) demonstrate that, in a growing economy, the capital stock depends on the interactions of saving behavior and investment decisions of firms, which are both influenced by capital taxation – and the property tax is part of the entire tax burden that falls on capital.

Second, it can be observed that jurisdictions do not choose the same property tax rates. This is recognized by the proponents of the new view, who argue that nonuniform tax rates could be regarded as a system of uniform taxation at an average rate, together with a system of jurisdiction-specific tax differentials. While the net return to capital falls by the average tax rate, the tax differentials across jurisdictions have an incidence similar to that derived by the traditional view. However, the concept of an average tax rate is problematic. Courant (1977) shows that there generally does not exist a uniform tax rate that generates the same national tax revenues as a given system of nonuniform rates and, at the same time, reduces the net return to capital equally. The net return can be lower or higher in the case of nonuniform tax rates, depending on the production technologies in the jurisdictions.

Despite both objections, the basic insight of the new view – that capital owners bear an essential part of the tax burden – remains a valid one.

4.5.3   The Benefit View

The third view does not consider the property tax to be on capital but rather on residential housing and regards it as a user charge for local public goods, similar to the head tax discussed in Chapters 2 and 3. In the literature, this opinion is (somewhat misleadingly) called the "benefit" view of the property tax. Although the property tax is not based on households' marginal willingness to pay for public services – the standard definition of a benefit tax – we will follow this convention.

Authors like Hamilton (1975a,b, 1976), Mills and Oates (1975), White (1975a,b), Mieszkowski (1976), and Mills (1979) (for an updated survey, see Fischel 1992) observe that head taxes on the local level used in the Tiebout world to achieve an efficient allocation are typically not available in existing federations. However, they argue that the property tax on residential property available to local governments can substitute for a head tax if it is combined with zoning arrangements requiring households living in a jurisdiction to consume a certain quantity of housing. Most notably, Hamilton (1975b, 1976) argues that, under such conditions, no household would build a house larger than the minimum requirement because this would result in higher taxes that are redistributed to residents consuming only the minimum amount of housing. Such households would choose to live in a homogeneous community with larger houses. Additionally, effective zoning requirements preclude the construction of houses with relatively low values, implying that poor individuals cannot move into wealthy communities in order to enjoy public services at subsidized prices (as pointed out by Wheaton 1975). This results in an equilibrium where zoning constraints are binding and communities are homogeneous with respect to house size. This conclusion is consistent with the results derived by McGuire (1974) and Berglas and Pines (1981) for club models, in which head taxes or user charges are the revenue source.

Although efficiency can be achieved by fiscal zoning, it is clear that the exclusion of poor households from wealthy communities raises certain equity concerns. Since public education is the local public good absorbing the highest revenue share – at least in the United States (Rosen 1995) – this implies that wealthy communities provide a better quality of education at lower property tax rates (higher per-capita tax bases) to the children of rich individuals. Such issues are discussed in Inman (1978), Rubinfeld (1979), and Inman and Rubinfeld (1979).

For a better understanding of how the property tax combined with zoning constraints works and may substitute for an efficiency-supporting head tax, let us recall the basic results derived in Chapter 3. There, it is shown that public expenditure and taxation decisions of small jurisdictions achieve an efficient allocation if local governments have both an undistortive land tax and a head tax available. The head tax is chosen so as to internalize marginal crowding costs of local public goods. Following Brueckner (1983) and Wildasin (1986), we suppose there is a local housing market and that each local resident consumes h_0 units of housing services at a (rental) price of p_0 at the initial efficient equilibrium, with a head tax τ. Now, let us assume that the local government has

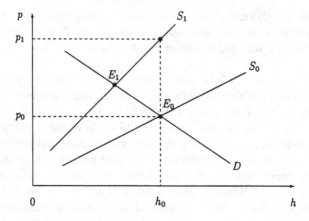

Figure 4.4. Zoning and housing market.

no head tax available but can levy a tax on residential property. Clearly, abolishing the head tax and introducing a property tax changes the equilibrium in the local housing market. Without any direct intervention in the demand for housing, the price increases and demand decreases. In Figure 4.4, housing is supplied under conditions of perfect competition; S denotes the upward sloping supply curve of housing services (marginal costs) and D the demand curve of individuals residing in the community. We normalize the efficient number of households residing in the community to 1. The initial equilibrium with head taxes is reached in E_0. If a property tax substitutes for the head tax, the owners of residential property face additional costs and the supply curve of housing services shifts upward. A new equilibrium is achieved in E_1. However, if the jurisdiction is able to impose an effective quantity constraint on the demand for housing at h_0, and if the property tax rate is chosen such that $p_1 h_0 = p_0 h_0 + \tau$, then the initial equilibrium is not distorted. Higher expenditures for housing, $(p_1 - p_0)h_0$, are just enough to internalize the congestion costs of supplying local public goods.

But what does the property tax rate that satisfies this requirement look like? To answer this question, we consider the way the property tax is usually implemented. Following Wildasin (1986), we define V as the value of the property that provides h units of housing and refer to r as the time-independent nationwide interest rate. Then, the property value in the case of head taxes is $V_0 = p_0 h_0 / r$ and, in the case of property taxes t, $V_1 = (p_1 h_0 - t V_1)/r = p_1 h_0 / (r + t)$. Setting the property tax rate such that $V_1 = V_0$, no change in the real equilibrium arises. The property tax rate that satisfies this condition can be derived by substituting $p_0 h_0 + \tau$ for $p_1 h_0$ into the expression for V_1, yielding $t = \tau / V_0$ or, alternatively, $t/r = \tau/(p_0 h_0)$. In other words, the present value of the property tax that perfectly substitutes for the efficiency-supporting head tax must be equal to the head tax per unit of housing expenditures.

4.5.4   Land Taxation

In our analysis so far, we have assumed that land in each jurisdiction is homogeneous and perfectly inelastic in supply. This has led us to conclude that local governments would favor land taxes (if available) over other taxes because taxes on land are *neutral* – avoiding any efficiency losses and any shifting of the tax burden. This conventional view about the properties of land taxes can be found in many textbooks (e.g. Rosen 1995, with some objections). The neutrality holds even if the tax is levied in future periods after the owner has sold the parcel of land. The owner must bear the burden of future taxes because they are capitalized into current values. To understand this, let us first assume that there are no taxes on land. The value of a parcel of land is equal to $V_0 = \rho/r$, that is, the capitalized value of an identical stream of land rents ρ. Now suppose that a tax t on the market value of land will be announced. This decreases the present value of the parcel of land to $V_1 = (\rho - tV_1)/r = \rho/(r + t)$, implying that each investor would pay less by the amount of the capitalized value of taxes, $V_1 - V_0 = -tV_1/r$.

However, these results have been challenged in the literature. First, traditional conclusions about the incidence of land taxes may be incorrect when intertemporal saving and investment decisions are taken into acount. Feldstein (1977) considers an overlapping generations framework where individuals are able to invest their savings into two assets – land and capital, both employed by firms. He shows that capital partly bears the burden of a land-rent tax because individuals will choose to hold larger amounts of capital in their portfolios. Thus, capital employment increases, dropping the return to capital. This also means that the marginal productivity and hence the gross return to other factors (including land) increases. Calvo, Kotlikoff, and Rodriguez (1979) show that the Feldstein result changes, and the classical result remains intact, if one assumes "rational bequest" behavior of individuals. Here, land taxes are fully capitalized into land values (as shown previously), and individuals adapt bequests so as to leave the equilibrium of the economy unchanged. Since collections of land taxes are given back to the private sector in a lump-sum fashion, the present value of the dynastic income does not change. With rational bequest behavior, this means that no member of a dynasty has incentives to reoptimize the consumption path and the portfolio choice. Moreover, Fane (1984) argues that even without rational bequest behavior, the government can ensure by its debt policy that land taxes are fully capitalized.[4] To do so, it must induce investors not to change their portfolio choice. If the government gives bonds to

---

[4]   See also Buiter (1989) and Bailey (1993) for a similar analysis.

initial land owners when a land tax is imposed and finances the new debt by future land tax collections, it preserves the equilibrium in the economy because the present value of these bonds is equal to the present value of future land taxes – the loss in land values.

Second, the basic reason why land taxes are considered to be an undistortive revenue source in the classical view is that land is fixed in supply. The implications of lifting this assumption have been discussed by various authors surveyed in Wildasin (1986, p. 115). Suppose that, after land has been developed, an investor receives a constant return of ρ_i for a parcel of land cultivated for some use i. If the tax is levied on the market value in each period, then the present market value of such a parcel of land is $V_i = (\rho_i - tV_i)/r = \rho_i/(r + t)$. As observed earlier, the tax increases the discount factor of evaluating a project. When two projects have the same before-tax present market value – the first by promising a steady flow of (nearly identical) returns, and the second by rather small returns in the first periods and high returns in more distant periods – it is clear that the tax drives a wedge in the choice between these projects, favoring the first one. However, as Wildasin (1982) points out, the distortive effect of land taxes can be traced to the fact that market values of land differ over time according to their use. Hence, land-value tax liabilities are not use-independent. Neutrality can be restored by taxes that do not depend on the specific use of the parcel of land – for instance, a tax per unit of land.

4.6   Appendix

The basic purpose of this appendix is to derive the responses $d\tau^K/dl$ and dc/dl set out in Section 4.4 and thus to prove Proposition 4.6. Total differentiation of (4.40) and (4.41) using (4.26) and (4.39) yields

$$\begin{pmatrix} G_{\tau^K} & G_c \\ H_{\tau^K} & H_c \end{pmatrix} \begin{pmatrix} d\tau^K \\ dc \end{pmatrix} = - \begin{pmatrix} G_l \\ H_l \end{pmatrix} dl, \tag{A.4.1}$$

with

$$G_{\tau^K} = \frac{dMRS}{d(z/x)} \left(\frac{k}{x} + \frac{z}{x^2} k \right) + \frac{1}{A^2} \frac{(1-l)}{\tau^K} \varepsilon, \qquad G_c = -\frac{dMRS}{d(z/x)} \frac{1}{x},$$

$$W_U H_{\tau^K} = (W_{cU} - U_z W_{UU})k(U_z - U_x) - W_U k(U_{zz} - U_{zx}),$$

$$W_U H_c = W_U U_{zz} + W_{cc} - W_{cU} \frac{W_c}{W_U} + U_z \left(W_{UU} \frac{W_c}{W_U} - W_{Uc} \right),$$

$$G_l = -\frac{1}{A^2} \varepsilon, \qquad H_l = 0, \qquad A \equiv [1 + (1-l)\varepsilon]. \tag{A.4.2}$$

Let D denote the 2×2 matrix on the left side of (A.4.1). It follows that $|D| > 0$ and that $G_{\tau^K} < 0$ and $H_c < 0$ to ensure stability of the system of equations (4.40) and (4.41). Solving (A.4.1) with the help of Cramer's rule and inserting (A.4.2) yields

$$\frac{d\tau^K}{dl} = \frac{1}{|D|}\frac{1}{A^2}\varepsilon H_c > 0, \tag{A.4.3}$$

$$\frac{dc}{dl} = -\frac{1}{|D|}\frac{1}{A^2}\varepsilon[(W_{cU} - U_z W_{UU})kU_x(MRS - 1)$$
$$- W_U k(U_{zz} - U_{zx})] > 0. \tag{A.4.4}$$

In order to sign (A.4.4), we have used the first-order conditions (4.37) and (4.38) and the assumptions that c and x are normal goods in the preference functions $W(c, U)$ and $U(x, z)$, respectively. The normality assumption implies $W_{UU}U_z - W_{cU} = W_{UU}W_c/W_U - W_{cU} < 0$ and $U_{zz} - U_{zx}MRS < 0$. However, if the last inequality holds, then it must be that $U_{zz} - U_{zx} < 0$, since $MRS \geq 1$. Equations (A.4.3) and (A.4.4) prove Proposition 4.6.

CHAPTER 5

Optimal Structure of Local Governments

The preceding chapters – most notably Chapter 2 – have studied whether an exogenously fixed number of mobile individuals in a federal state is allocated efficiently across a politically predetermined number of local jurisdictions. What the previous analysis has left out of consideration is determining the optimal size of individual jurisdictions or, in other words, the optimal number of individuals living in these jurisdictions. Of course, such questions concerning the optimal governmental structure in a federal state cannot be ignored when analyzing the problem of whether fiscal decentralization secures an optimal allocation. As long as utility of individuals can be increased by a restructuring of jurisdictional boundaries, there is scope for a Pareto improvement. There are several empirical examples of such a restructuring, indicating that costs and benefits of changes in jurisdictional boundaries are on the agenda of the political debate in federal states. For instance, the number of local governments in Germany was reduced significantly during the 1970s, and Henderson (1985) indicates that most American cities have grown through annexation. There is also an ongoing debate in Germany of integrating some small *Bundesländer* into a larger jurisdiction in order to reduce costs in the public sector.[1] It is therefore necessary to include another dimension in the characterization of an optimal allocation. We will speak of an *optimal allocation* in this chapter when, in addition to the efficient supply of local public goods and the efficient distribution of a certain number of individuals across jurisdictions, each jurisdiction has its optimal population size and thus there is an optimal number of jurisdictions in the federal state.

There are several important directions of research trying to determine the optimal structure of local governments in a federal state. In the original world of Tiebout (1956), there were no locationally fixed factors like land and hence

---

[1] In an election in late 1996, the *Bundesländer* Berlin and Brandenburg refused to become integrated, although the reduction of costs in both government sectors would have been significant. Here, as often is the case, historical reasons proved stronger than economic ones.

geography did not play any role. In this case, Berglas (1976) and Scotchmer and Wooders (1987), among others, use models of club theory to characterize the optimal allocation and study whether it can be decentralized. They establish that an optimal club membership size is achieved if the user charges imposed on members (to internalize marginal congestion costs) are just sufficient to cover all expenditures of providing club goods. This optimal allocation can be decentralized through a system of profit-maximizing clubs. The user charge is sufficient to induce the club board to supply club goods efficiently to the optimal number of members (residents).

When this world is extended by assigning fixed factors like land to clubs, the optimal allocation can no longer be sustained by user charges only. As explained by Stiglitz (1977), Arnott (1979), and Arnott and Stiglitz (1979), among others, the revenues created by user charges do not cover the expenditures of local public goods when the optimal number of residents is to be achieved. Rather, the aggregate land rent plus user charges must just equal government expenditures. This result is an extended version of the famous Henry George (1914) theorem derived for the case without congestion costs. In addition, if local governments maximize the rent of the land where the optimal number of residents live, and if they cannot affect the utility level of their mobile constituents, then they also have the correct incentives to choose the efficient supply of local public goods.

In an important article, Hochman, Pines, and Thisse (1995) observe that individuals must be supplied with various public goods, all of which are essential in the individual consumption basket – education, police and fire protection, electricity, streets, and many other public services. Any one local public good has a different market area on the strip of land where individuals live, so that market areas overlap. In the case of multiple local public goods there is a widespread belief, developed by Olson (1969) and advocated by Oates (1972), that each local public good should be provided by one layer of government – the *principle of fiscal equivalence*. Following this claim, two further problems arise when trying to achieve an optimal allocation. First, since several local governments have their jurisdiction over the same strip of land, the land rent must be divided among the various suppliers of local public goods if an optimal population size over the entire strip of land is to be achieved, according to the Henry George theorem. With such a revenue sharing, each supplier just breaks even. This can be achieved by an appropriate assignment of property rights in land to the individual jurisdictions. Second, and more severe, is the incentive problem of local governments. As emphasized in Chapter 3, local governments have the correct incentives to choose the efficient supply of local public goods and to internalize marginal congestion costs only if they maximize the *entire* rent over the strip of land where they have jurisdiction. Because market areas for various local public goods typically overlap, this incentive problem cannot be solved by one layer of government for each local public good – even with an appropriate division of property rights in land. As Hochman et al. (1995) point out, only *metropolitan* governments – supplying all essential public goods which, in addition, do not cause spillover effects – have the correct incentives to establish an efficient allocation, since they have jurisdiction over the entire land where residents live. However, as Chapter 3 has shown, efficiency also requires that regions must be small enough to ensure that local governments take the utility of mobile households as given. A fundamental question thus arises: Can metropolitan areas be *both* small and large enough?

In order to discuss the determination of the optimal structure of jurisdictions, Chapter 5 is organized as follows. Section 5.1 derives the basic elements of club theory in order to highlight Tiebout's conclusions in a world without fixed factors of production. In Section 5.2 we study the optimal allocation when jurisdictions are endowed with land and provide local public goods. Section 5.3 extends the analysis of Section 5.2 by assuming that there are several essential local public goods in each individual's consumption basket and that the market areas of local public goods overlap. We show that the optimal allocation can be decentralized only by metropolitan governments. Finally, Section 5.4 contains an appendix with some important proofs.

5.1   Tiebout and the Theory of Clubs

In his classic article, Tiebout (1956) assumes that a large number of local governments provide local public goods and finance them with user charges (head taxes). All individuals are endowed with location-independent incomes and are perfectly mobile. Moreover, Tiebout assumes that all communities are of optimal size and concludes that decentralization is efficient. Following McGuire (1974), Berglas (1976), Scotchmer and Wooders (1987), and Scotchmer (1994), one can use club theory (see Buchanan 1965) to describe what such an optimal allocation looks like and how it can be decentralized by competing clubs, which can be interpreted as local governments. Club theory is concerned with the optimal consumption of club goods, the optimal membership size of clubs, and the sustainability of clubs under a competitive market regime. To illustrate the basic pillars of club theory, let us assume that there are $\bar{N}$ identical individuals in the economy, each of them consuming a private numeraire good x and a club good z. The utility function of a representative individual is given by $U(x, z)$. Each individual is endowed with an exogenous income w. The costs of providing z units of the club good to N club members are equal to $C(z, N)$, expressed in units of the numeraire good. For any given level of z, we assume that the average cost curve C/N is a U-shaped function of the number of club members N.

The optimal allocation, including the optimal club membership size and the optimal supply of the club good, can be found by

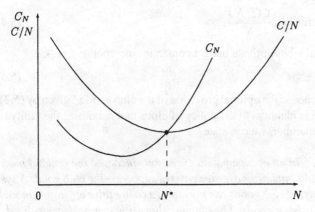

Figure 5.1. Optimal club size.

$$\text{maximizing } U\left(w - \frac{C(z, N)}{N}, z\right) \tag{5.1}$$

in the level of the club good z and the number of club members N. Thus, one has to maximize the utility of a representative individual, who must share the costs of providing the club good with all other members of the club. The first-order conditions of this problem are (with control variables shown in parentheses)

$$(z): \ N\frac{U_z}{U_x} = C_z, \tag{5.2}$$

$$(N): \ NC_N = C, \tag{5.3}$$

where subscripts again stand for partial derivatives.

Condition (5.2) is the Samuelson rule of providing the club good. Since the club good is collectively consumed, the sum of the *marginal benefits* of all club members must be equal to marginal costs. The optimal membership size of the club is characterized by condition (5.3). For any given provision of the club good z, the optimal number of users N^* minimizes average costs of supplying the club good. Accordingly, the optimal number of (identical) clubs supplying z is $\bar{N}/N^*$, where we ignore the integer problem.

Figure 5.1 depicts the optimal membership size of a club. Both condition (5.3) and Figure 5.1 show that, as in the problem of supplying private goods under conditions of perfect competition, each supplier of the club good just breaks even under marginal-cost pricing; that is, each individual pays an entrance fee in the amount of C_N.

Berglas (1976), Scotchmer and Wooders (1987), and Scotchmer (1994) have shown – in the spirit of Tiebout (1956) – that the optimal allocation characterized by (5.2) and (5.3) can be decentralized in a competitive market. If the entrance fee to a club providing the good z is equal to

$$\tau(z) \equiv \arg\min_{N} \frac{C(z, N)}{N}, \tag{5.4}$$

then an individual whose private budget constraint incorporates $\tau(z)$,

$$x = w - \tau(z), \tag{5.5}$$

would precisely choose the optimal provision of the club good z^* given by (5.2). Since this choice is identical to the policy of clubs that maximize the utility of a representative member, we can state

Proposition 5.1. *In an economy with exogenous incomes, the optimal membership size of clubs minimizes average costs of supplying the club good. A system of clubs supplying club goods can prevail in a competitive environment such as in the case of private goods. The optimal allocation can be decentralized.*

This analysis immediately extends to an economy wherein several club goods are essential in the households' preference structure. However, if one wants to apply the analysis with exogenous incomes to the provision of local public goods, a severe problem arises. Because there are also some immobile resources (like land) in fixed supply in the jurisdictions, the number of residents affects the average local rent to these fixed factors. Hence, in order to determine the optimal population size of a jurisdiction and thus the optimal number of jurisdictions in a federal state, two opposing effects must be taken into account. First, as derived in this section, an increasing number of residents decreases average costs of providing local public goods until minimum average costs are achieved. Second, if land rents are shared equally among old and new residents, the per-capita land rent declines with an increasing population. These opposing forces must be balanced in order to achieve the optimal local population size. As can intuitively be expected from this argument, we will demonstrate in the next section that this calls for a population size *lower* than the one that minimizes average costs of supplying local public goods.

5.2 The Henry George Theorem

Let us consider N identical individuals who inhabit a strip of land represented by the interval $[0, L]$, which can be interpreted as a metropolitan area. Land is used only for housing in this simple world. Each individual derives utility from consumption of a private numeraire good x, from housing h, and from a local public good z according to the well-behaved utility function $U(x, h, z)$. Each household is endowed with a fixed income w, which can be used for consumption of the private good and for producing the local public good. The costs of providing the local public good are given by the function $C(z, N)$, expressed in units of the private numeraire good.

Let us now characterize the optimal allocation, consisting of the efficient supply of the local public good and the optimal population size of the metropolitan area – that is, the number of metropolitan residents that maximizes the utility level of each individual living within this area. Thus, a metropolitan planner would have to

$$\text{maximize } U(x, h, z) \tag{5.6}$$

by choosing x, h, z and the number of residents N subject to the following constraints:

$$(\lambda): \; Nw - Nx - C(z, N) = 0, \tag{5.7}$$

$$(\mu): \; L - Nh = 0, \tag{5.8}$$

where the Lagrange multipliers associated with the constraints appear in parentheses. Constraint (5.7) states that each metropolitan area is a self-sufficient entity. Total income of residents must just cover total private consumption and the costs of providing the local public good. Moreover, condition (5.8) requires that the demand for housing must be equal to the metropolitan's endowment with land.

The first-order conditions of this problem become (with control variables shown in parentheses)

$$(x): \; U_x = \lambda N, \tag{5.9}$$

$$(h): \; U_h = \mu N, \tag{5.10}$$

$$(z): \; U_z = \lambda C_z, \tag{5.11}$$

$$(N): \; \lambda(w - x - C_N) = \mu h. \tag{5.12}$$

Dividing (5.11) by (5.9) yields the Samuelson condition of an efficient supply of the local public good:

$$N\frac{U_z}{U_x} = C_z. \tag{5.13}$$

Substituting (5.9) for λ and (5.10) for μ into (5.12) and inserting constraints (5.7) and (5.8) into the resulting expression, we obtain the necessary condition of an optimal population size in the metropolitan area:

$$C = L\frac{U_h}{U_x} + NC_N. \tag{5.14}$$

A simplified version of condition (5.14) is known in the literature as the *Henry George theorem*. If there are no congestion costs in the provision of the local public good, $C_N = 0$, then the Henry George theorem states that the optimal population size is achieved if the aggregate land rent in the metropolitan area on the right side is equal to total costs of supplying the local public good on the left side. Condition (5.14) presents a modified version of the Henry George theorem, including congestion costs that must be added to the land rent on the right side. Thus, we can state the modified Henry George theorem as

Proposition 5.2. *The utility-maximizing population size in a region (metropolitan area) is achieved if the aggregate land rent plus any user charges for internalizing marginal congestion costs of the local public good are equal to total costs of providing the local public good.*

In the next section, we show that this result extends to the case of several local public goods.

The modified Henry George theorem can be explained intuitively when we divide condition (5.14) by N. Then, the left side indicates the reduction in costs for all residents when a new individual enters the metropolitan area. The entrant takes on an equal share of the costs of supplying a certain amount of the local public good. The right side reflects the increase in costs that a new resident imposes on existing residents. These costs consist of two elements. First, the costs of providing a given amount of the local public good increase by marginal congestion costs. Second, as the entire land rent in the metropolitan area is equally divided among all residents, the share of all existing residents falls by the average aggregate land rent. The Henry George theorem suggests that an optimal population size is established when these opposing marginal costs and benefits are balanced. Since the costs of a new entrant include the decrease in the average land rent, it is clear from (5.14) that the optimal population size must be lower than the one that minimizes average costs of supplying local public goods. It is interesting to observe that – in the special case of constant per-capita costs of supplying the local public good, $C(z, N) = Nc(z)$ (with $c(\cdot)$ denoting the per-capita cost function) – the aggregate land rent should be zero. There is no reduction in the costs of supplying the local public good with an additional individual entering the metropolitan area. In this case, the new entrant merely decreases the average rent to land, and thus the optimal number of residents living in the metropolitan area should be zero.

Having derived the optimal population size in an urban area, the optimal structure of jurisdictions in a federal state is then achieved if the entire population $\bar{N}$ is divided among urban areas in such a way that conditions (5.13) and (5.14) hold in each urban area. Let us suppose that all urban areas are identical and that N^* indicates the optimal population size in each area. (We will assume that $\bar{N}/N^*$ is an integer number so that this is feasible.) Thus, a natural way to achieve the optimal structure of jurisdictions is to divide the entire land endowment of the federal state among the individual urban areas such that the optimal number of residents is established in each area.

Finally, we showed in Chapter 3 that governments of small jurisdictions have the correct incentives to supply local public goods (in accordance with the Samuelson condition) and to internalize marginal congestion costs *if* they maximize the net land rent in the jurisdiction. Thus, if the entire land in a federal state is divided among jurisdictions so that each jurisdiction is of optimal size, then the optimal allocation can be decentralized – provided each jurisdiction is still small enough to ensure that local governments take the utility level of mobile individuals as given. This potential trade-off between the optimal size of jurisdictions and the necessary incentive structure of local governments will play an important role in the next section, where we assume that local public goods have overlapping market areas.

5.3   Overlapping Market Areas of Local Public Goods

5.3.1   The Optimal Allocation

Let us now extend the analysis of Section 5.2 by assuming that the metropolitan area is made up of two suburbs, identified by the strips of land $L_1 = [0, L_1]$ and $L_2 =]L_1, L]$, where all variables relating to suburb i are subindexed by i. Land is used for housing only. Let N_i denote the number of individuals living in suburb i, with

$$N - \sum_{i=1,2} N_i = 0. \tag{5.15}$$

Each individual derives utility from consumption of a private numeraire good x, from housing h, and from two local public goods z^1 and z^2 according to the well-behaved utility function $U^i \equiv U(x_i, h_i, z^1, z_i^2)$. Both kinds of local public goods are essential, and we could think of z^1 as police protection and of z^2 as public education. The local public good police protection z^1 does not carry a suburb-specific index in the utility function U^i, since we assume that it can be consumed in the entire metropolitan area $[0, L]$. However, education can be consumed only in the suburb where the individuals live. In each suburb, education is provided to the amount of z_1^2 and z_2^2, respectively. Since police protection is provided for the entire area while education is restricted to the suburbs, the market areas of both kinds of public goods overlap. This is demonstrated in Figure 5.2.

In a spatial model, Hochman et al. (1995) explain the need for several suppliers of certain local public goods by transportation costs that individuals face to make a trip to a public facility. In our framework, we simply assume that there are no transportation costs when consuming public education within a suburb, while costs of consuming it in the other suburb are such that no individual makes the trip.

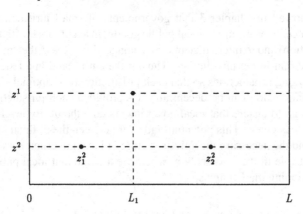

Figure 5.2. Market areas of local public goods in the metropolitan area.

The costs of providing local public goods are given by the functions $C^1(z^1, N)$ and $C^{2i} \equiv C^2(z_i^2, N_i)$ for $i = 1, 2$, expressed in units of the private numeraire good. We restrict our attention to the case where all individuals living in the metropolitan area receive the same utility level.

Let us now characterize the optimal allocation consisting of the efficient supply of local public goods, the efficient population distribution within the metropolitan area, and the optimal population size of the metropolitan area. Thus, a metropolitan planner would have to

$$\text{maximize} \quad U(x_1, h_1, z^1, z_1^2) \tag{5.16}$$

by choosing the vectors (x_i), (h_i), (z_i^2), (N_i) and the variables z^1 and N subject to the following constraints:

$$(\lambda): \quad U(x_1, h_1, z^1, z_1^2) - U(x_2, h_2, z^1, z_2^2) = 0, \tag{5.17}$$

$$(\gamma): \quad Nw - \sum_{i=1,2} [N_i x_i + C^2(z_i^2, N_i)] - C^1(z^1, N) = 0, \tag{5.18}$$

$$(\mu_i): \quad L_i - N_i h_i = 0, \quad i = 1, 2, \tag{5.19}$$

$$(\delta): \quad N - \sum_{i=1,2} N_i = 0, \tag{5.20}$$

where again the Lagrange multipliers associated with the constraints are set in parentheses. Constraint (5.17) indicates that all individuals in the metropolitan area receive the same utility level, regardless of the suburb in which they live. Moreover, condition (5.18) requires that total income of residents must just cover total private consumption and the costs of providing local public goods. Following (5.19), the demand for housing in each suburb must be equal to the suburb's endowment with land. Finally, (5.20) simply restates the population constraint (5.15) of the metropolitan area.

Solving this problem by standard Lagrangean techniques yields the following necessary conditions of an optimal allocation:

$$\sum_{i=1,2} N_i \frac{U_{z^1}^i}{U_x^i} = C_z^1, \tag{5.21}$$

$$N_i \frac{U_{z^2}^i}{U_x^i} = C_z^{2i}, \quad i = 1, 2, \tag{5.22}$$

$$x_i + \frac{U_h^i}{U_x^i} h_i + C_N^1 + C_N^{2i} = w, \quad i = 1, 2, \tag{5.23}$$

$$C^1 + \sum_{i=1,2} C^{2i} = \sum_{i=1,2} L_i \frac{U_h^i}{U_x^i} + N C_N^1 + \sum_{i=1,2} N_i C_N^{2i} \tag{5.24}$$

(see Section 5.4.1 for an explicit solution). Conditions (5.21) and (5.22) are the well-known Samuelson rules of supplying local public goods. Whereas condition (5.22) concerns public education and requires that the sum of the marginal willingness to pay in each suburb must be equal to marginal costs, condition (5.21) claims that, for police protection, all metropolitan residents' marginal willingness to pay counts. Condition (5.23) describes the efficient locational pattern of individuals across suburbs. The marginal costs of providing an individual with the metropolitanwide utility level must be equal to the income, which the individual brings along when entering the metropolitan area and which is the same across suburbs. The marginal costs on the left side include the value of the consumption bundle, consisting of the numeraire good and (the value of) housing and the marginal congestion costs of supplying local public goods. The income is given by the fixed endowment w on the right side. Finally, condition (5.24) characterizes the modified Henry George theorem of an economy with two local public goods and overlapping market areas. The aggregate land rent in both suburbs, plus marginal congestion costs on the right side, must be equal to the total costs of supplying all local public goods in the metropolitan area.[2] The optimal population size is again achieved if the costs and benefits of an additional individual in the metropolitan area are balanced. In contrast to

---

[2] In a model with transportation costs, in which the number of public facilities supplying local public goods is an endogenous variable, Hochman et al. (1995) show that the Henry George theorem must hold for any single local public good.

Section 5.2, however, the increase in congestion costs of supplying education z^2 is given by the average marginal crowding costs $(N_1/N)C_N^{21} + (N_2/N)C_N^{22}$, since the new entrant consumes public education in only one suburb.

Can the optimal allocation described by (5.21)–(5.24) be decentralized? Of particular interest is whether this implies one layer of government for each public good, as suggested by Olson (1969) and Oates (1972). This would require us to divide the metropolitan area into overlapping jurisdictions, where the jurisdiction over the entire metropolitan area provides police protection z^1 while the jurisdictions of the suburbs supply public education z_i^2.

5.3.2   Private Behavior

We now assume that each individual is endowed with an income $w + Y$, which is exogenously given from the viewpoint of the metropolitan area and consists of the fixed endowment w plus net land rents out of land ownership in all jurisdictions. As in Chapter 3, we assume that each individual in the federal state owns an equal share of the entire land in the economy. The individual must pay a head tax τ_i depending on the suburb where the individual lives. Let ρ_i denote the rental price of housing (here, in suburb i). The household uses its income for consuming the private numeraire good x_i and housing h_i. Moreover, all individuals are perfectly mobile across all metropolitan areas and, needless to say, among the suburbs in the urban areas. Let

$$V^i \equiv V(w + Y - \tau_i, \rho_i, z^1, z_i^2) \equiv \max U(x_i, h_i, z^1, z_i^2) \qquad (5.25)$$

in x_i and h_i, subject to

$$w + Y - \tau_i = x_i + \rho_i h_i, \qquad (5.26)$$

denote the indirect utility function of an individual living in suburb i. The properties of this indirect utility function imply that, for $i, j = 1, 2$,

$$-\frac{V_\rho^i}{V_w^i} = h_i, \quad V_\rho^i = -h_i U_x^i, \quad \frac{V_{z^j}^i}{V_w^i} = \frac{U_{z^j}^i}{U_x^i}. \qquad (5.27)$$

As a necessary incentive condition to choose an efficient allocation, we assume that each metropolitan area faces a given level of utility that its government cannot affect by own policy choices. This implies that there must be a huge number of urban areas in the federal state – each, on the one hand, large enough to supply all necessary local public goods and, on the other hand, small enough to take the utility level of mobile individuals as given. Therefore, we have

$$V(w + Y - \tau_i, \rho_i, z^1, z_i^2) = \bar{u}, \quad i = 1, 2; \qquad (5.28)$$

that is, the utility of individuals in each suburb must be equal to the economy-wide utility level $\bar{u}$, which is fixed from the metropolitan area's viewpoint. Finally, the market for housing services must be in equilibrium in each suburb,

$$-N_i \frac{V_\rho^i}{V_w^i} = L_i, \quad i = 1, 2. \tag{5.29}$$

5.3.3 Decentralization through Competing Metropolitan Governments

Now, let us suppose that there is only one jurisdiction over the entire metropolitan area and that the government of this jurisdiction – called metropolitan government – maximizes the aggregate net land rent,

$$R \equiv \sum_{i=1,2} [L_i \rho_i + N_i \tau_i - C^2(z_i^2, N_i)] - C^1(z^1, N_1 + N_2), \tag{5.30}$$

by choice of the vectors (τ_i), (z_i^2) and the variable z^1. Thus, we assume that the part of the costs of supplying local public goods that is *not* covered by head taxes is financed by a tax on land rents originated in the metropolitan area. This is why we have already inserted the budget constraint of the metropolitan government for the tax on land rents into the government's objective function. The choice of the objective function can once again be explained by the enormous interest that property owners have in influencing the political process. On the other hand, residents are not interested since they vote with their feet, and thus their utility level not affected by policy measures of a single government. Of course, locational choices of individuals cannot be controlled directly by the government.

Solving the government's problem, the first-order conditions are

$$\frac{dR}{d\tau_i} = [\tau_i - C_N^1 - C_N^{2i}] \frac{\partial N_i}{\partial \tau_i} = 0, \quad i = 1, 2, \tag{5.31}$$

$$\frac{dR}{dz^1} = \sum_{i=1,2} [\tau_i - C_N^1 - C_N^{2i}] \frac{\partial N_i}{\partial z^1} + \sum_{i=1,2} N_i \frac{U_{z^1}^i}{U_x^i} - C_z^1 = 0, \tag{5.32}$$

$$\frac{dR}{dz_i^2} = [\tau_i - C_N^1 - C_N^{2i}] \frac{\partial N_i}{\partial z_i^2} + N_i \frac{U_{z^2}^i}{U_x^i} - C_z^{2i} = 0, \quad i = 1, 2 \tag{5.33}$$

(see Section 5.4.2 for a detailed derivation). Following (5.31), a metropolitan government has incentives to internalize marginal congestion costs by choosing the marginal-cost pricing rule $\tau_i = C_N^1 + C_N^{2i}$. Inserting this result into the private budget constraint of individuals (5.26), noting that $\rho_i = U_h^i/U_x^i$, and comparing the resulting expression with (5.23) demonstrates that the efficient distribution of mobile individuals across suburbs is achieved. Note that $Y = 0$ when the optimal number of jurisdictions is established and when local public goods are financed by taxes on land rents and head taxes that serve as user charges. Substituting the marginal-cost pricing result into (5.32) and (5.33) shows that the metropolitan government also achieves the Samuelson conditions of supplying local public goods. Hence, if the entire land of the federal state is divided into different urban areas such that the aggregate net land rent surplus of each area (5.30) vanishes (also implying $Y = 0$), we obtain

Proposition 5.3.   *The optimal allocation can be sustained by competing metropolitan governments providing all necessary local public goods. If metropolitan areas are established over the entire land of the federal state such that the aggregate land rent surplus vanishes in each area, and if metropolitan governments are unable to affect the utility level of mobile residents, then metropolitan governments face the correct incentives to provide local public goods efficiently to the optimal number of residents, who are distributed efficiently across suburbs.*

Since the metropolitan area must be large enough to provide all essential local public goods, the assumption that it cannot affect the utility level of mobile individuals is critical. Do New York, London, Paris, or Tokyo have no market power in influencing the utility of individuals who vote with their feet? It is therefore interesting to know if efficiency can also be established by decentralizing the government functions further, that is, by establishing jurisdictions in the suburbs.

5.3.4   Decentralization with Smaller Jurisdictions

Let us suppose there is a metropolitan government that provides only local public goods, which can be consumed everywhere in the entire metropolitan area; that is, the metropolitan government supplies z^1. There is also a local government in each suburb i supplying public education z_i^2. Hence, the market areas of the governments supplying z_i^2 and of the metropolitan government overlap. Although problematic, we stick to the assumption that the metropolitan government cannot influence the utility of mobile households. Of course, the utility level is then also given for the local governments in the suburbs.

The first problem that arises is whether each government in the urban area can break even when (a) supplying the efficient amount of local public goods to the optimal number of metropolitan residents N^* and (b) financing the expenditures on local public goods by taxes on land rents and by head taxes that internalize marginal congestion costs. If this is possible for the entire metropolitan area by a division of land in the federal state (as assumed in the previous sections), then it is clear there exists a division of land rents among governments having their jurisdiction over the same territory that ensures each government will break even. Let $\sigma_i^{\,j}$ denote the fraction of land rents given to a government that provides the local public good $z_i^{\,j}$ ensuring such a division. Then, the following fundamental question arises. Does a local government that receives only part of the rent to land in its jurisdiction face the correct incentives to supply local public goods efficiently and to choose marginal-cost pricing so as to internalize congestion costs?

To answer this question, let us consider the problem of the local government in suburb i. We consider a Nash game among all governments in the metropolitan area, where each government takes the policy choices of its neighbors as given. Because the local government must share the land rent with the metropolitan government, its problem becomes to

$$\text{maximize } R_i \equiv \sigma_i^2 L_i \rho_i + N_i \tau_i - C^2(z_i^2, N_i) \tag{5.34}$$

by choosing its head tax τ_i and the level of public education z_i^2, thereby taking market clearing in the suburb's housing market (5.29) and the migration equilibrium (5.28) into account.[3] The first-order conditions of this problem become

$$\frac{dR_i}{d\tau_i} = N_i(1 - \sigma_i^2) + (\tau_i - C_N^{2i})\frac{\partial N_i}{\partial \tau_i} = 0, \tag{5.35}$$

$$\frac{dR_i}{dz_i^2} = (\tau_i - C_N^{2i})\frac{\partial N_i}{\partial z_i^2} + \sigma_i^2 N_i \frac{U_{z^2}^i}{U_x^i} - C_z^{2i} = 0. \tag{5.36}$$

As conditions (5.35) and (5.36) indicate, maximizing only part of the rent to land within a government's jurisdiction is insufficient to induce that government to choose an efficient allocation. When local public goods have overlapping market areas, the incentive problem cannot be solved by further decentralization of government functions from the metropolitan governments to the governments of each suburb. Thus, we can state

Proposition 5.4. *If several local governments share the land rent over a given territory according to some predetermined ratio, then competition between local governments is inefficient.*

---

[3] The migration equilibrium condition (5.28) changes a bit, since now there are head taxes collected by the suburb and the metropolitan government. However, since the head tax collected by the metropolitan government is taken as given in the choice problem of the suburb, the migration responses do not change.

This result can be contrasted to the principle of fiscal equivalence as derived by Olson (1969) and Oates (1972). According to this rule, each public good should be supplied by one layer of government. This conclusion is the compromise between two opposing forces. On the one hand, the government must be as small as possible, since smaller governments are more sensitive to the preferences of their constituents. On the other hand, spillover effects must be avoided and the government must be large enough to internalize the benefits of all consumers of the public good. The principle of fiscal equivalence balances these two opposing forces. However, the foregoing analysis suggests that this argument neglects one important aspect of decentralized government decision making: local governments must have the correct incentives to provide the efficient levels of local public goods to the optimal number of mobile individuals. When several local public goods are essential in each individual's consumption basket, the rule that each local public good must be supplied by one local government can no longer survive. Only metropolitan governments, providing all necessary local public goods, have sufficient incentives to choose the optimal allocation by maximizing net land rents over the entire territory of their jurisdiction. Any piece of land should be the tax base of only one local government.

However, even this conclusion hinges on strong assumptions that are somewhat questionable. Given the small number of metropolitan areas that we observe even in large countries like the United States, the utility-taking assumption may be too strong. If metropolitan governments have some market power to affect the economywide utility level, their policies may lead to efficiency losses similar to cases where countries rationally manipulate the international terms of trade in order to increase their income – the case of pecuniary externalities. Thus, there may be a trade-off between the efficiency loss of a further fragmentation of metropolitan areas (as discussed in this section) and the gain of decreasing the market power of any one local government. Whether regions indeed have incentives to employ a beggar-my-neighbor policy when they can affect the welfare of individuals living in other regions depends decisively on the degree of household mobility among regions. In the following chapters we shall analyze how mobility among larger jurisdictions influences the incentives of regional policy makers.

5.4   Appendix

5.4.1   Optimal Allocation with Overlapping Market Areas

The basic purpose of this appendix is to derive the first-order conditions (5.21)–(5.24) of the optimal allocation with overlapping market areas (reported without proof in the main text). The planner's problem stated by (5.16)–(5.20) can be solved by the Lagrange method, yielding the following first-order conditions (with choice variables shown in parentheses):

$$(x_i): \quad \lambda_i U_x^i - \gamma N_i = 0, \quad i = 1, 2, \tag{A.5.1}$$

$$(h_i): \quad \lambda_i U_h^i - \mu_i N_i = 0, \quad i = 1, 2, \tag{A.5.2}$$

$$(z^1): \quad \lambda_1 U_{z^1}^1 + \lambda_2 U_{z^1}^2 - \gamma C_z^1 = 0, \tag{A.5.3}$$

$$(z_i^2): \quad \lambda_i U_{z^2}^i - \gamma C_z^{2i} = 0, \quad i = 1, 2, \tag{A.5.4}$$

$$(N_i): \quad \gamma(x_i + C_N^{2i}) + \mu_i h_i + \delta = 0, \quad i = 1, 2, \tag{A.5.5}$$

$$(N): \quad \gamma(w - C_N^1) + \delta = 0, \tag{A.5.6}$$

where $\lambda_1 \equiv (1 + \lambda)$ and $\lambda_2 \equiv -\lambda$.

Solving (A.5.1) for λ_i/γ and inserting this into (A.5.3) and (A.5.4), respectively, yields the Samuelson conditions (5.21) and (5.22). Combining (A.5.1) and (A.5.2), we get an expression for the shadow price of housing, $\mu_i/\gamma = U_h^i/U_x^i$. Solving now (A.5.5) and (A.5.6) for δ, setting them equal to each other, and inserting the shadow price of housing yields

$$x_i + \frac{U_h^i}{U_x^i} h_i + C_N^1 + C_N^{2i} = w, \quad i = 1, 2, \tag{A.5.7}$$

that is, (5.23).

Multiplying (A.5.7) by N_i ($i = 1, 2$) and adding the expressions for both suburbs, we have

$$Nw - \sum_{i=1,2} \left[N_i x_i + N_i \frac{U_h^i}{U_x^i} h_i + N_i C_N^{2i} \right] - N C_N^1 = 0. \tag{A.5.8}$$

Comparing (A.5.8) with the self-sufficiency condition of the metropolitan area (5.18) and inserting the land market equilibrium in the suburbs (5.19) for $N_i h_i$ into (A.5.8), we obtain

$$\sum_{i=1,2} \left[L_i \frac{U_h^i}{U_x^i} + N_i C_N^{2i} \right] + N C_N^1 - C^1 - \sum_{i=1,2} C^{2i} = 0, \tag{A.5.9}$$

that is, the modified Henry George theorem.

5.4.2 Optimal Decentralization through Metropolitan Governments

We now want to prove that competing metropolitan governments choose the efficient allocation in their own interest and so derive conditions (5.31)–(5.33). From the migration equilibrium condition (5.28) and the properties of the indirect utility function, we first derive the following changes in the rental price of housing in the suburbs in response to policy changes of the metropolitan government for a given utility level:

$$\frac{d\rho_i}{d\tau_i} = \frac{V_w^i}{V_\rho^i} = -\frac{1}{h_i}, \quad i = 1, 2, \tag{A.5.10}$$

$$\frac{d\rho_i}{dz^1} = -\frac{V_{z^1}^i}{V_\rho^i} = \frac{U_{z^1}^i}{h_i U_x^i}, \quad i = 1, 2, \tag{A.5.11}$$

$$\frac{d\rho_i}{dz_i^2} = -\frac{V_{z^2}^i}{V_\rho^i} = \frac{U_{z^2}^i}{h_i U_x^i}, \quad i = 1, 2. \tag{A.5.12}$$

Next, the first-order conditions of the metropolitan government's problem (5.30) become

$$\frac{dR}{d\tau_i} = L_i \frac{d\rho_i}{d\tau_i} + N_i + [\tau_i - C_N^1 - C_N^{2i}] \frac{\partial N_i}{\partial \tau_i} = 0, \quad i = 1, 2, \tag{A.5.13}$$

$$\frac{dR}{dz^1} = \sum_{i=1,2} [\tau_i - C_N^1 - C_N^{2i}] \frac{\partial N_i}{\partial z^1} + \sum_{i=1,2} L_i \frac{d\rho_i}{dz^1} - C_z^1 = 0, \tag{A.5.14}$$

$$\frac{dR}{dz_i^2} = [\tau_i - C_N^1 - C_N^{2i}] \frac{\partial N_i}{\partial z_i^2} + L_i \frac{d\rho_i}{dz_i^2} - C_z^{2i} = 0, \quad i = 1, 2. \tag{A.5.15}$$

Inserting now (A.5.10) for $d\rho_i/d\tau_i$ into (A.5.13) and taking the land market equilibrium (5.29) in suburb i into account yields the first-order condition (5.31). Substituting then (A.5.11) for $d\rho_i/dz^1$ into (A.5.14) and (A.5.12) for $d\rho_i/dz_i^2$ into (A.5.15), and considering again the land market equilibrium (5.29), we achieve the first-order conditions (5.32) and (5.33), respectively.

If governments have to share the rent to land over their common territory (as studied in Section 5.3.4), then the first-order conditions (5.35) and (5.36) could also be derived by replacing L_i with $\sigma_i^j L_i$ in the first-order conditions (A.5.13) and (A.5.15), respectively, neglecting marginal crowding costs of police protection, $C_N^1 = 0$.

CHAPTER 6

Incentive Equivalence through Perfect Household Mobility

We now turn back to a federal state with fixed jurisdictional boundaries. In Chapter 3 we demonstrated that conditions of perfect interregional competition provide local governments with the correct incentives to choose an efficient allocation, provided they have a complete policy instrument set available. However, this result is restricted to small regions, and the question arises of whether there also exist conditions that take away all incentives for large regions to behave strategically. This chapter demonstrates that – under certain conditions – perfect household mobility may be such a mechanism, ensuring that noncooperative government policies of large regions result in an efficient allocation. Of course, this conclusion also holds only if regions have an efficiency-supporting instrument set available. It is of particular importance that regions can make an interregional transfer of resources. Without this instrument, it is generally not possible to achieve the efficient interregional population distribution.

Interregional household mobility is an incentive mechanism for regional governments to choose an efficient allocation because they become aware that any strategic behavior cannot be in the interest of their own residents. If regional governments act rationally, they must take into account migration responses of mobile households to government actions. Consequently, the migration equilibrium is an important and rational constraint on their behavior. By considering migration responses, regional governments take into account the effects of their actions – not only on their own residents' utility but also on the welfare of nonresidents. In the end, a beggar-my-neighbor policy would harm their own residents, since interregional utility differences are incompatible with perfect household mobility. For this reason, regions do not behave strategically. This general conclusion will be explained by using three examples that traditionally serve as classical cases to show why decentralized government policy fails (see Oates 1972; Gordon 1983; Boadway and Wildasin 1984). These examples are the interregional tax export, the existence of public good spillover effects, and interregional tax competition for scarce mobile capital. We show that these phenomena do not cause socially inefficient behavior of regional governments if the individual regions are connected by perfect household mobility.

The basic idea that perfect mobility of individuals takes away all incentives of regional governments for strategic behavior can be traced back to an article by Boadway (1982). He emphasizes the importance of the migration equilibrium for decentralized government activities. Myers (1990a,b) extends this model and shows that regions voluntarily make an interregional transfer of resources in order to avoid migration distortions. Krelove (1992) demonstrates that an interregional export of land taxes can be efficiency-enhancing because it allows regions to achieve the efficient population distribution. Myers and Papageorgiou (1993) and Wellisch (1993) make clear that regions internalize even those spillover effects associated with their supply of public goods when they take migration responses into account.[1]

In order to explain the power of household mobility to coordinate the behavior of self-interested regional governments, this chapter is divided into three sections. Section 6.1 confirms the result of Section 2.2 that an interregional export of taxes on land rents is necessary to ensure the efficient locational pattern of mobile individuals, and it additionally shows that regions do not respond by oversupplying public goods as a result of the shift in tax burden to nonresidents. This section also demonstrates that regions internalize public good spillover effects in their own interest. Section 6.2 shows that an interregional competition for the scarce mobile tax base capital does not result in an underprovision of local public goods if households are perfectly mobile across the regions of a federation. Finally, Section 6.3 contains proofs of the basic results reported in Sections 6.1 and 6.2.

6.1   Tax Export and Spillover Effects with Household Mobility

6.1.1   Private Behavior

The analysis in this section uses a simplified version of the model introduced in Section 2.2. We first turn to the behavior of households and firms. The federal state consists of two regions in which N identical mobile households reside. Households living in region i derive utility from consumption of the private numeraire goods x_i, from consuming the public good z_i supplied by region i, and from using the public good z_j provided by region j. Hence, the last assumption makes clear that there are interregional spillover effects in the provision of public goods. The utility function of a representative household residing in

---

[1] Henderson (1994) is another study analyzing the role of household mobility for coordination of regional government decisions.

region i is $U^i \equiv U(x_i, z_i, z_j)$. There are no migration costs, so a migration equilibrium can be characterized by identical utility levels across regions:

$$U(x_i, z_i, z_j) = U(x_j, z_j, z_i). \tag{6.1}$$

In equilibrium, N_i mobile households reside in region i. Households have identical preferences and are also equally endowed with one unit of labor, which is supplied inelastically in their region of residence, and with the immobile factor land in both regions. These assumptions about endowment imply that the budget constraint of a representative household living in region i is

$$x_i = w_i + \sum_{j=1,2} \frac{L_j \rho_j (1 - t_j)}{N}, \tag{6.2}$$

where w_i stands for the regional wage rate, L_j denotes region j's land endowment, ρ_j is the land rent, and t_j is the proportional source-based tax on land rents. It follows from the budget constraint (6.2) that households attain the same net land rent income regardless of the region in which they reside. Since they also own land in the neighboring region and since land rents are taxed, each region can shift part of the tax burden to nonresidents. In other words, there is an interregional export of taxes. We shall explain that this interregional tax export leads precisely to the necessary interregional resource transfer that sustains the efficient locational pattern of households. An implicit assumption made in (6.2) is that regional governments do not collect residence-based taxes from households.

Each region uses its tax revenues to finance public goods. The costs of providing public goods, measured in units of the private numeraire good, are $C^i(z_i)$ and depend only on the level of z_i (not on the number of users). Hence, we ignore crowding costs in this section. This also explains why we have assumed that regions do not collect a direct household tax. Since there are no crowding costs to be internalized, the efficient allocation can be achieved simply by levying a tax on land rents. The budget restriction of the regional government then becomes

$$t_i \rho_i L_i = C^i(z_i). \tag{6.3}$$

Finally, each region produces the private numeraire good by using the linear homogeneous production function $F^i(L_i, N_i)$. Firms choose the employment of land L_i and of workers N_i so as to maximize profits

$$F^i(L_i, N_i) - \rho_i L_i - w_i N_i, \tag{6.4}$$

taking all prices as given. The resulting behavioral rules are described by

$$F_N^i = w_i, \tag{6.5}$$

$$F_L^i = \rho_i; \tag{6.6}$$

that is, marginal factor products must be equal to factor prices.

For the following analysis, it is important to derive the regional resource constraint. Inserting (6.3)–(6.6) into (6.2), we obtain

$$x_i = \frac{1}{N_i}\left[F^i - \frac{N_j}{N}L_iF_L^i + \frac{N_i}{N}L_jF_L^j - \frac{N_iC^i(z_i) + N_iC^j(z_j)}{N}\right]. \tag{6.7}$$

We have already derived (in Section 2.1) the first-order conditions of the efficient allocation. However, in order to evaluate the outcome of regional government decisions, let us recall the relevant conditions. Since crowding costs are absent, the necessary condition of the efficient population distribution becomes

$$F_N^1 - x_1 = F_N^2 - x_2; \tag{6.8}$$

that is, the marginal social benefits of households to regions must be equalized across regions. Public goods generate spillover effects such that the Samuelson condition reads as

$$N_i\frac{U_{z_i}^i}{U_x^i} + N_j\frac{U_{z_i}^j}{U_x^j} = C_z^i. \tag{6.9}$$

In other words, marginal costs of providing a public good must be identical to the marginal willingness to pay of all individuals living in the federal state.

Before explaining the behavior of regional governments, we should recall an important result derived in Section 2.2. By assumption, regions do not levy potentially distorting residence-based taxes on mobile households. Moreover, there are no crowding costs in the provision of public goods, and households are equally endowed with land in both regions independent of their residence. Consequently, the first-order condition of the efficient interregional allocation of mobile households is always satisfied. The interregional transfer of resources necessary to achieve the efficient locational pattern is obtained by the export of land taxes. Inserting (6.5) into (6.2) yields

$$F_N^1 - x_1 = -\sum_{j=1,2}\frac{L_j\rho_j(1-t_j)}{N} = F_N^2 - x_2, \tag{6.10}$$

and hence, as claimed, (6.8).

6.1.2   Regional Government Behavior

Let us now turn to the behavior of regional governments. Since all regional residents are identical, it seems natural to suppose that the government in i maximizes the utility of a representative resident living in i by choosing z_i. Following (6.3), this choice also determines t_i indirectly. The region acts under the Nash assumption that the other region does not change its public good level

z_j in response. In choosing z_i, the government must, however, take into account that households make their residential choices dependent on z_i. The N_i term is determined implicitly by the migration equilibrium (6.1) as a function of z_i and z_j,

$$G(N_i, z_i, z_j) \equiv U(x_i, z_i, z_j) - U(x_j, z_j, z_i) = 0, \tag{6.11}$$

where x_i and x_j must be inserted from (6.7) and where $F^i = F^i(L_i, N_i)$ and $N_j = N - N_i$ must be taken into account.

The problem of the regional government is thus to

$$\text{maximize } U(x_i, z_i, z_j) \tag{6.12}$$

by choosing z_i, where x_i must be substituted by (6.7) and N_i depends on z_i so as to satisfy (6.11). If one takes $dN_j = -dN_i$ into account, it follows as a first-order condition of the optimal regional government behavior that

$$\frac{dU^i}{dz_i} = -\frac{U^i_x}{N} C^i_z + U^i_N \frac{\partial N_i}{\partial z_i} + U^i_{z_i} = 0, \tag{6.13}$$

with

$$U^i_N \equiv U^i_x \frac{\partial x_i}{\partial N_i}.$$

Before deriving the migration response $\partial N_i/\partial z_i$, let us first illustrate why previous contributions expected an inefficient allocation as a result of an interregional tax export and public good spillover effects. These studies ignored any migration responses by assuming that $\partial N_i/\partial z_i = 0$.[2] Consequently, (6.13) reduces to

$$N_i \frac{U^i_{z_i}}{U^i_x} = \frac{N_i}{N} C^i_z. \tag{6.14}$$

The first-order condition of an optimal regional government behavior (6.14) reveals two distortions. The left side makes clear that regions have no incentive to internalize the marginal willingness to pay of nonresidents when providing public goods that also offer consumption possibilities for residents living

---

[2] Gordon (1983) is the standard reference for describing potential externalities of decentralized government decision making. In a model incorporating household mobility, he concludes that spillover effects and tax export are important reasons why regional government decisions fail to ensure an efficient allocation. However, he does not explicitly derive migration responses and, even more importantly, assumes that regional governments maximize a utilitarian welfare function consisting of the sum of residents' utilities. Both differences to the present approach explain why Gordon derives an inefficient result. Pauly (1970) and Boskin (1973) also conclude (in a model with household mobility) that decentralized government decisions result in an inefficient allocation when there are public good spillover effects.

in neighboring regions. The right side of (6.14) indicates the problem caused by an interregional tax export. The regional government internalizes only the fraction N_i/N of the costs of supplying the public good, since the fraction N_j/N is shifted to nonresidents by taxing land rents. Whereas the left side of (6.14) indicates an inefficiently low provision of public goods generating positive spillovers, the right side points in the direction of an oversupply of (local) public goods due to an export of taxes.

However, if regions act in a rational way then they must take migration responses into account. Locational responses can be derived by implicit differentiation of (6.11). Inserting them into the first-order condition (6.13) yields, after a few algebraic steps,

$$N_i \frac{U_{z_i}^i}{U_x^i} + N_j \frac{U_{z_i}^j}{U_x^j} = C_z^i \tag{6.15}$$

(see Section 6.3.1). Following (6.15), both regions have incentives to supply public goods in a socially efficient way, although public goods generate spillovers and part of the tax burden is shifted to nonresidents.

This result can be summarized as

Proposition 6.1. *If all households are identical and perfectly mobile across the regions of a federal state, then regional governments completely internalize public good spillover effects and do not export taxes in a socially inefficient way.*

The export of the land-rent tax is necessary to achieve the efficient allocation, since regions must have a revenue source to finance public goods without distorting the interregional population distribution. If public goods were financed by a residence-based direct tax on mobile households, then migration decisions would be distorted because tax rates must differ between regions in order to provide the efficient level of public goods (Flatters et al. 1974). Only the taxation of land offers regions the possibility of providing public goods in a socially efficient way without causing locational distortions. Note that there are no crowding costs to be internalized. The basic reason for this efficiency result is that each region, by taking the migration equilibrium into account, in effect maximizes the utility of all households living in the federal state. Therefore, each region is endowed with the correct incentives to provide public goods in line with the Samuelson condition, even if nonresidents can use them and even if the tax burden is partly shifted to nonresidents. Central government intervention is not necessary in this case. This result is in sharp opposition to the traditional view that it is especially the presence of spillover effects and tax export that causes distortions.

6.2 Tax Competition and Household Mobility

If households are immobile then the interregional tax competition for mobile capital results in an underprovision of local public goods. This conclusion was derived in Section 4.1. Let us now extend the model set out in Chapter 4 by introducing household mobility in order to demonstrate that local public goods are no longer undersupplied owing to interregional tax competition for capital. To make the argument as clear as possible, we again assume that regions are identical. The reason for making this assumption in Chapter 4 was to exclude at the outset the possibility that regions may strategically influence the interregional interest rate by choice of their tax policy, and to exclude that they choose different capital tax rates leading to an inefficient interregional capital allocation. As can be expected from the analysis of Section 6.1, the threat of strategic behavior is not present when households are perfectly mobile. Here, then, the essential reason for introducing the assumption of identical regions is to ensure that a source-based capital tax as the single source of regional revenue raising (as in Chapter 4) is a complete tax instrument set for achieving the efficient allocation. Hence, the following analysis can concentrate on incentive effects of household mobility.[3]

6.2.1 Private Behavior

As in Section 6.1, we consider a federal state consisting of two regions in which N identical and perfectly mobile households reside. Households living in region i derive their utility from the consumption of private goods x_i and from the use of the local public good z_i, so that the utility function of a representative household living in region i is $U^i \equiv U(x_i, z_i)$. Since migration costs are still being neglected, a migration equilibrium is further characterized by identical utility levels across regions:

$$U(x_1, z_1) = U(x_2, z_2). \tag{6.16}$$

In addition to having identical preferences, households are equally endowed with labor and capital. Each household supplies one homogeneous unit of labor in its region of residence. Moreover, each household owns the fraction $k \equiv K/N$ of the entire capital stock K and allocates the capital so as to maximize its return. Therefore, a uniform interest rate r prevails in both regions in an arbitrage equilibrium. However, contrary to Section 6.1, let us now assume that region i's land endowment L_i is publicly owned by the regional government

---

[3] Notice that an interregional transfer of resources is not necessary to achieve the efficient population distribution in the case of identical regions.

in i and that the government divides the land rent ρ_i (per unit of land) equally among all regional residents. We introduce this assumption since it makes this section directly comparable to Chapter 4. If households were immobile, this assumption ensures that the first-order condition characterizing the Nash equilibrium would be identical to condition (4.15) although there are three factors of production in the present section.[4] With these assumptions about the ownership distribution of production factors, the budget constraint of a representative household living in region i becomes

$$x_i = w_i + \frac{L_i \rho_i}{N_i} + kr, \tag{6.17}$$

where w_i denotes the wage rate and N_i the population size (labor supply) in region i.

The regional government in i has only one revenue source: it levies a source-based tax on capital τ_i^K and uses the tax proceeds to provide the local public good. Let us assume, as in Chapter 4, that the consumption of z_i is completely rival. The costs for providing z_i are described by the function $C^i(z_i, N_i) = N_i z_i$, expressed in units of the private numeraire good, and the budget constraint of the regional government reads as

$$K_i \tau_i^K = N_i z_i, \tag{6.18}$$

where K_i is the amount of capital employed in region i. Firms in region i produce the private numeraire good x_i using the linear homogeneous production function $F^i(L_i, K_i, N_i)$. Their profits can be written as

$$F^i(L_i, K_i, N_i) - \rho_i L_i - w_i N_i - (r + \tau_i^K) K_i, \tag{6.19}$$

where, in particular, the costs of employing one further unit of capital consist of the interest rate plus the capital tax rate. In choosing L_i, K_i, and N_i, firms maximize their profits by taking all prices and the capital tax rate as given. They behave according to the following rules:

$$F_L^i = \rho_i, \tag{6.20}$$

$$F_N^i = w_i, \tag{6.21}$$

$$F_K^i = r + \tau_i^K. \tag{6.22}$$

Conditions (6.20)–(6.22) can now be inserted into the budget constraint of private households (6.17) in order to derive the regional resource restriction

$$x_i = \frac{F^i}{N_i} + \frac{1}{N_i} E_i F_K^i - k\tau_i^K, \tag{6.23}$$

with $E_i \equiv kN_i - K_i$ denoting the net capital export of region i. In principle, a positive E_i means that region i is a net exporter of capital. However, in this

---

[4] Making the alternative assumption – that all households are equally endowed with land in both regions – would not change any of the results derived in this section.

section we are assuming identical regions, which are neither net exporters nor net importers of capital in a symmetric equilibrium; that is, $E_i = 0$ holds in equilibrium.

In order to derive a reference situation for evaluating the outcome of unco-ordinated regional decisions, let us briefly turn to the conditions of an efficient allocation. Since both regions are identical, we need not fear there is an inefficient interregional allocation of mobile capital or mobile households in a symmetric equilibrium. The first-order conditions of the efficient capital allocation, $F_K^1 = F_K^2$, and the efficient population distribution, $F_N^1 - x_1 - z_1 = F_N^2 - x_2 - z_2$, are satisfied. Since the public good does not cause spillover effects (and since use of the local public good is completely rival), its efficient supply is characterized by the Samuelson condition

$$\frac{U_z^i}{U_x^i} \equiv MRS_i = 1. \tag{6.24}$$

The basic purpose of the following analysis is to examine whether regional governments in fact provide local public goods in accordance with (6.24).

6.2.2   Regional Government Behavior

The behavior of the regional government in i is again simply described by max-imizing the utility of a representative household by choice of the capital tax rate τ_i^K. In order to meet the budget constraint of the regional government (6.18), the choice of τ_i^K determines z_i. The government acts under the Nash assumption that the other region does not change its tax rate τ_j^K in response. A rationally acting regional government takes into account that a change in τ_i^K induces migration responses of mobile households and capital. These responses can be derived from the migration equilibrium and from the arbitrage equilibrium of capital owners. Inserting (6.18) for z_i into the migration equilibrium (6.16), and taking the necessary condition of an optimal demand for capital by firms (6.22) into account, allows us to derive N_i and K_i as implicit functions of the regional control variables τ_i^K and τ_j^K from the following two-equation system:

$$G(N_i, K_i, \tau_i^K, \tau_j^K) \equiv U\left(x_i, \frac{K_i \tau_i^K}{N_i}\right) - U\left(x_j, \frac{K_j \tau_j^K}{N_j}\right) = 0, \quad (6.25)$$

$$H(N_i, K_i, \tau_i^K, \tau_j^K) \equiv F_K^i(L_i, K_i, N_i) - \tau_i^K$$
$$- F_K^j(L_j, K_j, N_j) + \tau_i^K = 0, \tag{6.26}$$

where x_i and x_j must be substituted by (6.23) and where $F^i = F^i(L_i, K_i, N_i)$, $N_j = N - N_i$, and $K_j = K - K_i$ must be taken into account.

The problem of the regional government is thus to

$$\text{maximize } U\left(x_i, \frac{K_i \tau_i^K}{N_i}\right) \tag{6.27}$$

by choosing τ_i^K, where again x_i must be substituted from (6.23) and where N_i and K_i depend on τ_i^K so as to satisfy (6.25) and (6.26). The first-order condition for solving this problem becomes

$$\frac{dU^i}{d\tau_i^K} = -U_x^i \frac{K}{N} + U_N^i \frac{\partial N_i}{\partial \tau_i^K} + U_K^i \frac{\partial K_i}{\partial \tau_i^K} + U_z^i \frac{K_i}{N_i} = 0, \tag{6.28}$$

with

$$U_N^i \equiv U_x^i \frac{\partial x_i}{\partial N_i} - U_z^i \frac{z_i}{N_i},$$

$$U_K^i \equiv U_x^i \frac{E_i}{N_i} F_{KK}^i + U_z^i \frac{\tau_i^K}{N_i}.$$

Let us now transform (6.28) into an expression that makes it comparable to the Samuelson condition (6.24). Implicit differentiation of (6.25) and (6.26) yields the migration responses $\partial N_i / \partial \tau_i^K$ and $\partial K_i / \partial \tau_i^K$. By inserting them into (6.28), it follows as a necessary condition of the optimal behavior of regional governments that

$$\left| \begin{array}{cc} \dfrac{(F_N^i - x_i) - (F_N^j - x_j) - (MRS_i z_i - MRS_j z_j)}{U_N^j} & \dfrac{MRS_i \tau_i^K - MRS_j \tau_j^K}{U_K^j} \end{array} \right|$$

$$+ (MRS_i - 1)K_i \left| \begin{array}{cc} \dfrac{(F_{KN}^i + F_{KN}^j)}{U_N^j} & \dfrac{(F_{KK}^i + F_{KK}^j)}{U_K^j} \end{array} \right| = 0 \tag{6.29}$$

(see Section 6.3.2 for the derivations).

In a symmetric equilibrium – that is, for $F_N^i - x_i = F_N^j - x_j$, $MRS_i = MRS_j$, $z_i = z_j$, and $\tau_i^K = \tau_j^K$ – the first determinant in (6.29) vanishes. If the locational equilibrium characterized by (6.25) and (6.26) is to be locally stable, then the second determinant in (6.29) is negative. Therefore, in the case of perfect household mobility, the symmetric equilibrium is characterized by the efficient provision of local public goods,

$$MRS_i = 1. \tag{6.30}$$

Thus, we can state

Proposition 6.2.   *If all households are identical and perfectly mobile, then financing local public goods by a tax on the mobile capital factor does not result* *in an underprovision of local public goods. The symmetric Nash equilibrium among identical regions is socially efficient.*

Tax competition does not matter in the case of household mobility, since each region considers the welfare of nonresidents by taking the migration equilibrium into account. As explained in Section 4.1, an inefficient interregional tax competition can be traced back to the existence of fiscal externalities in the case of identical regions. Because each region completely internalizes the effects of its own actions on the welfare of nonresidents in order to conjecture migration responses, there are no external effects. Notice again that, in the case of identical regions, a tax on mobile capital as the sole source of revenue raising of regions is sufficient to achieve the efficient allocation. The condition of having a complete instrument set is satisfied. Moreover, since each region in effect maximizes the welfare of all households living in the federal state, it also has incentives to avoid any allocative distortions. In particular, local public goods are supplied in line with the Samuelson rule.

6.3   Appendix

6.3.1   Tax Export and Spillover Effects

The basic purpose of this section is to derive the first-order condition (6.15). The first step is to calculate the migration response $\partial N_i / \partial z_i$ by implicit differentiation of (6.11):

$$\frac{\partial N_i}{\partial z_i} = -\frac{G_z^i}{G_N^i}, \tag{A.6.1}$$

with

$$G_N^i = U_N^i + U_N^j, \quad G_z^i = -\frac{U_x^i}{N} C_z^i + U_{z_i}^i + \frac{U_x^j}{N} C_z^i - U_{z_i}^j,$$

$$U_N^i \equiv \frac{U_x^i}{N_i} \left[F_N^i - x_i + \frac{L_i F_L^i + L_j F_L^j}{N} - \frac{1}{N} (L_i N_j F_{LN}^i + L_j N_i F_{LN}^j) \right]$$

$$- \frac{U_x^i}{N_i} \left[\frac{C^i(z_i) + C^j(z_j)}{N} \right]. \tag{A.6.2}$$

Inserting (A.6.1) into the first-order condition (6.13) and using the first two equalities set out in (A.6.2) yields

$$\frac{dU^i}{dz_i} = 0 \iff U_N^j \left(U_{z_i}^i - \frac{U_x^i}{N} C_z^i \right) + U_N^i \left(U_{z_i}^j - \frac{U_x^j}{N} C_z^i \right) = 0. \tag{A.6.3}$$

Using U_N^i and U_N^j from (A.6.2) in (A.6.3) and taking (6.10) into account yields the first-order condition (6.15).

6.3.2   Tax Competition

This section derives the first-order condition (6.29) set out in Section 6.2. Let us first calculate from (6.25) and (6.26) the locational responses $\partial N_i/\partial \tau_i^K$ and $\partial K_i/\partial \tau_i^K$. Total differentiation of (6.25) and (6.26) yields

$$\begin{pmatrix} G_N^i & G_K^i \\ H_N^i & H_K^i \end{pmatrix} \begin{pmatrix} dN_i \\ dK_i \end{pmatrix} = -\begin{pmatrix} G_{\tau^K}^i \\ H_{\tau^K}^i \end{pmatrix} d\tau_i^K, \tag{A.6.4}$$

with

$$G_N^i = U_N^i + U_N^j, \qquad G_K^i = U_K^i + U_K^j,$$

$$H_N^i = F_{KN}^i + F_{KN}^j, \qquad H_K^i = F_{KK}^i + F_{KK}^j,$$

$$G_{\tau^K}^i = -\frac{U_x^i}{N_i}E_i + \frac{U_x^i}{N_i}K_i(MRS_i - 1), \qquad H_{\tau^K}^i = -1,$$

$$U_N^i \equiv \frac{U_x^i}{N_i}\left[F_N^i - x_i + E_i F_{KN}^i + \frac{K}{N}(F_K^i - \tau_i^K)\right] - U_z^i \frac{z_i}{N_i},$$

$$U_K^i \equiv \frac{U_x^i}{N_i}E_i F_{KK}^i + U_z^i \frac{\tau_i^K}{N_i}. \tag{A.6.5}$$

Applying Cramer's rule to (A.6.4), it follows that

$$\frac{\partial N_i}{\partial \tau_i^K} = \begin{vmatrix} -G_{\tau^K}^i & G_K^i \\ -H_{\tau^K}^i & H_K^i \end{vmatrix} |A|^{-1} \tag{A.6.6}$$

and

$$\frac{\partial K_i}{\partial \tau_i^K} = \begin{vmatrix} G_N^i & -G_{\tau^k}^i \\ H_N^i & -H_{\tau^K}^i \end{vmatrix} |A|^{-1}, \tag{A.6.7}$$

with

$$|A| \equiv \begin{vmatrix} G_N^i & G_K^i \\ H_N^i & H_K^i \end{vmatrix}.$$

Inserting (A.6.6) and (A.6.7) into (6.28) and using the definition of MRS_i yields

$$\left(\frac{U_x^i}{N_i}K_i(MRS_i - 1) - \frac{U_x^i}{N_i}E_i\right)\begin{vmatrix} (F_{KN}^i + F_{KN}^j) & (F_{KK}^i + F_{KK}^j) \\ U_N^j & U_K^j \end{vmatrix}$$

$$+ \begin{vmatrix} U_N^i & U_K^i \\ U_N^j & U_K^j \end{vmatrix} = 0. \tag{A.6.8}$$

Adding both expressions implies

$$
\begin{vmatrix}
\left(\frac{U_x^i}{N_i} K_i (MRS_i - 1) - \frac{U_x^i}{N_i} E_i \right) & \left(\frac{U_x^i}{N_i} K_i (MRS_i - 1) - \frac{U_x^i}{N_i} E_i \right) \\
\times (F_{KN}^i + F_{KN}^j) + U_N^i & \times (F_{KK}^i + F_{KK}^j) + U_K^i \\
U_N^j & U_K^j
\end{vmatrix} = 0. \qquad (A.6.9)
$$

Multiplying the first line by N_i / U_x^i and the second line by N_j / U_x^j, subtract-ing the second from the first line, and finally using the explicit expressions for $U_N^i, U_N^j, U_K^i, U_K^j$ from (A.6.5), the necessary condition (6.29) follows.

CHAPTER 7

Efficiency and the Degree of
Household Mobility

In Chapter 6, we explained that perfect interregional household mobility may
serve as an incentive mechanism for regional governments to abstain from
strategic behavior and to internalize all interregional externalities. However,
this efficiency result hinges on strong assumptions. We have assumed that only
one group of perfectly mobile and identical households lives in the federal state,
and that regional governments maximize the utility of a representative resident.
Deviations from these assumptions are impediments to an efficient allocation.

There are at least five deviations from this basic model that merit discussion here owing to previous study in the literature and because they either better
characterize the situation in federal states or describe the behavior of regional
governments at least equally well. First, regions might maximize a utilitarian
welfare function consisting of the sum of residents' utilities (Bentham welfare
function). Second, there could be several types of mobile households, with all
members of one type identical and perfectly mobile but with types differing
with respect to preferences and endowments. Third, households could have
identical preferences yet differ in their endowments; for example, native residents living in a region usually own a larger fraction of the regional property
than nonnative households living in the same region. Fourth, all households
may not be equally mobile; there are contributions in the literature studying
the extreme scenario of two groups of households – one group with perfectly
mobile members and the other with immobile members. Finally, the different
degrees of household mobility can also be modeled by costly migration, where
migration costs may differ among households.

We will briefly refer to some of the contributions using these alternative
assumptions and discuss the consequences of such deviations from the basic
model of Chapter 6; a more formal analysis of some deviations can be found
in Mansoorian and Myers (1997). If regional governments maximize a utilitarian social welfare function of the Bentham type and the population is mobile
(see Gordon 1983), then the value of their objective function increases directly
with a rising number of residents. As a consequence, each region wants to have

a population greater than the efficient size within its boundaries, even if there exists only one type of identical households. This is problematic, since a net interregional transfer must be made in order to achieve the efficient population distribution. However, any interregional transfer of resources decreases the regional population size and will therefore not be made if welfare increases directly with population size. Hence, a regional welfare function that depends directly on population interferes with the requirement that regions voluntarily choose the efficient net interregional transfer of resources.

If there are several types of mobile households, then benevolent regional governments must maximize a social welfare function depending at least on the respective utility levels of representative members of each type (see Burbidge and Myers 1994b; Wellisch 1996). Even if all households of one type are identical and perfectly mobile, regional welfare functions may differ, expressing different regional views about redistribution between rich and poor households. In this case, different regional governments try to favor a different household type. In the end, these attempts must fail, since all households of a certain type attain the same utility level as a consequence of free migration. However, these attempts lead to strategic behavior and so result in an inefficient allocation.[1]

Furthermore, Bucovetsky (1995) studies the case where perfectly mobile households differ in their endowment with land. More specifically, households essentially own land in the region where they are born. As a consequence, natives and nonnatives living and working together in a region are not equally endowed with land in that region. For instance, Italian guest workers in Germany own property in Sicily but not in Germany, while their German colleagues own most of the German property. Because of this difference, the utilities of natives and nonnatives differ, since only part of the income is equalized interregionally via migration. If regional governments maximize the utility of natives, then taking the migration equilibrium into account no longer entails maximizing the welfare of nonnatives, too. Hence, free and costless migration is no longer a perfect mechanism for ensuring incentive equivalence among different regional governments. This leads to strategic behavior of regions, resulting in distortions.

A further impediment to efficiency is the existence of immobile households. Because household mobility serves as the internalization mechanism, it is clear that regions behave strategically if there are both immobile residents and mobile residents. We shall forgo discussing this problem until Chapters 8–10, where decentralized redistribution policy is studied in a framework that allows for both mobile and immobile households.

---

[1] The various distortions that result from such behavior are analyzed by Wellisch (1996), who also discusses a simple central government intervention method for coordinating regional government decisions.

In existing federations, households are neither perfectly immobile nor perfectly mobile; the truth lies somewhere between both extreme scenarios. Consequently, in this chapter we assume that migration of households is costly. Then the question arises of how migration costs affect the efficiency properties of decentralized government activities or, more generally, how the degree of interregional household mobility influences the outcome of regional government policy. Migration costs are modeled by psychic attachment of households to their home regions, and we assume that this psychic attachment differs among households. In doing so, this chapter builds on studies by Mansoorian and Myers (1993, 1996), Burbidge and Myers (1994b), and Wellisch (1994, 1995c) in which the outcome of regional fiscal and environmental policy with imperfectly mobile households is analyzed. Hercowitz and Pines (1991) study the efficiency implications of alternative degrees of household mobility in a different framework. Because mobility differs in various federal states, it is more than an academic exercise to differentiate between various degrees of household mobility. In heterogeneous federal states such as Canada or the EU, cultural and social attachment of households to their home region might play an important role; different languages alone contribute to the fact that household mobility is far from perfect. However, cultural ties are less important in homogeneous federal states like Germany or the United States.

In order to study how the outcome of decentralized government decisions depends on the degree of household mobility, this chapter is organized as follows. Section 7.1 derives the necessary conditions of an efficient allocation. They differ from the conditions derived in Chapter 2, since alternative degrees of mobility are considered. Although individuals may be imperfectly mobile (or even immobile), capital is always perfectly mobile. Section 7.2 goes one step further by analyzing the Nash equilibrium outcome of regional government policy. Whereas this section derives general behavioral rules for regional governments, Section 7.3 investigates in detail the outcome of regional government policy for different degrees of household mobility. Section 7.3 also analyzes how the outcome depends on the available tax instruments for any given degree of mobility. Finally, Section 7.4 proves some important results which are reported in Sections 7.2 and 7.3.

7.1   Efficient Allocation

7.1.1   The Model

Let us once again consider a federal state consisting of two regions, 1 and 2. There live N mobile households in this system of regions, who differ only in their psychic attachments to their home region. Let us suppose that there is one household of each type, indexed by n. Then, n varies between 0 and N.

Furthermore, we assume that the utility function of a household is additively separable with respect to the psychic utility component expressing attachment to a region. The utility function of a type-n household $V(n)$ reads as

$$V(n) = \begin{cases} U(x_1, z_1, z_2) + a(N - n) & \text{if } n \text{ lives in 1,} \\ U(x_2, z_2, z_1) + an & \text{if } n \text{ lives in 2.} \end{cases} \tag{7.1}$$

We use $U^i \equiv U(x_i, z_i, z_j)$ to denote the *pecuniary* part of the utility function, increasing in the consumption of the private numeraire good x_i and in the consumption of public goods z_i and z_j, respectively. Since both z_i and z_j enter the utility function, the provision of public goods generates spillover effects. Note that all households have the same pecuniary utility function $U(\cdot)$. The parameter n measures the psychic utility a household derives from living in region 2, and $(N - n)$ expresses the psychic utility derived from residing in region 1. Households with a relatively small n are at home in 1 and households with a high n are born in region 2. The parameter a ($a \geq 0$) measures the degree of heterogeneity in tastes for a region, the *degree of household mobility*. If $a = 0$ then there is no attachment to home, and we are back in the economy of Chapter 6 with perfect household mobility. The case of imperfect household mobility is characterized by $a > 0$. If, finally, $a \to \infty$, then households are perfectly immobile. Neither a central planner nor regional governments can affect the psychic benefit a household derives from a particular region.

Households are free to choose their location, and they choose the region where they attain the highest utility. Households differ in their attachment to a region, so the migration equilibrium must be characterized by the marginal household, identified by $n = N_1$, being indifferent between locating in either region:

$$U(x_1, z_1, z_2) + a(N - N_1) = U(x_2, z_2, z_1) + aN_1, \tag{7.2}$$

$$U(x_1, z_1, z_2) + a(N - n) > U(x_2, z_2, z_1) + an \quad \forall\, n < N_1,$$

$$U(x_1, z_1, z_2) + a(N - n) < U(x_2, z_2, z_1) + an \quad \forall\, n > N_1.$$

Hence, N_1 is also the number of households residing in region 1. Households with n less than N_1 locate in region 1, and households with n greater than N_1 live in region 2. If households are perfectly mobile ($a = 0$), then (7.2) reduces to the well-known migration equilibrium condition (6.1).

Each household is endowed with one unit of labor, which is inelastically supplied in the region where the household resides. The private numeraire good is produced by the linear homogeneous production function $F^i(L_i, N_i, K_i, g_i)$, using four factors of production. Here L_i stands for the regional endowment with land, N_i denotes regional labor (population), K_i stands for mobile capital employed in region i, and g_i is the local public input provided by the region. The costs of providing public goods and factors are measured in units of the private good and are described by the functions $C^i(z_i)$ and $H^i(g_i)$, respectively. These costs depend only on the amount of services provided. In order to concentrate on other problems, in this chapter we ignore crowding costs of supplying public services.

The federal state is endowed with a fixed capital stock K that must be allocated across regions, $K = K_1 + K_2$. By making use of the population and the capital constraint, the private good constraint for the entire federal state becomes

$$F^1(L_1, N_1, K_1, g_1) + F^2(L_2, N - N_1, K - K_1, g_2) - N_1 x_1 - (N - N_1)x_2$$
$$-C^1(z_1) - C^2(z_2) - H^1(g_1) - H^2(g_2) = 0. \quad (7.3)$$

7.1.2   First-Order Conditions

The central planner is constrained by free locational choices of households (7.2) and by the private good constraint (7.3) of the federal state. An efficient allocation is defined as a subset of feasible allocations, satisfying (7.2) and (7.3), at which it is impossible to raise the utility of one household in the federal state without reducing the utility of another household. For the problem stated here, this means that efficient allocations are achieved if it is impossible to increase U^1 without reducing U^2 and vice versa. Equivalently, all efficient allocations can be characterized by maximizing a linear combination of U^1 and U^2, or $\beta U^1 + (1 - \beta)U^2$ for all $\beta \in [0, 1]$. Although these subutilities ignore locational tastes, any locational change that accompanies a change in U^1 and U^2 must further raise total utilities. This is a *revealed preference* argument: if a change in location did not increase utility, it would not be made. Thus, if $\beta U^1 + (1 - \beta)U^2$ is not maximized, the allocation cannot be efficient. Therefore, the set of efficient allocations can be achieved as a solution, for all $\beta \in [0, 1]$, of the problem to

$$\text{maximize} \quad \beta U(x_1, z_1, z_2) + (1 - \beta)U(x_2, z_2, z_1) \quad (7.4)$$

by choosing (x_i), (z_i), (g_i), N_1, and K_1 subject to (7.2) and (7.3).

When there is perfect household mobility $(a = 0)$, for any β the problem reduces to the standard efficiency problem, discussed in Section 2.1, of maximizing the common utility of all households. For imperfect household mobility $(a > 0)$, maximizing U^1 no longer means maximizing U^2 as well since, according to (7.2), both pecuniary utility levels differ where the wedge depends on the planner's choice variable N_1. Therefore, there is a set of efficient allocations differing in the choice of the weight $\beta \in [0, 1]$.

Defining λ and μ as the Lagrange multipliers associated with the migration equilibrium (7.2) and the private good constraint (7.3), respectively, the following first-order conditions (with instruments shown in parentheses) characterize an efficient allocation:

(x_1): $[\beta + \lambda]U_x^1 - \mu N_1 = 0,$ (7.5)

(x_2): $[(1 - \beta) - \lambda]U_x^2 - \mu N_2 = 0,$ (7.6)

(z_1): $[\beta + \lambda]U_{z_1}^1 + [(1 - \beta) - \lambda]U_{z_1}^2 - \mu C_z^1 = 0,$ (7.7)

(z_2): $[\beta + \lambda]U_{z_2}^1 + [(1 - \beta) - \lambda]U_{z_2}^2 - \mu C_z^2 = 0,$ (7.8)

(g_1): $F_g^1 - H_g^1 = 0,$ (7.9)

(g_2): $F_g^2 - H_g^2 = 0,$ (7.10)

(N_1): $-2a\lambda + \mu[F_N^1 - x_1 - (F_N^2 - x_2)] = 0,$ (7.11)

(K_1): $F_K^1 - F_K^2 = 0.$ (7.12)

Some of the necessary conditions are well known from our discussion in Chapter 2 of an efficient allocation. For example, condition (7.12) requires that we equate the marginal products of capital across regions in order to achieve the efficient interregional capital allocation. Moreover, conditions (7.9) and (7.10) can be summarized by

$$F_g^i = H_g^i, \quad i = 1, 2,$$ (7.13)

indicating the first-order conditions of the efficient supply of local public factors. The marginal product of public factors on the left side must be equal to the marginal costs of providing public inputs on the right side. Next, inserting (7.5) and (7.6) into (7.7) and (7.8) allows us to derive the Samuelson condition of an efficient supply of public goods:

$$N_i \frac{U_{z_i}^i}{U_x^i} + N_j \frac{U_{z_i}^j}{U_x^j} = C_z^i, \quad i, j = 1, 2, \ i \neq j.$$ (7.14)

Conditions (7.12)–(7.14) do not differ from the corresponding first-order conditions with perfect household mobility because they are determined for a given population distribution N_1. However, the necessary condition of an efficient population distribution differs from the condition derived in Chapter 2. Using (7.5) and (7.6) to solve for λ and μ, then inserting the expressions for λ and μ into (7.11) and allowing β to take all values from 0 to 1 yields, for the set of efficient population distributions,

$$-\frac{2aN_2}{U_x^2} \leq (F_N^1 - x_1) - (F_N^2 - x_2) \leq \frac{2aN_1}{U_x^1}.$$ (7.15)

Turning first to the case of immobile households ($a \to \infty$), condition (7.15) places no restriction on the population distribution; all population distributions are efficient. When households are perfectly mobile ($a = 0$), the well-known condition $F_N^1 - x_1 = F_N^2 - x_2$ of the unique efficient population distribution results. If households are imperfectly mobile ($a > 0$), there is a range of efficient population distributions. This interval begins at $(F_N^1 - x_1) - (F_N^2 - x_2) = -2aN_2/U_x^2$ for $\beta = 1$ and ends at $(F_N^1 - x_1) - (F_N^2 - x_2) = 2aN_1/U_x^1$ for $\beta = 0$. According to (7.2), households living in region 1 prefer a larger N_1 than households living in region 2. A planner who attaches a higher weight to households residing in 1 (i.e., decides for a high β) must choose a large N_1, thereby reducing the utility of households living in region 2.

7.2   Decentralized Nash Equilibrium

7.2.1   Private Behavior

We now turn to a decentralized economy. Before describing the behavior of regional governments, we first have to explain the behavior of firms and households. There is perfect competition in the private sector of the economy. Let us suppose that owners of land run the regional firms. This assumption implies that land owners receive not only land rents but also the return to the public factor. Firms in region i produce the private numeraire good and (on behalf of land owners) maximize the surplus

$$R_i \equiv F^i(L_i, N_i, K_i, g_i) - w_i N_i - (r + \tau_i^K) K_i \qquad (7.16)$$

by choosing N_i and K_i. As always, w_i denotes the regional wage rate and r the interregional interest rate; τ_i^K stands for the source-based capital tax. Expression (7.16) indicates that regional governments interfere in two ways with the behavior of firms: they increase the firms' productivity by providing local public factors, and they raise the costs of using private capital by levying the capital tax. In solving this problem, firms take the regional wage rate w_i and the interest rate r, as well as the amount of public factors g_i and the source-based capital tax τ_i^K, as given. The first-order conditions of an optimal demand for private factors are

$$F_N^i = w_i, \qquad (7.17)$$

$$F_K^i = r + \tau_i^K. \qquad (7.18)$$

Inserting (7.17) and (7.18) into (7.16), the entire rent generated in region i becomes

$$R_i = F^i - N_i F_N^i - K_i F_K^i. \qquad (7.19)$$

Households differ only in their attachment to a region. Each household is endowed, independently of the region in which it resides, with one unit of labor, with $k \equiv K/N$ units of capital, and with L_i/N units of land in region i. In their role as owners of capital, households seek to maximize their returns. They allocate the capital stock across regions so that its rate of return r becomes equal in both regions. Gross and net income of households differ because of the collection of taxes. The regional government collects a direct residence-based tax τ_i^N from households living in the region and a proportional source-based tax $t_i \leq 1$ on the entire rent generated in the region. The budget constraint of each household living in region i becomes

$$x_i = w_i - \tau_i^N + \sum_{j=1,2} \frac{R_j(1 - t_j)}{N} + kr. \tag{7.20}$$

The regional government uses its tax revenues to finance public goods and factors. In order to analyze whether regions make an interregional transfer of resources, it is useful to define $\theta_i \equiv 1 - t_i \geq 0$ as the nonnegative tax factor on regional rents and to choose θ_i instead of t_i as the government's decision variable. Using this definition, the budget constraint of the regional government reads as

$$N_i \tau_i^N + R_i(1 - \theta_i) + K_i \tau_i^K = C^i(z_i) + H^i(g_i). \tag{7.21}$$

It is also helpful for the following analysis to derive the regional feasibility restriction. Using the definition of θ_i and inserting (7.17)–(7.19) as well as the government constraint (7.21) for τ_i^N into the private budget restriction (7.20) yields, as the regional resource constraint,

$$x_i = \frac{1}{N_i}\left[F^i - \frac{N_j}{N} R_i \theta_i + \frac{N_i}{N} R_j \theta_j \right.$$

$$\left. + E_i(F_K^i - \tau_i^K) - C^i(z_i) - H^i(g_i) \right], \tag{7.22}$$

with $E_i \equiv N_i k - K_i$ again denoting region i's net capital export.

Rationally acting regional governments must consider locational responses of mobile households and capital when choosing their instruments. Since we have substituted the government's budget constraint for τ_i^N into the private budget restriction, N_i and K_i can be derived as implicit functions of the remaining government choice variables (z_i), (g_i), (τ_i^K), and (θ_i) from the following two-equation system:

$$G(N_i, K_i, z_i, z_j, g_i, g_j, \tau_i^K, \tau_j^K, \theta_i, \theta_j)$$

$$\equiv F_K^i(L_i, N_i, K_i, g_i) - \tau_i^K - F_K^j(L_j, N_j, K_j, g_j) + \tau_j^K = 0, \tag{7.23}$$

$$P(N_i, K_i, z_i, z_j, g_i, g_j, \tau_i^K, \tau_j^K, \theta_i, \theta_j)$$

$$\equiv U(x_i, z_i, z_j) - U(x_j, z_i, z_j) + aN - 2aN_i = 0, \tag{7.24}$$

where x_i and x_j must be replaced with (7.22) and where we must take $F^i = F^i(L_i, N_i, K_i, g_i)$, $N_j = N - N_i$, and $K_j = K - K_i$ into account.

7.2.2 Regional Government Behavior

Because households living in the same region differ, at first sight it seems less straightforward to decide for a certain behavioral assumption on behalf of regional governments. However, since residents differ only in their attachment to the region, we assume that the regional government in i maximizes $U(x_i, z_i, z_j)$. By maximizing U^i, the government maximizes the utility of each household living in i, since the psychic attachment n is a parameter. In choosing z_i, g_i, τ_i^K, and θ_i, the region acts under the Nash assumption that its choices are the best response to given z_j, g_j, τ_j^K, and θ_j. Its problem becomes to

$$\text{maximize } U(x_i, z_i, z_j) \tag{7.25}$$

by choosing z_i, g_i, τ_i^K, and $\theta_i \geq 0$, where x_i must be replaced with (7.22) and N_i and K_i depend on the government's instruments according to (7.23) and (7.24). Taking $dN_i = -dN_j$ and $dK_i = -dK_j$ into account yields the following first-order conditions of the simultaneous Nash equilibrium:

$$\frac{dU^i}{dz_i} = -\frac{U_x^i}{N_i} C_z^i + U_N^i \frac{\partial N_i}{\partial z_i} + U_K^i \frac{\partial K_i}{\partial z_i} + U_{z_i}^i = 0, \tag{7.26}$$

$$\frac{dU^i}{dg_i} = \frac{U_x^i}{N_i}\left[F_g^i - H_g^i - \frac{N_j}{N} R_{ig}\theta_i + E_i F_{Kg}^i \right]$$

$$+ U_N^i \frac{\partial N_i}{\partial g_i} + U_K^i \frac{\partial K_i}{\partial g_i} = 0, \tag{7.27}$$

$$\frac{dU^i}{d\tau_i^K} = -\frac{U_x^i}{N_i} E_i + U_N^i \frac{\partial N_i}{\partial \tau_i^K} + U_K^i \frac{\partial K_i}{\partial \tau_i^K} = 0, \tag{7.28}$$

$$\frac{dU^i}{d\theta_i} = -\frac{U_x^i}{N_i} \frac{N_j}{N} R_i + U_N^i \frac{\partial N_i}{\partial \theta_i} + U_K^i \frac{\partial K_i}{\partial \theta_i} \leq 0,$$

$$\theta_i \geq 0, \quad \theta_i \frac{dU^i}{d\theta_i} = 0, \tag{7.29}$$

with

$$U_N^i \equiv U_x^i \frac{\partial x_i}{\partial N_i}, \qquad U_K^i \equiv U_x^i \frac{\partial x_i}{\partial K_i}. \tag{7.30}$$

Our basic analytical objective is to rewrite the conditions of the optimal government behavior (7.26)–(7.29) so that they become comparable with the first-order conditions of an efficient allocation (7.12)–(7.15). Total differentiation of (7.23) and (7.24) allows us to derive the locational responses $\partial N_i/\partial *$ and $\partial K_i/\partial *$ for $* \in \{z_i, g_i, \tau_i^K, \theta_i\}$ (see Section 7.4.1). Inserting them into (7.26)–(7.29) and taking (7.30) into account yields, as necessary conditions of the optimal behavior of region i's government,

$$\frac{dU^i}{dz_i} = 0 \iff N_i \frac{U_{z_i}^i}{U_x^i} + N_j \frac{U_{z_i}^j}{U_x^j} \frac{(N_i/U_x^i)|A_i|}{(N_j/U_x^j)|A_j|} = C_z^i, \tag{7.31}$$

$$\frac{dU^i}{dg_i} = 0 \iff$$

$$F_g^i = H_g^i + \frac{N_j}{N} R_{ig}\theta_i \left(1 - \frac{(N_i/U_x^i)|A_i|}{(N_j/U_x^j)|A_j|}\right)$$

$$+ \frac{F_{Kg}^i}{F_{KK}^i + F_{KK}^j} \left(\left[-E_i F_{KK}^j + \tau_j^K + \frac{N_j R_{iK}\theta_i + N_i R_{jK}\theta_j}{N}\right]\right.$$

$$\times \left.\left[1 - \frac{(N_i/U_x^i)|A_i|}{(N_j/U_x^j)|A_j|}\right] + \tau_i^K - \tau_j^K\right), \tag{7.32}$$

$$\frac{dU^i}{d\tau_i^K} = 0 \iff \tau_j^K - \tau_i^K = \left[-E_i F_{KK}^j + \tau_j^K + \frac{N_j R_{iK}\theta_i + N_i R_{jK}\theta_j}{N}\right]$$

$$\times \left[1 - \frac{(N_i/U_x^i)|A_i|}{(N_j/U_x^j)|A_j|}\right], \tag{7.33}$$

$$\frac{dU^i}{d\theta_i} \leq 0 \iff \frac{N_j}{U_x^j}|A_j| - \frac{N_i}{U_x^i}|A_i| \leq 0, \tag{7.34}$$

with

$$|A_i| \equiv \begin{vmatrix} (F_{KN}^i + F_{KN}^j) & (F_{KK}^i + F_{KK}^j) \\ U_N^i & U_K^i \end{vmatrix},$$

$$|A_j| \equiv \begin{vmatrix} (F_{KN}^i + F_{KN}^j) & (F_{KK}^i + F_{KK}^j) \\ U_N^j - 2a & U_K^j \end{vmatrix}. \tag{7.35}$$

7.2.3 Transfer-Constrained Region

In the next section it will turn out that the efficiency properties of the decentralized Nash equilibrium hinge crucially on whether regions voluntarily make an interregional transfer of resources. It is therefore useful to introduce the concept of a transfer-constrained region. Note that the only possibility of an interregional transfer of resources is an outflow of land rents, and that a region's choice of θ_i determines whether it allows a rent outflow or not. If it chooses $\theta_i = 0$, then it avoids any interregional transfer through an outflow of land rents.

Definition. A region is called *transfer-constrained* if its first-order condition with respect to θ_i, (7.34), holds with strict inequality.

Hence, if region i is transfer-constrained, then it would like to make a negative interregional transfer but is bound by the nonnegativity constraint of θ_i. The basic reason why regions make transfers is to restrict immigration. They compare the direct loss of resources from making the transfer (choosing $\theta_i > 0$) with the gain in per-capita consumption from decreasing the regional population size. Whether regions are transfer-constrained depends on the degree of household mobility. To see this more directly, we insert the explicit expressions for $|A_i|$ and $|A_j|$ into (7.34) and collect terms to achieve a first-order condition of choosing θ_i as follows:

$$(F_N^j - x_j) - (F_N^i - x_i) - \frac{2aN_j}{U_x^j} \le 0. \tag{7.36}$$

If households are immobile ($a \to \infty$) then both regions are obviously transfer-constrained, since a positive interregional transfer only lowers regional resources without affecting the population distribution (nor thus the capital allocation). To see this, divide (7.36) by a and take the limit $a \to \infty$. It follows that the first-order condition (7.34) must hold with strict inequality for both regions. In the case of perfect household mobility ($a = 0$), (7.36) can hold for both regions simultaneously only with strict equality. Hence, no region is transfer-constrained in equilibrium. If households are imperfectly mobile ($0 < a \ll \infty$), then at least one region must be transfer-constrained. Suppose that region i is not transfer-constrained, $(F_N^j - x_j) - (F_N^i - x_i) = 2aN_j/U_x^j$. Then region j must be transfer-constrained, since its first-order condition (7.36) becomes $(F_N^i - x_i) - (F_N^j - x_j) = -2aN_j/U_x^j < 2aN_i/U_x^i$. An obvious case where both regions are transfer-constrained is a symmetric equilibrium of identical regions, $F_N^i - x_i = F_N^j - x_j$. Let us summarize these results in

Proposition 7.1. *If households are perfectly mobile, then no region is transfer-constrained. If households are imperfectly mobile, then at least one region is transfer-constrained. If households are immobile, then both regions are transfer-constrained. Whenever a region is transfer-constrained, it avoids any outflow of land rents by choosing $\theta_i = 0$.*

In the case of perfect household mobility, the migration equilibrium ensures that all households living in the federal state attain the same utility level. Since the migration equilibrium is taken into account by both governments, they agree on the net interregional transfer that maximizes the common utility level of all households. Hence, no region would like to have more resources by making a negative interregional transfer. If households are imperfectly mobile then both regions disagree on their desired population size, since – according to (7.2) – the pecuniary utility levels differ in both regions, where the wedge depends on the regional population size. Hence, if one region is not transfer-constrained then the other region must necessarily be constrained. We must therefore ask under which conditions regions are transfer-constrained. If the production functions are the same in both regions, then interregional differences can only be attributed to different land endowments. The greater the interregional differences in land endowments and the smaller the heterogeneity of tastes for a region (the smaller a), the more likely it is that the region with the higher land endowment will make the transfer.

Let us now investigate the first-order conditions (7.31)–(7.34) and hence the outcome of regional decision-making for different degrees of household mobility.

7.3 Different Degrees of Household Mobility

7.3.1 Perfect Household Mobility

As demonstrated in Chapter 6, perfect interregional household mobility ($a = 0$) serves as an incentive mechanism for regional governments to choose the efficient allocation. In this case, Proposition 7.1 makes clear that no region is transfer-constrained. Using this result to insert the necessary condition (7.34) of strict equality into (7.31)–(7.33) and taking (7.36) for $a = 0$ into account, we can state

Proposition 7.2. *When households are perfectly mobile, the decentralized Nash equilibrium is socially efficient and characterized by the following conditions:*

(i) $\quad N_i \dfrac{U^i_{z_i}}{U^i_x} + N_j \dfrac{U^j_{z_i}}{U^i_x} = C^i_z, \quad i, j = 1, 2, \ i \neq j,$

(ii) $\quad F^i_g = H^i_g, \quad i = 1, 2,$

(iii) $\quad F^i_K = F^j_K,$

(iv) $\quad F^i_N - x_i = F^j_N - x_j.$

In Chapter 6 we have already discussed the power of the equal utility migration equilibrium for coordinating self-interested regional behavior. Once again, we should emphasize that an interregional transfer of resources is necessary to achieve the efficient population distribution across regions. In other words, a complete instrument set must include the possibility to make a transfer. This could be, as in our case, a source-based tax on land rents when regional land is also owned by households living in other regions, or (alternatively) a direct interregional cash transfer such as foreign aid.

7.3.2   Perfect Immobility of Households

If households are immobile ($a \to \infty$) then neither region can influence the interregional labor allocation and thus neither has an incentive to make a transfer. The regions therefore tax land rents confiscatorily, $\theta_i = 0$, in order to avoid an outflow of rents. As $a \to \infty$, the fraction $(N_i/U_x^i)|A_i|/[(N_j/U_x^j)|A_j|]$ becomes zero. Using these results in the first-order conditions (7.31)–(7.33) allows us to state

Proposition 7.3. *Suppose households are perfectly immobile across regions. Then the Nash equilibrium among regions is inefficient and is characterized by the following conditions:*

(i) $N_i \dfrac{U_{z_i}^i}{U_x^i} = C_z^i, \quad i = 1, 2,$

(ii) $F_g^i = H_g^i + \dfrac{F_{Kg}^i}{F_{KK}^i + F_{KK}^j}[-E_i F_{KK}^j + \tau_j^K + \tau_i^K - \tau_j^K],$

   $i, j = 1, 2, \ i \neq j,$

(iii) $\tau_j^K - \tau_i^K = -E_i F_{KK}^j + \tau_j^K, \quad i, j = 1, 2, \ i \neq j.$

Because households are immobile and regional governments are interested in the welfare of residents only, the welfare of nonresidents is completely ignored. According to condition (i), only the marginal willingness of residents to pay is considered when providing public goods. Regions undersupply public goods relative to the Samuelson condition when there are spillover effects. Another consequence of this self-interested behavior is that regions try to increase their interregional income share by choice of their policy instruments. If a source-based tax on capital is available, it is levied to influence the interregional allocation of capital in order to increase the regional interest income. In this case, the provision of public factors is not used as a strategic instrument and is therefore not distorted. Inserting condition (iii) into (ii) shows that regions provide local public factors in line with the Samuelson rule. Following (iii), the net capital exporter, $E_i > 0$, chooses a negative capital tax rate (subsidizes capital) in order to attract capital so as to increase the interregional interest rate. The other region chooses a positive capital tax rate in order to decrease the demand for capital by its firms. Since this region is a net capital importer, it has incentives to reduce the entire demand for capital and therefore the interest rate. This policy reduces its interest liabilities to nonresidents. Of course, such strategic behavior distorts the interregional capital allocation.

If regions have no capital tax available ($\tau_i^K = \tau_j^K \equiv 0$) – because, for example, the central government has taken away from the regions the responsibility to levy source-based taxes on capital – then the supply of local public factors partly takes over the task of influencing the interregional capital allocation. According to condition (ii), if a region is a net capital exporter and if the marginal productivity of capital rises by an increase in the provision of public factors, $F_{Kg}^i > 0$, then this region has incentives to oversupply local public inputs relative to the Samuelson rule in order to increase the net interest income from abroad.

7.3.3 Imperfect Household Mobility

Imperfect household mobility ($0 < a \ll \infty$) is the case with the broadest applicability, and Proposition 7.1 states that either region 1, region 2, or both regions must be transfer-constrained. This implies

Proposition 7.4. *If households are imperfectly mobile, then the Nash equilibrium among regions is characterized by an inefficient allocation. Only the region that is not transfer-constrained (e.g., region i) has incentives to avoid distortions, and it behaves according to the following conditions:*

(i) $\quad N_i \dfrac{U_{z_i}^i}{U_x^i} + N_j \dfrac{U_{z_i}^j}{U_x^j} = C_z^i,$

(ii) $\quad F_g^i = H_g^i,$

(iii) $\quad \tau_i^K = \tau_j^K,$

(iv) $\quad F_N^j - x_j - \dfrac{2aN_j}{U_x^j} = F_N^i - x_i.$

At least one region (e.g., region j) is transfer-constrained, and its behavior can be described by the following rules:

(v) $\quad N_j \dfrac{U_{z_j}^j}{U_x^j} + N_i \dfrac{U_{z_j}^i}{U_x^i} \dfrac{(N_j/U_x^j)|A_j|}{(N_i/U_x^i)|A_i|} = C_z^j,$

(vi) $\quad F_g^j = H_g^j + \dfrac{F_{Kg}^j}{F_{KK}^j + F_{KK}^i}\left([-E_j F_{KK}^j + \tau_i^K] \right.$

$$\left. \times \left[1 - \dfrac{(N_j/U_x^j)|A_j|}{(N_i/U_x^i)|A_i|} \right] + \tau_j^K - \tau_i^K \right),$$

(vii) $(\tau_i^K - \tau_j^K) = [-E_j F_{KK}^i + \tau_i^K]\left[1 - \dfrac{(N_j/U_x^j)|A_j|}{(N_i/U_x^i)|A_i|}\right]$,

(viii) $(F_N^i - x_i) - (F_N^j - x_j) - \dfrac{2aN_i}{U_x^i} < 0$.

Conditions (i), (ii), and (iii) are derived by inserting (7.34) with strict equality into (7.31)–(7.33). The behavioral rules (v)–(viii) restate conditions (7.31)–(7.33) and (7.36), where we have used that $\theta_j = 0$ in a transfer-constrained region. Proposition 7.4 states that the decentralized Nash equilibrium is generally socially inefficient.

However, there is one important exception for which noncooperative government activities result in an efficient allocation even when households are imperfectly mobile. If there are no interregional spillover effects in the provision of public goods ($U_{z_j}^i = 0$) and if one region (say, i) is not transfer-constrained, Proposition 7.4 shows that there are no distortions. Local public goods and – as can be seen by inserting (vii) into (vi) – local public factors are provided in line with the Samuelson rule. Moreover, the region that is not transfer-constrained can achieve its desired interregional resource distribution and therefore has no incentive to manipulate the interregional capital allocation in order to change the interest income from abroad. Hence, such a region chooses the efficient interregional capital allocation by setting $\tau_i^K = \tau_j^K$ (see (iii)). According to (vii), the region (here, j) that *is* transfer-constrained chooses $\tau_j^K = E_j F_{KK}^i$. In summary, if there are no public good spillover effects then there is no pure efficiency reason for a central government to intervene. According to condition (iv), an efficient allocation with a distribution weight of $\beta = 1$ for the unconstrained region is achieved. A central government intervention can only be justified if the center prefers a different interregional resource distribution. Hence, there is room only for a redistributive central government intervention.

If there are public good spillover effects or if both regions are transfer-constrained, then the allocation is inefficient. Following (v)–(viii), the single sources of inefficiency are the same as for perfect immobility. However, the size of the distortions is reduced since the following relation holds:

$$0 < \dfrac{(N_j/U_x^j)|A_j|}{(N_i/U_x^i)|A_i|} < 1$$

(see Section 7.4.2). For instance, a transfer-constrained region takes partly into account the marginal willingness of nonresidents to pay for providing public goods. Even a transfer-constrained region must consider the welfare effects of its actions on nonresidents in order to assess migration responses and so derive all effects of its policy on its own residents. As in the case of immobile households, if transfer-constrained regions have a capital tax available then they supply local public factors in line with the Samuelson condition. The chosen capital tax rate is either positive or negative, depending on whether the region is a net exporter or importer of capital. More specifically, if region i is not transfer-constrained then it chooses $\tau_i^K = \tau_j^K = E_i F_{KK}^j$.

The predicted behavior of regional governments has consequences for a central government aiming at correcting inefficient regional policies. The center must first observe whether regions make a transfer (directly or via an outflow of land rents) before it can decide to intervene. Even if it concludes that there is no migration-related transfer, the center must adapt its optimal intervention scheme to the environment of household mobility. Compared to the well-known corrective devices for the case of immobile households, the Pigouvian remedies must be reduced. Regions internalize part of the externalities they cause in their own interest.

However, before this prediction of the model can become policy advice for existing federations, it must be tested empirically for regions that are linked by labor mobility and that may make interregional transfers. The assertion is that such regions have a greater trust in decentralized governmental decisions than those other regions that rely on supranational coordination. Candidates for testing are countries that give interregional aid – partly to restrict immigration, as with the massive transfer from West Germany to East Germany, the transfers from the EU to the former Soviet Union since its breakdown, the U.S. transfer to Mexico during the peso crisis, and foreign aid from the industrialized world to less developed countries.

7.4 Appendix

7.4.1 First-Order Conditions

The basic purpose of this appendix is to derive the first-order conditions (7.31)–(7.34). As a first step, the migration responses must be calculated from (7.23) and (7.24). Total differentiation of (7.23) and (7.24) yields

$$
\begin{pmatrix} G_N^i & G_K^i \\ P_N^i & P_K^i \end{pmatrix} \begin{pmatrix} dN_i \\ dK_i \end{pmatrix} = - \begin{pmatrix} G_z^i & G_g^i & G_{\tau^K}^i & G_\theta^i \\ P_z^i & P_g^i & P_{\tau^K}^i & P_\theta^i \end{pmatrix} \begin{pmatrix} dz_i \\ dg_i \\ d\tau_i^K \\ d\theta_i \end{pmatrix}, \tag{A.7.1}
$$

with

$$G_N^i = F_{KN}^i + F_{KN}^j, \qquad G_K^i = F_{KK}^i + F_{KK}^j,$$

$$P_N^i = U_N^i + U_N^j - 2a, \qquad P_K^i = U_K^i + U_K^j,$$

$$G_z^i = 0, \quad G_g^i = F_{Kg}^i, \quad G_{\tau^K}^i = -1, \quad G_\theta^i = 0,$$

$$P_z^i = -\frac{U_x^i}{N_i}C_z^i + U_{z_i}^i - U_{z_i}^j,$$

$$P_g^i = \frac{U_x^i}{N_i}\left(F_g^i - H_g^i - \frac{N_j}{N}\theta_i R_{ig} + E_i F_{Kg}^i\right) - \frac{U_x^j}{N_j}\frac{N_j}{N}R_{ig}\theta_i,$$

$$P_{\tau^K}^i = -\frac{U_x^i}{N_i}E_i, \quad P_\theta^i = -\frac{U_x^i}{N_i}\frac{N_j}{N}R_i - \frac{U_x^j}{N_j}\frac{N_j}{N}R_i,$$

$$U_N^i \equiv \frac{U_x^i}{N_i}\left\{(F_N^i - x_i) + \frac{R_i\theta_i + R_j\theta_j}{N} - \frac{N_j}{N}R_{iN}\theta_i\right.$$

$$\left. - \frac{N_i}{N}R_{jN}\theta_j + E_i F_{KN}^i + \frac{K}{N}(F_K^i - \tau_i^K)\right\},$$

$$U_K^i \equiv \frac{U_x^i}{N_i}\left\{-\frac{N_j}{N}\theta_i R_{iK} - \frac{N_i}{N}\theta_j R_{jK} + E_i F_{KK}^i + \tau_i^K\right\}. \tag{A.7.2}$$

Let $A = A_i + A_j$ denote the 2×2 matrix on the left side of (A.7.1), with A_i and A_j as defined in (7.35). Local stability of the locational equilibrium (7.23) and (7.24) requires that $|A|$ be negative. Applying Cramer's rule to (A.7.1) yields

$$\frac{\partial N_i}{\partial z_i} = \begin{vmatrix} -G_z^i & G_K^i \\ -P_z^i & P_K^i \end{vmatrix}|A|^{-1}, \tag{A.7.3}$$

$$\frac{\partial K_i}{\partial z_i} = \begin{vmatrix} G_N^i & -G_z^i \\ P_N^i & -P_z^i \end{vmatrix}|A|^{-1}, \tag{A.7.4}$$

$$\frac{\partial N_i}{\partial g_i} = \begin{vmatrix} -G_g^i & G_K^i \\ -P_g^i & P_K^i \end{vmatrix}|A|^{-1}, \tag{A.7.5}$$

$$\frac{\partial K_i}{\partial g_i} = \begin{vmatrix} G_N^i & -G_g^i \\ P_N^i & -P_g^i \end{vmatrix}|A|^{-1}, \tag{A.7.6}$$

$$\frac{\partial N_i}{\partial \tau_i^K} = \begin{vmatrix} -G_{\tau^K}^i & G_K^i \\ -P_{\tau^K}^i & P_K^i \end{vmatrix}|A|^{-1}, \tag{A.7.7}$$

$$\frac{\partial K_i}{\partial \tau_i^K} = \begin{vmatrix} G_N^i & -G_{\tau^K}^i \\ P_N^i & -P_{\tau^K}^i \end{vmatrix}|A|^{-1}, \tag{A.7.8}$$

$$\frac{\partial N_i}{\partial \theta_i} = \begin{vmatrix} -G_\theta^i & G_K^i \\ -P_\theta^i & P_K^i \end{vmatrix}|A|^{-1}, \tag{A.7.9}$$

$$\frac{\partial K_i}{\partial \theta_i} = \begin{vmatrix} G_N^i & -G_\theta^i \\ P_N^i & -P_\theta^i \end{vmatrix}|A|^{-1}. \tag{A.7.10}$$

Inserting (A.7.3) and (A.7.4) into (7.26), collecting terms, and multiplying the entire expression by $N_i N_j / (U_x^i U_x^j)$ yields

$$N_i \frac{U_{z_i}^i}{U_x^i} \frac{N_j}{U_x^j} |A_j| + N_j \frac{U_{z_i}^j}{U_x^j} \frac{N_i}{U_x^i} |A_i| = C_z^i \frac{N_j}{U_x^j} |A_j|. \qquad (A.7.11)$$

Dividing (A.7.11) by $(N_j / U_x^j) |A_j|$ yields the first-order condition (7.31).

Inserting (A.7.5) and (A.7.6) into (7.27) and collecting terms, it follows that

$$(F_g^i - H_g^i) \frac{U_x^i}{N_i} |A_j| + \frac{N_j}{N} \theta_i R_{ig} \left(\frac{U_x^j}{N_j} |A_i| - \frac{U_x^i}{N_i} |A_j| \right)$$

$$+ F_{Kg}^i \begin{vmatrix} (U_x^i/N_i) E_i G_n^i - U_N^i & (U_x^i/N_i) E_i G_K^i - U_K^i \\ U_N^j - 2a & U_K^j \end{vmatrix} = 0. \quad (A.7.12)$$

Multiplying the entire expression by $N_i N_j / (U_x^i U_x^j)$, adding the second row of the determinant in the second line to the first row, then using the full expressions from (A.7.2) in this determinant and collecting terms yields

$$(F_g^i - H_g^i) \frac{N_j}{U_x^j} |A_j| = \frac{N_j}{N} \theta_i R_{ig} \left(\frac{N_j}{U_x^j} |A_j| - \frac{N_i}{U_x^i} |A_i| \right)$$

$$- \frac{F_{Kg}^i}{F_{KK}^i + F_{KK}^j} \left[\frac{N_j}{U_x^j} U_K^j \left(\frac{N_j}{U_x^j} |A_j| - \frac{N_i}{U_x^i} |A_i| \right) \right.$$

$$\left. + (\tau_i^K - \tau_j^K) \frac{N_j}{U_x^j} |A_j| \right]. \qquad (A.7.13)$$

Inserting the full expression of U_K^j from (A.7.2) and dividing the entire term by $(N_j / U_x^j) |A_j|$, the first-order condition (7.32) follows.

Substituting (A.7.7) and (A.7.8) into (7.28), it follows that

$$-\frac{U_x^i}{N_i} E_i |A_j| + \begin{vmatrix} U_N^i & U_K^i \\ U_N^j - 2a & U_K^j \end{vmatrix} = 0. \qquad (A.7.14)$$

Both expressions can be collected by adding the elements in the first row:

$$\begin{vmatrix} (N_i/U_x^i) U_N^i - E_i (F_{KN}^i + F_{KN}^j) & (N_i/U_x^i) U_K^i - E_i (F_{KK}^i + F_{KK}^j) \\ (N_j/U_x^j) U_N^j - (N_j/U_x^j) 2a & (N_j/U_x^j) U_K^j \end{vmatrix} = 0.$$

$$(A.7.15)$$

Subtracting the second row from the first row, inserting the full expressions of U_N^i, U_N^j, U_K^i, and U_K^j, and making use of the definitions of A_i and A_j from (7.35) yields the first-order condition (7.33).

Finally, substituting (A.7.9) and (A.7.10) into (7.29), collecting terms, and dividing the entire expression by $(U_x^i U_x^j / N_i N_j)(N_j / N) R_i$ yields the first-order condition (7.34). Using the explicit expressions of U_N^i, U_N^j, U_K^i, and U_K^j in (7.34), (7.36) follows.

7.4.2   *Expressions of a Transfer-Constrained Region*

It remains only to prove that, for a transfer-constrained region i, the expression $(N_j/U_x^j)|A_j|$ is negative and the fraction $(N_i/U_x^i)|A_i|/[(N_j/U_x^j)|A_j|]$ is positive but less than unity. Stability of the migration equilibrium requires that

$$|A_i| + |A_j| < 0. \tag{A.7.16}$$

For a transfer-constrained region, the first-order condition (7.34) must hold with strict inequality, implying

$$\frac{N_j}{U_x^j}|A_j| < \frac{N_i}{U_x^i}|A_i|. \tag{A.7.17}$$

If (A.7.16) and (A.7.17) hold then the following inequality must also hold:

$$|A_i|\left(1 + \frac{N_j}{U_x^j}\frac{U_x^i}{N_i}\right) < 0. \tag{A.7.18}$$

Hence, $|A_i| < 0$. Together with (A.7.17), this yields

$$0 > \frac{N_i}{U_x^i}|A_i| > \frac{N_j}{U_x^j}|A_j|, \tag{A.7.19}$$

which completes the proof.

CHAPTER 8

Decentralized Redistribution Policy

In addition to its allocative function, the government must redistribute income between poor and rich households in order to ensure a fair income distribution. Here, the question once again arises of how to delegate this function to different governmental levels. The prevailing view is that redistribution policy is best administered by the central government (see Stigler 1957; Musgrave 1971; Oates 1972; Brown and Oates 1987). According to this opinion, decentralized redistribution policy causes some kind of adverse selection. It is argued that regional redistribution programs (a) attract poor households from neighboring regions by increasing their net income via transfers and (b) repel rich households, who have to pay for the program. From the viewpoint of a single region, the marginal costs of providing additional transfer payments to poor residents exceed the social marginal costs, since other regions benefit from the induced migration responses by losing beneficiaries of and gaining contributors to their welfare system. However, this is not taken into account by the region that enacts the program. As the analysis of Chapter 3 reveals, perfect interregional competition for mobile households results in a policy optimum where regional governments have no incentive to redistribute income among the owners of mobile and immobile factors of production. This adverse selection problem arises to a far less pronounced extent when the redistribution function is assigned to the central government, since the degree of household mobility decreases with the size of the jurisdiction.

There is another, quite different opinion on this problem. Pauly (1973) rejects the idea of assigning the redistribution branch of the government to the central level. He argues that only a regional responsibility for redistribution policy can be Pareto-efficient. If rich households are altruistic and are interested in the well-being of their poor neighbors, then only diverse regional redistribution programs can be efficient, since regional preferences for redistribution differ among rich households living in different regions – at least in general. Redistributive payments derived from altruistic motives can be regarded as a local public good, so the same problems arise as with a central provision of local

137

public goods. A national responsibility for redistribution policy lacks the sensitivity to different tastes for redistribution in the individual regions and would therefore imply uniform tax–transfer programs across all regions of a federal state. This causes efficiency losses.

However, taking a closer look, Pauly's argument can be supported only if individuals are immobile. To see this as clearly as possible, recall the basic result of Chapter 6 that perfect interregional household mobility serves as an incentive mechanism for regional governments to choose the efficient allocation. Even under these ideal circumstances, Burbidge and Myers (1994a) and Wellisch (1996) derive that regional redistribution policies are efficient and ensure a socially optimal degree of redistribution between rich and poor individuals if (and only if) regional preferences for redistribution are the same. If regions have diverse preferences for redistribution then they choose different tax–transfer policies and so distort migration decisions. These contributions reveal that Pauly's argument turns to just the opposite if households are mobile. If all households are mobile, it is especially the existence of different views about redistribution among regions that causes distortions.

Rather than follow the studies by Burbidge and Myers (1994a) or Wellisch (1996), in this chapter we wish to incorporate an important phenomenon of existing federations in the model: not all households are perfectly mobile across regions. This chapter will therefore assume that there exist immobile and mobile households and that regional governments redistribute income between both groups. In contrast to Chapter 3, we now assume that regions are large, thereby following studies by Wildasin (1991) and Wellisch and Wildasin (1995, 1996a,b). The subsequent analysis confirms the expectations about decentralized redistribution policy stated at the beginning, and it shows that there are two basic problems involved. First, regions choose different tax–transfer levels when their redistributive activities are not coordinated, and this results in migration distortions. Second, in choosing its policy, each region ignores that the costs of redistribution programs of the other regions decrease. When a region increases the transfer payments, it attracts mobile low-income households by increasing their net income, creating a positive externality on other regions. Therefore, regional redistribution programs lead to a positive but suboptimally low degree of redistribution.[1]

To illustrate the problems arising from regional redistribution policy and to outline an intervention method that helps to overcome these problems, Chapter 8 is divided into three sections. Section 8.1 derives the necessary conditions of a socially optimal income distribution and an efficient population distribution among regions, and it discusses the properties of the noncooperative Nash equilibrium in redistribution policies between two competing regions. A corrective

---

[1] Epple and Romer (1991), Wildasin (1992, 1994a), and Wellisch and Walz (1998) arrive at similar conclusions.

central government intervention scheme is derived in Section 8.2. Finally, the appendix in Section 8.3 proves some important results reported in Sections 8.1 and 8.2.

8.1 Uncoordinated Regional Redistribution Policy

8.1.1 Private Behavior

Let us again consider a federal state consisting of two regions denoted by $i = 1, 2$. Each region produces a homogeneous output, which is taken as numeraire in the following analysis. The output in each region is produced using two (types of) inputs. The first input is called the fixed factor, assumed to be immobile and inelastically supplied in each region. It may represent land or other natural resources, but it should be interpreted to include any other immobile factors as well. The precise definition of these other factors depends on the intended application, but could include immobile labor (e.g., the old, or workers in particular skill or occupational categories). The variable L_i stands for the amount of the fixed factor. We assume that the fixed factor is owned by a representative immobile resident, indexed by A.[2]

The second input is mobile labor, which refers to a class of identical workers who are mobile among regions; this group is indexed by B. Each worker is assumed to provide one unit of labor in the region of that worker's residence. The variable N_i stands for the size of the mobile labor force in region i, consisting of the exogenously given original residents plus any workers who enter from the other region.

Regional production takes place by a linear homogeneous production function $F^i(L_i, N_i)$. We assume competitive factor markets, so that workers living in region i attain a wage equal to their marginal product F_N^i. However, gross and net incomes may diverge because of redistributive policy conducted by the government of region i. The government may provide a transfer to (resp., levy a tax on) mobile workers $\tau_i^B > 0$ (< 0), which must be financed by collecting a tax from (granting a subsidy to) the fixed factor. Hence, the net income of a mobile worker living in region i is equal to $x_i^B = F_N^i + \tau_i^B$, while the net income of the owner of the fixed factor amounts to $x_i^A = F^i - N_i x_i^B$. In deriving the budget constraint of the owner of the fixed factor, the budget restriction of the regional government has already been inserted for the tax this household must pay. It is important to note that all members of the mobile work force in a region not only have the same wage but also are treated identically with respect to transfers and taxes. This assumption depicts the situation in the EU, where the Treaty of Rome (Article 48) guarantees all EU citizens an identical treatment in all member states with respect to wages, taxation, and fiscal benefits.

---

[2] The results derived in this chapter would not change if the fixed factor were owned by many residents, as long as they are immobile.

It should (again) be emphasized that the fiscal variables are not restricted to sign, and they should be interpreted very broadly. The notational treatment of taxes and transfers as cash or cash equivalents simplifies the analysis considerably but should not be taken too literally. Rather, the variable τ_i^B should stand for the net fiscal benefit, per mobile worker, of the totality of government tax, transfer, and expenditure policies. Public expenditures for rival public services to mobile workers should also be included in τ_i^B. Pure cash transfers are the most obvious and easily measured examples of government provision of rival goods to households, but any public goods or services for which it makes sense to construct cash equivalents will fit the model equally well.

All members of the mobile work force are assumed to be able to costlessly migrate from one region to the other. A migration equilibrium in the federal state requires that no worker has an incentive to move from one region to another. Hence, a migration equilibrium is characterized by identical net incomes of mobile workers,

$$x_1^B = x_2^B = x^B, \tag{8.1}$$

with x^B being the common net income level.

Moreover, total employment in the two regions must be equal to total supply of labor:

$$N = N_1 + N_2, \tag{8.2}$$

where N is the entire work force of the federal state. Substituting $x_i^B = F_N^i + \tau_i^B$ into (8.1), conditions (8.1) and (8.2) can be used to determine the equilibrium allocation N_i of labor as a function of the redistributive transfers (τ_i^B) in each region. Hence, N_i is implicitly given as a function of the transfer levels by the equation

$$G(N_i, \tau_i^B, \tau_j^B) \equiv F_N^i(L_i, N_i) + \tau_i^B - F_N^j(L_j, N - N_i) - \tau_j^B = 0. \tag{8.3}$$

Defining $D \equiv F_{NN}^i + F_{NN}^j < 0$ and implicitly differentiating (8.3) yields the following migration responses:

$$\frac{\partial N_i}{\partial \tau_i^B} = -\frac{\partial N_i}{\partial \tau_j^B} = -\frac{1}{D} > 0. \tag{8.4}$$

Two general properties of the system (8.1) and (8.2) can be seen by considering (8.4). First, a higher level of transfers toward workers in one region increases its equilibrium labor force and reduces that of the other region. Second, the equilibrium allocation of labor, factor prices, or welfare depends only on the difference between the level of transfers to mobile workers, $\tau_i^B - \tau_j^B$, and not on each of them separately.

Given any redistributive policies (τ_i^B) for both regions, the equilibrium labor allocation, equilibrium factor prices, and net incomes are determined. Then, we can define the functions

$$x_i^B(\tau_i^B, \tau_j^B) \equiv F_N^i(L_i, N_i[\tau_i^B - \tau_j^B]) + \tau_i^B, \tag{8.5}$$

$$x_i^A(\tau_i^B, \tau_j^B) \equiv F^i(L_i, N_i[\tau_i^B - \tau_j^B]) - N_i(\tau_i^B - \tau_j^B)F_N^i(L_i, N_i[\tau_i^B - \tau_j^B])$$
$$- N_i(\tau_i^B - \tau_j^B)\tau_i^B. \tag{8.6}$$

Let us assume that each region determines its redistributive policy by maximizing a social welfare function defined over the net income of its immobile factor owner and the net income of a representative native worker, $W^i(x_i^A, x_i^B)$, and let us define

$$MRS_i \equiv \frac{\partial W^i}{\partial x_i^B} \Big/ \frac{\partial W^i}{\partial x_i^A}$$

as the marginal social rate of substitution between the consumption of workers and the immobile factor owner in region i.[3] Both x_i^A and x_i^B are normal goods in the preference structure W^i. The social welfare function in one region may differ from that in the other, so that the model is quite general with respect to preferences for redistribution.

Note that there is another common interpretation of each region's redistribution policy. One might interpret the welfare function W^i as a form of an interdependent utility function whereby redistribution follows from altruistic motives between donors and recipients (see Hochman and Rodgers 1969; Pauly 1973; Orr 1976). For instance, it is possible to assume that the immobile factor owner derives utility both from own consumption and from that of workers, as reflected by the utility function $W^i(x_i^A, x_i^B)$, and that this household chooses the transfer payments to workers τ_i^B in order to maximize this function.

8.1.2   Socially Optimal Allocation

Before detailing the behavior of regional governments in a noncooperative equilibrium, it is instructive to recall the condition of the efficient labor allocation across regions and to derive the necessary condition of a socially optimal income distribution.[4] Since mobile workers derive utility only by consuming private goods and migrate until $x_1^B = x_2^B$, the first-order condition of the efficient population distribution set out in Chapter 2, (2.10), reduces to

---

[3] Note that the welfare function does not depend on the number of mobile workers (native workers plus immigrants from the other region) directly. If this were the case then the analysis would change, making immigration more desirable. However, it is always problematic to define social welfare with changing population sizes, whether the change is due to natural increase (Nerlove, Razin, and Sadka 1985) or migration (Gordon 1983; Cukierman, Hercowitz, and Pines 1994; Mansoorian and Myers 1997). The analysis would *not* change if the number of native workers entered the welfare function, since that number is exogenously given.

[4] The first-order conditions (8.7) and (8.8) follow from maximizing the social welfare function $W^1(x_1^A, x^B) + W^2(x_2^A, x^B)$ by choosing x_1^A, x_2^A, x^B, and N_1 subject to the resource constraint $F^1(L_1, N_1) + F^2(L_2, N - N_1) - x_1^A - x_2^A - Nx^B = 0$.

$$F_N^1 = F_N^2. \tag{8.7}$$

Hence, the efficient locational pattern requires identical marginal products of labor. This means that the transfers chosen by both regions must be identical in order to avoid migration distortions in a free migration equilibrium.

Since the net income of mobile workers is identical and enters the welfare functions in both regions, a socially optimal redistribution policy must satisfy the Samuelson condition

$$MRS_1 + MRS_2 = N. \tag{8.8}$$

The social benefit of increasing the net income of mobile workers by one unit on the left side must be equal to the social costs on the right side. Since all mobile workers receive the same net income, social costs are equal to the entire number of mobile workers living in the federal state. For later reference, it is important to note that the condition of a socially optimal income distribution reduces to $MRS_i = N/2$ for each region if both regions are perfectly symmetric.

8.1.3   Regional Government Policy

Let us now turn to decentralized redistribution policies in both regions. Regions choose their redistributive measures noncooperatively and find a Nash equilibrium in the levels of per-worker transfers (τ_i^B). Nash behavior implies that region i chooses its transfer variable τ_i^B in order to

$$\text{maximize } W^i(x_i^A, x_i^B) \tag{8.9}$$

subject to (8.5), (8.6), and the assumption that region j does not change τ_j^B in response. Defining $d\mu_i \equiv MRS_i \, dx_i^B + dx_i^A$ as the change in social welfare in region i measured in terms of real income of the fixed factor (the equivalent variation), the first-order condition of this problem is

$$\frac{d\mu_i}{d\tau_i^B} = (MRS_i - N_i)\left(1 + F_{NN}^i \frac{\partial N_i}{\partial \tau_i^B}\right) - \tau_i^B \frac{\partial N_i}{\partial \tau_i^B} = 0. \tag{8.10}$$

Inserting the migration response $\partial N_i / \partial \tau_i^B$ derived in (8.4) into (8.10), collecting terms, and multiplying by D yields

$$MRS_i = N_i - \frac{\tau_i^B}{F_{NN}^j}, \quad i, j = 1, 2, \ i \neq j. \tag{8.11}$$

In the Nash equilibrium, (8.11) holds simultaneously for both regions. The left side reflects the benefit of increasing the net income of mobile workers living in the region by one unit. The regional government balances this marginal benefit with the marginal costs of redistribution; from its viewpoint, marginal costs are composed of two elements. Note that $-1/F_{NN}^j$ reflects the change in net migration from region j to region i resulting from an increase in the net income of workers living in i. Then, the right side of (8.11) shows that marginal costs are equal to the number of workers N_i plus the costs of extending the benefits τ_i^B to those additional workers attracted to region i as real income there rises, $-1/F_{NN}^j$. The equilibrium transfer levels (τ_i^B) are implicitly determined by both first-order conditions.

The first problem of decentralized redistribution policy can be identified by inspection of (8.11). If regions differ, there is no mechanism ensuring an equalization of transfer levels chosen by the regions in a noncooperative Nash equilibrium. However, this would be necessary to avoid migration distortions. Our first result is thus

Proposition 8.1. *Suppose that regional governments redistribute income among immobile and mobile residents. Then, uncoordinated regional redistribution policies result in migration distortions because regions choose different tax–transfer levels for mobile individuals.*

The second problem of regional redistribution policy is too low a level of redistribution. In order to isolate this problem from other motives for strategic regional behavior, let us assume (as in Chapter 4) that both regions are identical. Using this assumption, regions have no incentives to use their tax–transfer policy to manipulate the interregional resource distribution. In a symmetric equilibrium they are aware that they cannot increase their income by a strategic choice of τ_i^B. Hence, symmetry allows us to concentrate on the problem of whether decentralization of the redistributive branch itself leads to a suboptimally low degree of redistribution. With symmetric regions, the first-order condition (8.11) becomes

$$MRS_i = \frac{N}{2} - \frac{\tau_i^B}{F_{NN}^j}, \quad i, j = 1, 2, \ i \neq j. \tag{8.12}$$

Comparing (8.12) with the first-order condition of a social optimum (8.8), it becomes clear that the degree of redistribution is suboptimally low in a noncooperative equilibrium. Social costs of redistribution in each region are equal to $N/2$. However, each region conjectures that the costs exceed $N/2$, since it anticipates that an increase in τ_i^B attracts mobile workers from the other region. But in equilibrium both regions choose the same transfer level and the interregional labor allocation is, in effect, independent of the common level of τ_i^B. Since each region conjectures too high costs of redistributing income toward the mobile population in a decentralized equilibrium, there are no incentives

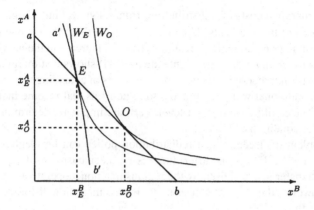

Figure 8.1. Regional income redistribution.

to choose the socially optimal tax–transfer policy. This argument holds in a similar way when mobile households are net contributors to the redistribution program rather than net beneficiaries, $\tau_i^B < 0$ for $i = 1, 2$. By increasing the tax on mobile residents in order to finance transfers to the immobile population, each region conjectures that mobile taxpayers will leave the region in order to reduce their tax burden. This makes the redistribution program rather costly from the region's viewpoint.

The problem of a suboptimally low level of redistribution can be illustrated very instructively with the help of Figure 8.1, which concentrates on the case where mobile households are recipients of the welfare program. The figure depicts the situation in one of the two symmetric regions and ignores region-specific indices. The line ab is the locus of all possible net income distributions between the fixed factor and a representative mobile worker in equilibrium. Line ab could be called the *social distribution possibility curve*. Since both regions choose the same transfer level, ab has a constant slope of $-N/2$, identical to the social costs of increasing the net income level of mobile workers by one unit. The socially optimal degree of redistribution must be located on ab; it is depicted by O, where an indifference curve of the preference structure W (i.e., W_O) is tangent to ab. From the region's viewpoint, however, the situation is different. It conjectures higher costs of redistribution due to the expected inflow of workers from the neighboring region. Hence, the region's cost line of redistribution is depicted by $a'b'$, which is steeper than ab. The curve $a'b'$ may be referred to as the *regional distribution possibility curve*. The region chooses the income distribution where an indifference curve of W (i.e., W_E) is tangent to $a'b'$. Since ab depicts all possible income distributions in equilibrium, the regional distribution optimum must also be located on ab. Hence, the regional income distribution resulting from uncoordinated redistribution policy is achieved in E where $a'b'$ intersects with ab. The equilibrium point E indicates that the net income of workers is suboptimally low – as is the level of welfare – since W_E intersects with ab in E. A coordinated increase in τ^B would increase social welfare, since it reflects a move from E toward O along ab.

These results can be summarized in

Proposition 8.2. *Suppose that regions are identical. Then, uncoordinated regional redistribution policy results in a suboptimally low degree of redistribution between mobile and immobile residents. A coordinated increase in the redistributive tax–transfer levels in all regions would increase social welfare.*

In Section 4.1 we attributed the underprovision of local public goods caused by interregional tax competition to the existence of fiscal externalities (in the case of identical regions). Here, too, we can explain the suboptimality of regional redistribution policy by fiscal external effects that a region imposes on its neighbor. If a region increases its transfers to mobile residents then it attracts mobile recipients of that program, given the redistribution policy in the other region. As the neighboring region loses beneficiaries of the welfare program, the costs of its transfer program decrease. Since the acting region ignores this effect when choosing its transfer level, it creates a positive externality.

To see this, let us derive the effect of an increase in τ_i^B on region j's welfare (see Section 8.3.1):

$$\frac{d\mu_j}{d\tau_i^B} = -\frac{\tau_j^B}{F_{NN}^i}. \tag{8.13}$$

Because $F_{NN}^i < 0$, an increase in τ_i^B generates a positive external effect on region j whenever it chooses a positive transfer, $\tau_j^B > 0$. Equation (8.13) also demonstrates that the external effect is a pure fiscal externality. If it were optimal for region j not to redistribute at all – that is, to decide for $\tau_j^B = 0$ in equilibrium – then there would be no external effect. However, when regions decide to redistribute in favor of the mobile work force, there is a positive external effect that is ignored by region i. From a social point of view, region i thus conjectures too high costs of redistributing income toward mobile workers and therefore chooses too low a transfer level.

In contrast to Section 4.1, the expression "fiscal externalities" now relates to the regional welfare functions and not to individual utility, except for the case in which W^i is interpreted as the altruistic utility function of the immobile resident. Moreover, if W^i is interpreted as a regional welfare function and if regions are identical so that there are no migration distortions, then the allocation is efficient. A central government intervention to stimulate regional redistribution efforts would not be a Pareto improvement, since immobile residents become worse off. This should be kept in mind when considering a corrective central government policy, to which we now turn.

8.2   Internalizing Fiscal Externalities

8.2.1   Central Government Intervention

The analysis of Section 8.1 has shown that decentralized redistribution policy causes two problems. First, since regions generally differ, they choose different tax–transfer levels and so cause migration distortions. Second, since regions ignore the positive external effects of their redistribution programs on other regions, they decide for a suboptimally low degree of redistribution.

There are several ways for a central government to overcome these problems. The most immediate method is to take on the responsibility for redistribution policy in the federal state. By choosing an economywide tax–transfer level for the mobile population, the central government could avoid migration distortions. Because it takes into account the welfare in all regions, there would be no external effects of redistribution programs either, leading to a socially optimal degree of redistribution. A more indirect way for the central government is to accept the regions' basic redistribution policy but to correct regional behavior by developing a system of interregional grants in the spirit of Pigouvian corrective subsidies. This indirect method seems to be more appropriate in the EU case, since one can hardly imagine that member states would be willing to give up their responsibility for redistribution issues to a supranational institution. The following analysis concentrates on such a grant system, starting from the insight that regional redistribution policies create externalities.

Suppose that the central government collects taxes from each of the two regions and uses the proceeds to implement a system of matching grants that finance some fraction s_i of each region i's expenditures on redistributive transfers to workers. Let T_i denote the lump-sum tax imposed by the center on region i. Without loss of generality, it may be assumed that this tax falls entirely on the income of the immobile factor owner.[5] The policy of the central government must satisfy the constraint

$$\sum_{i=1,2} s_i \tau_i^B N_i = \sum_{i=1,2} T_i; \qquad (8.14)$$

the net income accruing to the immobile factor owner in region i is given by

[5] More directly, the center collects taxes (T_i) from regional governments – as, for example, the VAT-financed contributions by EU member states to EU expenditure programs like the European Regional Development Fund, the European Social Fund, and the Common Agricultural Fund. We have substituted the regional government constraints for the taxes levied by regions on immobile residents into the budget restriction of this household group, so (8.15) follows, too.

$$x_i^A = F^i - N_i F_N^i - (1 - s_i) N_i \tau_i^B - T_i. \tag{8.15}$$

Condition (8.15) reflects the fiscal contribution of immobile factor owners to the central government, as well as the fiscal relief that they obtain from grants received by their regional governments.

How do central government grants and taxes affect the level of redistribution chosen by each jurisdiction? There are several possible modeling approaches, but it is traditional to assume that individual regions take central government policies as parametrically given. Thus, as in Section 4.1.3, the center acts as a Stackelberg leader. Matching grants lower the relative price of redistributive expenditures – as well as easing the fiscal burdens of recipient governments – while taxes paid to the center lower each region's net income. Following this traditional approach, each region i chooses τ_i^B, subject to (8.5) and (8.15), to maximize social welfare, taking the other region's redistributive transfer level (as well as central government variables) as given. This yields the first-order condition

$$MRS_i = N_i - \frac{(1 - s_i)\tau_i^B}{F_{NN}^j} - \frac{Ds_i N_i}{F_{NN}^j}, \quad i, j = 1, 2, \ i \neq j \tag{8.16}$$

(see Section 8.3.1 for a derivation). This is clearly a generalization of (8.11).

In order to derive how the central government must choose its policy instruments so as to achieve a social optimum, it is important to be aware that each region i now creates two kinds of external effects when choosing τ_i^B. The first one is the fiscal externality on the other region, which we emphasized in the previous section. In the presence of a corrective matching grant scheme, this external effect becomes

$$\frac{d\mu_j}{d\tau_i^B} = -\frac{(1 - s_j)\tau_j^B}{F_{NN}^i} - \frac{F_{NN}^j s_j N_j}{F_{NN}^i}. \tag{8.17}$$

This is still a fiscal externality since in the absence of any central government correction, $s_j = 0$, it would vanish if it were optimal for region j to choose $\tau_j^B = 0$. However, in the presence of central government intervention, the external effect a region creates is not restricted to (8.17). Since each region influences the interregional labor allocation by choosing its transfer, it affects the budget of the central government. This changes the necessary taxes the center must collect in order to balance its budget, taxes that must be paid by the immobile factor owners in both regions. However, each region takes T_i ($i = 1, 2$) as given when choosing the redistributive transfer and thereby creates a second external effect. Region i influences the central government's budget by

$$\frac{d\left(\sum_k T_k\right)}{d\tau_i^B} = s_i N_i + s_i \tau_i^B \frac{\partial N_i}{\partial \tau_i^B} + s_j \tau_j^B \frac{\partial N_j}{\partial \tau_i^B}, \tag{8.18}$$

and it causes external effects equal to the sum of (8.17) and (8.18). If the central government's objective is to achieve a social optimum, then it must choose the matching grant rates (s_i) so as to internalize the external effects caused by uncoordinated regional redistribution policy. In other words, it must choose s_1 and s_2 in order to solve the two-equation system

$$\frac{d\mu_j}{d\tau_i^B} - \frac{d\left(\sum_k T_k\right)}{d\tau_i^B} = 0, \tag{8.19}$$

$$\frac{d\mu_i}{d\tau_j^B} - \frac{\left(d\sum_k T_k\right)}{d\tau_j^B} = 0, \tag{8.20}$$

where (8.17) and (8.18) must be inserted.

8.2.2   *Corrected Equilibrium*

We now define a *corrected Nash equilibrium* in redistributive transfers as a vector (s_i) of matching grants and a vector (τ_i^B) of transfers such that $d\mu_i/d\tau_i^B = 0$ for $i = 1, 2$ and (8.19) and (8.20) hold. Section 8.3.2 shows that such a corrected equilibrium is characterized by the following conditions:

$$\tau_1^B = \tau_2^B, \tag{8.21}$$

$$MRS_1 + MRS_2 = N. \tag{8.22}$$

According to (8.21), regions have incentives to choose the same transfer level and thus avoid any migration distortions. The intuition behind this result is straightforward. If the transfer levels differ across regions then there are pure fiscal reasons to migrate, and this distorts the interregional allocation of mobile labor. Any given degree of redistribution can be achieved with less cost simply by subsidizing redistribution more heavily in regions with small redistributive transfers. Furthermore, the efficiently achieved degree of redistribution is, following (8.22), the socially optimal one. These results allow us to state

Proposition 8.3.   *If the central government internalizes all external effects of regional redistributive policies by an appropriate matching grant scheme, then it can achieve the optimal allocation including the socially optimal income distribution.*

Note that the central government ensures (8.21) and (8.22) by choosing the matching grant rates (s_i) alone. Since it needs only one tax for budget-clearing reasons, the central government has a degree of freedom in choosing T_i. This can be used by the center to achieve the optimal interregional resource distribution, requiring equalization of the marginal social benefit of expanding the consumption of the immobile factor owners across regions, $\partial W^1/\partial x_1^A = \partial W^2/\partial x_2^A$, as a complete solution to the problem outlined in footnote 5.

A final question concerns the determination of the subsidy level chosen by the central government. In general, matching grant rates must vary across regions so that regional governments will be induced to equalize their transfer levels. In the special case discussed in the second part of Section 8.1, where regions are identical, it can be shown (see Section 8.3.2) that the identical matching grant rates become

$$ s = \frac{1}{1 - NF_{NN}/\tau^B} \tag{8.23} $$

(indices omitted); that is, s is positive and less than unity. Because regions decide for suboptimally low redistributive transfers in a noncooperative equilibrium, the central government must decrease the regional price of redistributive expenditures in order to induce regions to choose the socially optimal degree of income distribution. In terms of Figure 8.1, by choosing the positive matching grant rate set out in (8.23), the central government provides regional governments with the correct incentives to implement a transfer that results in the income distribution characterized by point O.[6]

8.3 Appendix

8.3.1 Derivation of Welfare Effects

The purpose of this section is to derive the fiscal externality (8.13) and the first-order condition (8.16). Differentiating W^j with respect to τ_i^B and using the definition of $d\mu_j$ yields

$$ \frac{d\mu_j}{d\tau_i^B} = [(MRS_j - N_j)F_{NN}^j - \tau_j^B]\frac{\partial N_j}{\partial \tau_i^B}. \tag{A.8.1} $$

Inserting the first-order condition (8.11) of region j and the migration response derived in (8.4) into (A.8.1) and then collecting terms gives (8.13). Solving the problem (8.9) when the central government implements a corrective matching grant scheme (x_i^A is given by (8.15)) yields

$$ \frac{d\mu_i}{d\tau_i^B} = (MRS_i - N_i)\left(1 + F_{NN}^i \frac{\partial N_i}{\partial \tau_i^B}\right) $$

$$ - (1 - s_i)\tau_i^B \frac{\partial N_i}{\partial \tau_i^B} + s_i N_i = 0. \tag{A.8.2} $$

---

[6] Note that, owing to symmetry of both regions in Figure 8.1, central government intervention has no income effect on any region.

Inserting the migration response (8.4) into (A.8.2), collecting terms, and multiplying the entire expression by D yields the first-order condition (8.16).

8.3.2 Central Government Intervention

The basic objectives of this section are (a) to prove that the central government ensures (8.21) and (8.22) by designing a matching grant scheme that internalizes redistribution externalities and (b) to derive the socially optimal matching grant rate in the case of identical regions.

Inserting the expressions on the right side of (8.17) and (8.18) into condition (8.19) yields

$$-\frac{(1-s_j)\tau_j^B}{F_{NN}^i} - s_j N_j \frac{F_{NN}^j}{F_{NN}^i} - s_i N_i - s_i \tau_i^B \frac{\partial N_i}{\partial \tau_i^B} - s_j \tau_j^B \frac{\partial N_j}{\partial \tau_i^B} = 0. \qquad (A.8.3)$$

Substituting the migration responses derived in (8.4) into (A.8.3) and collecting terms gives

$$\tau_j^B = s_j F_{NN}^j \left(\frac{\tau_j^B}{D} - N_j \right) + s_i F_{NN}^i \left(\frac{\tau_i^B}{D} - N_i \right). \qquad (A.8.4)$$

Condition (A.8.4) holds in a corrected equilibrium. Since the right side of (A.8.4) is independent of the region causing the externality and therefore holds for both regions, we have

$$\tau_i^B = \tau_j^B, \qquad (A.8.5)$$

that is, condition (8.21).

Next, substituting

$$\frac{d\mu_j}{d\tau_i^B} = [(MRS_j - N_j)F_{NN}^j - (1-s_j)\tau_j^B]\frac{\partial N_j}{\partial \tau_i^B}$$

and the right side of (8.18) into (8.19), it follows that

$$[(MRS_j - N_j)F_{NN}^j - (1-s_j)\tau_j^B]\frac{\partial N_j}{\partial \tau_i^B}$$

$$- N_i s_i - s_i \tau_i^B \frac{\partial N_i}{\partial \tau_i^B} - s_j \tau_j^B \frac{\partial N_j}{\partial \tau_i^B} = 0. \qquad (A.8.6)$$

Adding now (A.8.2) and (A.8.6), inserting the migration responses, collecting terms, and multiplying by D/F_{NN}^j yields

$$MRS_1 + MRS_2 = N, \qquad (A.8.7)$$

or condition (8.22).

To derive the optimal matching grant rate in the case of identical regions, we use the symmetry property in (8.17). After dropping all indices, we achieve

$$\frac{d\mu_j}{d\tau_i^B} = -\frac{(1-s)\tau^B}{F_{NN}} - s\frac{N}{2}.$$ (A.8.8)

Moreover, from (8.18) it follows that

$$\frac{d\left(\sum_k T_k\right)}{d\tau_i^B} = s\frac{N}{2}.$$ (A.8.9)

Inserting both (A.8.8) and (A.8.9) into (8.19) and solving for s yields (8.23), as was to be proved.

CHAPTER 9

Decentralization and Intergenerational Problems

This chapter studies whether a decentralization of certain government functions can better protect the interests of future generations than a central responsibility. It concentrates on two areas of government activities – environmental and public debt policies. According to orthodox neoclassical reasoning, public debt policies and the control over long-lived pollutants are related by the joint problem of intergenerational externalities. Currently living generations extend their consumption at the expense of their descendants, since they tend to ignore the costs which their descendants must bear without being asked to do so. Long-lived pollutants and debt differ only in that the former results in technological externalities and the latter in fiscal externalities.[1] However, owing to this difference, each issue must be treated analytically as a separate problem.

An implicit and rarely recognized assumption of the externality problem is that future generations cannot escape the undue burden: they cannot emigrate because the economy is assumed to be closed. The purpose of this chapter is instead to allow for migration and to analyze the externality problem from the perspective of regional economics. Emissions will only harm the local environment and debt will always refer to the local jurisdiction. Regions are small and households are perfectly mobile. Households live for two periods. They are mobile when young and stick to their locational choice when old.[2] The basic question then arises: Do regional authorities have any incentive to internalize intergenerational externalities caused by the emission of long-lived pollutants and by local public debt? In other words, are regional governments better qualified to take the interests of future generations into account than their national counterpart?

---

[1] One of the most prominent critics of the orthodox neoclassical view of public debt is Barro (1974). That people make bequests is interpreted by him as evidence for operative altruism. Altruistic parents anticipate that public debt simply results in shifting tax payments to their children; parents will find it optimal to neutralize any income effect by increasing bequests.

[2] Empirical studies by Topel (1986) and LaLonde and Topel (1991) confirm the view that the degree of household mobility is age-dependent. Old households are less mobile than young households.

For the case of local public debt, this question has been analyzed by Daly (1969) and Oates (1972). The basic message of their analysis is that local public debt policies leave the net wealth of local property owners unchanged. A current reduction in tax payments for local property owners that is accompanied by an increase in future taxes (so as to balance the intertemporal budget constraint of the local government) causes emigration of households who would otherwise live in future periods in the region.[3] Emigration reduces future rents of local property, and the present value of local property declines by an amount that leaves the net wealth of property owners unchanged – although their tax payments decrease. The same result is derived by Buiter (1989) and by Bailey (1993). They assume that taxes are levied on immobile factors such as land and demonstrate that any intertemporal change in the time pattern of these taxes leaves the property value of the taxed immobile factors unchanged. In the Buiter–Bailey world, it is the arbitrage behavior of investors that leaves the property value unchanged; in the Daly–Oates approach, it is the perfect interregional mobility of households that ensures the neutrality of any intertemporal shifts in local taxes. Daly (1969, p. 48) claims that this result applies to all kinds of local taxes: "The critical factor is not the type of the tax but the basis on which a person is ruled liable for the tax. So long as this basis is the individual's residence in the particular community then the burden will not be shifted to future generations."

If this view were true then one could derive an important implication for the problem of harmonizing public debt and pension policies in the EU. Given that regional authorities take the interests of local property owners into account, this view would imply that they had no incentive to engage in intergenerational redistribution by issuing public debt or financing pensions with a pay-as-you-go system. Consequently, they would not need to levy residence-based taxes to service the debt (resp., to enforce residence-based contributions to the pension scheme) that distort locational choices of mobile households – the basic efficiency problem of uncoordinated public debt policies (pension policies) in a federal state.

One basic purpose of this chapter is to show that this neutrality result does not hold if local taxes are residence-based taxes on mobile individuals. Contrary to the intuition developed by Daly and Oates, debt finance has income effects – at least in general. Local debt must be serviced by taxes that distort locational choices of mobile households. Because of this distortion, a change in the intertemporal time pattern of local taxes creates income effects. The neutrality thesis only holds in a weak form. If no debt is accumulated that must be serviced by distortionary taxes, then a marginal increase in local public debt leaves the net wealth of local property owners unchanged. In summary, the neutrality

---

[3] The possibility of tax-driven emigration was already seen by Ricardo (1817) and was emphasized in Tiebout's (1956) seminal paper on local public goods.

thesis of Daly and Oates generally holds only if local taxes are source-based taxes on immobile factors such as land.[4] This result implies that, even under ideal conditions of perfect interregional competition for mobile households, regions may have incentives to issue local public debt, making it necessary to tax mobile households to service the public debt. Since these taxes differ among regions, there are pure fiscal reasons to relocate. The resulting migration distortions provide a strong efficiency argument for harmonization of public debt policies in the EU: under all other, less than ideal conditions, different regional debt policies (accompanied by different residence-based taxes) become even more likely.

The result that local public debt is not neutral if nonmarginal residence-based taxes on mobile households are used to service the debt is reminiscent of conclusions derived in the "endogenous fertility" literature. Wildasin (1990) and Lapan and Enders (1990) show that, although parents are assumed to be altruistic toward their children in the Barro (1974) sense, public debt is not neutral insofar as head taxes on children (levied to service the accumulated debt) distort fertility decisions.

We cannot derive that regional governments have sufficient incentives to avoid public debt and thus the imposition of distortionary residence-based taxes on mobile households, but the results for local control of long-lived pollutants are more optimistic. If the regional environmental agency controls pollution by means of a regulatory approach, then it does not generate revenues that must be distributed among mobile residents. Contrary to the case of local public debt, migration decisions of households are therefore not distorted. Moreover, if the environmental agency maximizes the utility of old households living in the region, and if the implicit rent of immobile factors such as land and waste emissions are appropriated by residents living in the region, then the environmental agency has incentives to fully internalize all intergenerational externalities caused by long-lived pollutants. Increased pollution causes emigration of individuals in future periods and reveals the marginal willingness to pay of mobile households for avoiding current pollution. Emigration thus reduces the future land rents and therefore the current asset value of land. Since the environmental agency takes changes in the current value of local land into account when choosing its optimal emission level, it is forced to internalize all welfare effects on future mobile households.

Note that this internalization of intergenerational pollution externalities is *not* the result of any altruism toward future generations; rather, it is the mobility of households that forces regional authorities to take the effects of long-lived pollutants into account when making current decisions. Since the mobility of

---

[4] The immobile factor of land can be used for housing as in Wildasin (1987) or in Brueckner and Yoo (1991), and the source-based tax may be interpreted as a property tax on residential property.

households tends to be higher in smaller regions, regional governments may be better qualified than the national government to control long-lived local pollutants like hazardous and toxic waste. However, the important assumption for this result to hold is that pollution externalities must be local. Interregional spillovers must be excluded so that descendant generations have a chance to escape.[5]

In deriving the basic results, this chapter follows Wellisch and Richter (1995) and is organized as follows.[6] Section 9.1 introduces the model, which incorporates endogenous household mobility and pollution externalities into a standard overlapping generations framework. We then derive the first-order conditions of an efficient allocation. Section 9.2 examines regional environmental policy under conditions of perfect interregional competition. It shows that decentralized environmental decisions internalize all intergenerational externalities, provided (a) that the implicit rent of immobile factors (such as pollution) is fully appropriated by households living inside the region and (b) that locational choices of mobile households are not distorted. In Section 9.3, the model will be changed slightly by ignoring pollution externalities and introducing local public debt into the analysis. This section demonstrates that changes in public debt are not neutral if nonmarginal residence-based taxes are imposed to service the debt. Finally, Section 9.4 proves some important results reported in Sections 9.2 and 9.3.

9.1 Efficient Allocation

9.1.1 The Model

We set forth a model that combines the notion of perfect household mobility with a standard overlapping generations structure. Households live for two periods. The members of generation t are young in period t and old in period $t + 1$, choosing their region of residence $i = 1, \ldots, I$ when young and sticking to their choice when old. Generation t consists of $\bar{N}_t = \sum_i N_t^i$ identical members, where N_t^i is the number of individuals living in region i. The exogenously given cohort size $\bar{N}_t$ and the regional population size N_t^i are treated as real numbers, as in the preceding chapters. Young individuals inelastically supply

---

[5] Chapter 6 emphasized that perfect interregional household mobility provides an incentive mechanism for regional governments to internalize all interregional spillover effects. Whether perfect mobility is also an incentive mechanism for local authorities to internalize intergenerational externalities when local pollution crosses regional boundaries remains an unsolved problem.

[6] For a similar analysis of local government policy in an overlapping generations framework, see Oates and Schwab (1996). Schweizer (1996), Wildasin and Wilson (1996), and Brueckner (1997) are other recent studies investigating economies with local public goods in overlapping generations models.

one unit of labor in the region of their residence. Hence, N_t^i denotes local labor supply as well. Each region produces a private numeraire good by the production function $F^{ti}(L^i, N_t^i, e_t^i)$, where output increases in land L^i, labor N_t^i, and emissions e_t^i. The regional endowment with land is assumed to be independent of time. There may be additional factors, such as mobile capital, that are not made explicit in the notation. Emissions affect the local state of pollution a_t^i according to

$$a_t^i = (1 - \alpha)a_{t-1}^i + e_t^i. \tag{9.1}$$

Hence, there is a geometric decay, and α denotes the decay rate. Note also that there are no spillovers; that is, e_t^i has no impact on a_t^j for $j \neq i$. Members of generation t living in region i are characterized by the utility function $U^{ti} \equiv U^t(x_t^i, y_{t+1}^i, a_t^i, a_{t+1}^i)$, where x_t^i stands for their consumption when young and y_{t+1}^i for their consumption when old. Households suffer from pollution in the sense that the marginal utility $U_j^{ti} \equiv \partial U^{ti}/\partial a_{t+j}^i$ ($j = 0, 1$) is negative with respect to the state of pollution in their youth a_t^i and in their old age a_{t+1}^i. Needless to say, $U_x^{ti} \equiv \partial U^{ti}/\partial x_t^i$ and $U_y^{ti} \equiv \partial U^{ti}/\partial y_{t+1}^i$ are positive, and all standard assumptions ensuring second-order conditions are assumed to hold in deriving the efficient allocation.

9.1.2   First-Order Conditions

When characterizing an efficient allocation, we take a central planner's perspective in period $t = 1$. At that time, x_0^i, a_0^i, and N_0^i are predetermined, implying that households which are currently old are immobile in contrast to young and unborn individuals. To derive an efficient allocation, the planner would have to

$$\text{maximize } U^0(x_0^1, y_1^1, a_0^1, a_1^1) \tag{9.2}$$

in $(x_t^i, y_t^i, a_t^i, e_t^i, N_t^i)_{t \geq 1, i=1,\dots,I}$ subject to

$$U^0(x_0^i, y_1^i, a_0^i, a_1^i) = \bar{u}_0^i, \quad i = 2, \dots, I, \tag{9.3}$$

$$U^t(x_t^i, y_{t+1}^i, a_t^i, a_{t+1}^i) = \bar{u}_t, \quad t \geq 1, \ i = 1, \dots, I, \tag{9.4}$$

$$a_t^i = (1 - \alpha)a_{t-1}^i + e_t^i, \quad t \geq 1, \ i = 1, \dots, I, \tag{9.5}$$

$$(\mu_t): \ \sum_i [F^{ti}(L^i, N_t^i, e_t^i) - N_t^i x_t^i - N_{t-1}^i y_t^i] = 0, \quad t \geq 1, \tag{9.6}$$

$$(\lambda_t): \ \bar{N}_t - \sum_i N_t^i = 0, \quad t \geq 1. \tag{9.7}$$

The variables μ_t und λ_t denote Lagrange multipliers, where only those used in the following analysis are made explicit. Condition (9.3) is a utility constraint of the old immobile households living in regions $i \neq 1$. Similarly, condition

(9.4) requires that the utility of young and unborn individuals must reach a predetermined level. Once again, the implicit assumption is that the planner is unable to discriminate mobile households by their region of residence. Individuals would respond by migrating if the planner tried to ignore the equal utility constraint. Condition (9.5) simply restates (9.1), while (9.6) is the federal state's feasibility constraint of the private good in period t. Aggregate output $\sum_i F^{ti}$ must cover aggregate consumption in period t. Condition (9.7) finally requires that all households must locate somewhere in the economy. Solving this system by standard Lagrangean techniques yields three first-order conditions ($i = 1, \ldots, I; t \geq 1$):

$$\frac{U_y^{ti}}{U_x^{ti}} = \frac{\mu_{t+1}}{\mu_t}, \tag{9.8}$$

$$F_N^{ti} - x_t^i - \frac{U_y^{ti}}{U_x^{ti}} y_{t+1}^i = \frac{\lambda_t}{\mu_t}, \tag{9.9}$$

$$S^{ti} \equiv -N_t^i \frac{U_0^{ti}}{U_x^{ti}} - N_{t-1}^i \frac{U_1^{(t-1)i}}{U_y^{(t-1)i}}$$

$$= F_e^{ti} - (1 - \alpha) \frac{U_y^{ti}}{U_x^{ti}} F_e^{(t+1)i} \equiv H^{ti}, \tag{9.10}$$

with subindexes on F^{ti} again denoting marginal products, $F_e^{ti} \equiv \partial F^{ti}/\partial e_t^i$ and $F_N^{ti} \equiv \partial F^{ti}/\partial N_t^i$. Condition (9.8) describes *consumption efficiency*, requiring that the marginal rate of intertemporal substitution must be equal for all members of a generation. Condition (9.9) characterizes *locational efficiency*. Mobile households are efficiently distributed across regions if the net social benefit of adding one further household to region i is interregionally equalized. The net social benefit is obtained by subtracting the household's value of consumption in i from its marginal product. Finally, condition (9.10) characterizes the efficient level of local pollution a_t^i. *Pollution efficiency* requires that the Samuelson expression S^{ti} equal the Hotelling expression H^{ti}. Whereas S^{ti} measures the local sum of the marginal willingness to pay for a marginal reduction of pollution, H^{ti} measures the marginal costs of reducing pollution. For fixed states of pollution a_s^i ($s \neq t$), a marginal decrease of a_t^i requires a concurrent decrease $de_t^i = da_t^i$ and a delayed increase $de_{t+1}^i = -(1 - \alpha)da_t^i$ of emissions. Hence H^{ti} is the net present value of the resulting output variations. The fraction of today's emissions that is not absorbed by the environment's self-cleaning mechanism (i.e., the decay rate) rivals tomorrow's emissions. Note that, because condition (9.10) holds for all periods, $F_e^{(t+1)i}$ represents the marginal willingness to pay of all future generations affected by the change in emission allowances in period t.

9.2   Decentralized Environmental Policy

In order to avoid problems caused by strategic interactions among regions, we assume conditions of perfect competition throughout the economy. This implies that regions are small. As a consequence of this assumption, it is possible to concentrate on a representative region in order to analyze the efficiency properties of decentralized environmental policy, so we may drop the regional index i from the notation. Local emissions are controlled by a local environmental agency, and the question arises of whether the local authority has any incentive to internalize intergenerational externalities generated by local emissions. Before describing the behavior of the local environmental authority, let us turn to decentralized decisions of households and firms.

9.2.1   Private Behavior

Young households have to make two kinds of decisions. Within their region of residence, they must divide their wage income w_t between current and future consumption so as to maximize their utility. Let r denote the interregional interest rate, which (for expository ease) is assumed to be constant over time.[7] Households take w_t and r as given. Then, a young household's indirect utility function is given by

$$V^t(w_t, r, a_t, a_{t+1}) \equiv \max U^t(x_t, y_{t+1}, a_t, a_{t+1}) \tag{9.11}$$

in x_t and y_{t+1}, subject to

$$x_t + \frac{y_{t+1}}{1+r} = w_t. \tag{9.12}$$

The optimal choice of the intertemporal consumption pattern and the properties of the indirect utility function imply that

$$\frac{U_y^t}{U_x^t} = \frac{1}{1+r} \quad \text{and} \quad \frac{V_j^t}{V_w^t} = \frac{U_j^t}{U_x^t} \quad (j = 0, 1), \tag{9.13}$$

where

$$V_j^t \equiv \frac{\partial V^t}{\partial a_{t+j}} \quad \text{and} \quad V_w^t \equiv \frac{\partial V^t}{\partial w_t}.$$

The second household decision concerns the locational choice. Only young households are mobile, and they will reside in the region under consideration

---

[7] Notice again that we have suppressed the mobile factor capital in the production function only for notational convenience. However, r can be interpreted as the return to this suppressed factor. If one additionally assumes that capital is internationally mobile, and that the considered federal state is a price taker in the international capital market, then it makes sense to assume that r is time-independent.

if they attain their reservation utility $\bar{u}_t$. Hence, the migration equilibrium can be characterized by

$$V^t(w_t, r, a_t, a_{t+1}) = \bar{u}_t \quad \text{for } t \geq 1. \tag{9.14}$$

We further assume (as in Chapter 7) that production decisions are made by land owners. Hence, they are not only owners of the production factor land but also are entrepreneurs. However, they need only choose the number of workers employed since it will be assumed that the environmental agency controls the number of permissible local emissions by using a regulatory approach. Let us suppose that land owners maximize the surplus,

$$R_t \equiv F^t - N_t w_t, \tag{9.15}$$

and that they take r and w_t as given when choosing N_t. Hence, they choose N_t so as to satisfy

$$F_N^t = w_t. \tag{9.16}$$

Note that the implicit factor reward for emissions is left to land owners because firms do not have to pay for their emissions. Therefore, the income of local land owners includes not only the direct factor reward for land but also the implicit rent to local waste emissions. Hence, R_t simply stands for the *local rent* in the following analysis.

Young households of generation $t - 1$ must save in order to finance their old-age consumption, and they can invest their savings in one of two ways: they can either buy assets in the capital market carrying the interest rate r, or they can acquire property rights in land. When they buy a plot of land in region i, they acquire a claim on the following period's rent R_t and on the resale value of the plot q_t. By arbitrage, both investment possibilities must have the same return. Hence, rents and resale values are connected via the arbitrage condition

$$q_t = \frac{R_{t+1} + q_{t+1}}{1+r} = \sum_{s>t}^{\infty} \frac{R_s}{(1+r)^{s-t}}. \tag{9.17}$$

Taking both investment possibilities into account, the budget constraint of a representative old household living in the region reads as

$$y_t = \frac{\delta}{N_{t-1}}[R_t + q_t] + Y_t, \tag{9.18}$$

where Y_t is the household's capital income and δ is the share of property claims on local land that is held by old households living in the region. (It is simply a matter of notational convenience that δ is carrying no index t.) Local rents are fully appropriated by the region if $\delta = 1$. The case of incomplete rent appropriation is characterized by $0 < \delta < 1$ and is generally not excluded.

Competition among regions is expressed by the assumption that each single region takes the reservation utility $\bar{u}_t$ and the interregional interest rate r as given. Note that this also implies the exogeneity of Y_t from the region's viewpoint.

9.2.2   Local Government Behavior

Finally, it is necessary to make an assumption about the behavior of the local environmental agency. Since it cannot affect the utility level of young households, we naturally assume that the agency chooses e_t so as to maximize the utility of a representative household of the older generation living in the region. Formally, the objective of the local environmental authority in period t is to

$$\text{maximize } U^{t-1}(x_{t-1}, y_t, a_{t-1}, a_t) \tag{9.19}$$

by choosing e_t and taking x_{t-1} and a_{t-1} as predetermined. The local state of pollution a_t and old-age consumption y_t are determined by (9.1) and (9.18), respectively. Furthermore, the environmental agency is assumed to act under the Nash assumption that local environmental agencies in subsequent periods stick to their respective choices e_s, $s > t$.

Because of its intertemporal structure, the model considered in this chapter differs substantially from the static models studied so far. Having specified the behavior of all agents, it is therefore instructive to summarize again how an equilibrium allocation is defined.

Definition 9.1.   The allocation $(x_t, y_t, a_t, e_t, N_t, w_t)_{t \geq 1}$ is called an *equilibrium allocation* if

(i) x_t, y_{t+1} maximize young households' utility according to (9.11)–(9.13),
(ii)   young households attain their reservation utility (9.14),
(iii) N_t satisfies (9.16),
(iv) e_t maximizes old households' utility according to (9.19), and
(v)   (9.17) and (9.18) hold.

In what follows, we analyze whether the equilibrium allocation is efficient. According to condition (iv), the decentralized equilibrium is characterized by the following first-order condition:

$$-N_{t-1}\frac{U_1^{t-1}}{U_y^{t-1}} = \delta\left(F_e^t + N_t\frac{U_0^t}{U_x^t} - \frac{1-\alpha}{1+r}F_e^{t+1} + \frac{\delta-1}{\delta}\frac{1-\alpha}{1+r}N_t\frac{U_1^t}{U_y^t}\right) \tag{9.20}$$

(see Section 9.4.1 for derivation of this first-order condition as well as a proof of Proposition 9.1).

The properties of an equilibrium allocation, and especially condition (9.20), allow us to state the basic result:

Proposition 9.1. *Equilibrium allocations are efficient if*

  (i) *local rents are fully appropriated within the region, $\delta = 1$, or if*
  (ii) *old households do not suffer from pollution, $U_1^s = 0$ for all s.*

Proposition 9.1 invites us to take a closer look at possible sources of inefficiencies. The first important point to note is that locational efficiency of mobile households can be ensured if the local environmental agency conducts its policy by using direct controls. If the environmental authority instead uses price instruments – emission taxes or marketable pollution permits – and distributes the revenues equally among old households living in the region (or among young households), then migration decisions are distorted because per-capita emission tax revenues differ interregionally. This causes an inefficient interregional allocation of mobile households (as noted by Henderson 1977a,b) and also prevents local authorities from internalizing all intergenerational pollution externalities in a socially efficient way. Thus, if local authorities cannot avoid all distortions, they prefer several distortions over one big inefficiency (locational distortion).

Second, if local land is partly in the hands of nonresidents, $\delta < 1$, then decentralized environmental policy is inefficient, in general. The local environmental agency internalizes the marginal willingness to pay for avoiding emissions of the old generation living in the region, but the implicit factor reward on local pollution is left partly with nonresident owners of local land. However, this does not necessarily imply – as it does in static models (see Wellisch 1995b) – that the local emission level is inefficiently low. The reason for possible ambiguity is that, contrary to static models, the environmental agency must take into account changes in the resale value of land plots. Suppose that the resale value declines as a consequence of higher local emission levels. Then the decline is smaller if local land is partly in the hands of nonresidents, $\delta < 1$. Therefore, the total increase in the implicit rent of pollution in response to higher emissions is greater if $\delta < 1$ and, on balance, optimally chosen emissions can deviate from the efficient level in both directions. However, it is straightforward to show that the emission-reducing effect dominates in stationary equilibria, which are characterized by

$$N_{t-1} = N_t = N \quad \text{and} \quad N_{t-1}\frac{U_1^{t-1}}{U_y^{t-1}} = N_t\frac{U_1^t}{U_y^t} = N\frac{U_1}{U_y}.$$

Adding $N_{t-1}U_1^{t-1}/U_y^{t-1}$ to both sides of (9.20) and making use of the stationary state properties, the first-order condition of an optimal stationary regional environmental policy reads as

$$-N_{t-1}\frac{U_1^{t-1}}{U_y^{t-1}} - N_t\frac{U_0^t}{U_x^t} - F_e^t + (1-\alpha)\frac{U_y^t}{U_x^t}F_e^{t+1}$$

$$= N_t\frac{U_1^t}{U_y^t}\left(1 - \frac{1}{\delta}\right)\frac{1-\alpha}{1+r} - N_{t-1}\frac{U_1^{t-1}}{U_y^{t-1}}\left(1 - \frac{1}{\delta}\right)$$

$$= N\frac{U_1}{U_y}\left(1 - \frac{1}{\delta}\right)\left(\frac{1-\alpha}{1+r} - 1\right). \tag{9.21}$$

Assuming $\alpha, \delta < 1$ and $r > 0$, the right side of (9.21) is negative. Hence, the pollution level tends to be inefficiently low if local land is partly owned by non-residents.

Third, if no old household suffers from pollution, $U_1^s = 0$ for all s, then regional environmental policy is socially efficient. This is the case if, for example, individuals tend to spend their old days in resort areas like Florida or Spain. Old households are no longer assumed to be immobile. They leave pollution areas as soon as they retire, and the local environmental agency is assumed only to maximize the rents and resale values of land plots. Because changes in rents and resale values reflect all social costs and benefits of higher local pollution, including the marginal willingness to pay of future young households living in the region, it follows that the environmental agency internalizes all costs and benefits of local pollution and has incentives to choose the efficient local pollution level.

It should be emphasized (see Richter and Wellisch 1994) that no local environmental agency is necessary to choose an efficient emission level in the case where old households live in clean retirement areas. Assume that land owners maximize rents and resale values $R_t + q_t$ by choosing the labor employment N_t and the emission level e_t. Assume further that land owners make the Nash assumption that, for all $s > t$, N_s and e_s do not change in response but must meet the migration equilibrium (9.14) when choosing the number of workers. Then, land owners (in their roles as entrepreneurs) have incentives to choose the efficient pollution level in order to attract their optimal number of mobile workers.

9.3   Local Public Debt

This section examines the thesis, expounded by Daly (1969) and Oates (1972), that local public finance is irrelevant given conditions of perfect interregional competition. More precisely, this thesis states that it is impossible to change the net wealth of local property owners by reducing their taxes and running a budget deficit. In this view, local public debt is neutral in that there are no incentives for local authorities to run budget deficits. Consequently, there is no need to levy taxes to service the debt that could distort locational choices of households.

We demonstrate that this irrelevance thesis holds only in a very weak form. Suppose that local property owners fully internalize current tax reductions, and that any local debt must be serviced by residence-based taxes that distort locational choices of households. Given conditions of perfect interregional competition, local public debt is neutral only if it does not lead to the imposition of distortionary taxes. Taxes need not be imposed if there is no debt to be serviced. In this case, any decision to increase the debt marginally is irrelevant. There would be no change in the net wealth of local property owners, and locational choices would remain undistorted. If, however, a nonzero debt level must be serviced by distortionary residence-based taxes, then tax–debt decisions are no longer irrelevant.

9.3.1 Private Behavior

In proving these claims we shall basically use the model introduced in the preceding sections, changing it only in two respects. We first disregard technological intergenerational externalities by eliminating the pollution variables a_t and e_t from the model specification. Second, we allow for fiscal intergenerational externalities by considering a poll tax τ_t. By assumption, this tax is levied on old immobile households and is rationally anticipated by young households when making their migration decision.[8] With these changes, the migration equilibrium condition can be written as

$$V^t\left(w_t - \frac{\tau_{t+1}}{1+r}, r\right) = \bar{u}_t. \tag{9.22}$$

Tax revenues are used only for servicing the local public debt, since (for simplicity) in this section we disregard real public expenditures. The budget constraint of the regional government requires revenues and expenditures to be balanced,

$$\tau_t N_{t-1} + b_t N_t = (1+r)b_{t-1}N_{t-1}, \tag{9.23}$$

where b_t measures local public debt per young household. The budget constraint of old households now becomes

$$y_t = \frac{\delta}{N_{t-1}}(R_t + q_t) + Y_t - \tau_t, \tag{9.24}$$

where R_t is given by (9.15) and q_t denotes the present value of all future land rents R_s, as stated in (9.17).

---

[8] The conclusions drawn in this section would not change if young households had to pay the tax. Moreover, similar results can be derived if each regional government redistributes income between the young and the old generation living together in the same region using a pay-as-you-go pension system.

9.3.2   *Local Government Behavior*

Let us further assume that the local government chooses per-capita debt b_t in order to maximize old residents' welfare. Since there is no pollution in this section, this objective reduces to

$$\text{maximizing } y_t = \frac{\delta}{N_{t-1}}(R_t + q_t) + Y_t - \tau_t \tag{9.25}$$

by choice of b_t. The local government is assumed to act under the Nash assumption that b_t is the best response to given b_s, $s > t$.

As in Section 9.2, it is instructive to define an equilibrium allocation.

Definition 9.2. The allocation $(x_t, y_t, N_t, w_t, b_t, \tau_t)_{t \geq 1}$ is called an *equilibrium allocation* if

   (i) x_t, y_{t+1} maximize young households' utility,
   (ii) young households attain their reservation utility (9.22),
   (iii) N_t satisfies (9.16), and
   (iv) b_t maximizes old households' consumption according to (9.25).

The irrelevance thesis of local public debt states that a marginal increase in local public debt does not affect the net wealth of local property owners if the current reduction in tax payments is restricted to this group. In terms of the equilibrium defined here, the neutrality thesis states that all debt paths b_s $(s \geq 1)$ constitute a Nash equilibrium if rents do not leave the region – that is, if $\delta = 1$. Let us now analyze whether this assertion can be supported. Inserting (9.15) and (9.17) into (9.25), the first-order condition of an optimal regional debt policy becomes

$$0 = \frac{dy_t}{db_t} = \frac{\delta}{N_{t-1}} \left[-N_t \frac{dw_t}{db_t} - \frac{N_{t+1}}{1+r} \frac{dw_{t+1}}{db_t} - \cdots \right] - \frac{d\tau_t}{db_t}. \tag{9.26}$$

The wage response dw_s/db_t $(s \geq t)$ must satisfy the migration equilibrium condition (9.22),

$$\frac{dw_s}{db_t} = \frac{1}{1+r} \frac{d\tau_{s+1}}{db_t}, \quad s \geq t. \tag{9.27}$$

From the optimal labor demand of firms (9.16) and from the migration equilibrium (9.22), it follows that

$$\frac{dN_t}{d\tau_{t+1}} = \frac{1}{(1+r)F_{NN}^t}. \tag{9.28}$$

Inserting (9.27) into (9.26), the first-order condition becomes

$$0 = \frac{\delta}{N_{t-1}} \left[-\frac{N_t}{1+r}\frac{d\tau_{t+1}}{db_t} - \frac{N_{t+1}}{(1+r)^2}\frac{d\tau_{t+2}}{db_t} - \cdots \right] - \frac{d\tau_t}{db_t}. \qquad (9.29)$$

Condition (9.29) shows that the change in net wealth of local property owners is equal to today's value of all current and future tax changes if the current tax reduction is restricted to this group ($\delta = 1$).

The tax reactions $d\tau_s/db_t$ are derived from the requirement that the local government's budget remain balanced. They must therefore solve the following system of equations, which can be obtained by implicit differentiation of (9.23) and inserting (9.23) again in the resulting expressions:

$$N_t + b_t \frac{dN_t}{d\tau_{t+1}}\frac{d\tau_{t+1}}{db_t} = -\frac{d\tau_t}{db_t}N_{t-1}, \qquad (9.30)$$

$$b_{t+1}\frac{dN_{t+1}}{d\tau_{t+2}}\frac{d\tau_{t+2}}{db_t} = \left[(1+r) - \frac{d\tau_{t+1}}{db_t}\right]N_t + \frac{b_{t+1}N_{t+1}}{N_t}\frac{dN_t}{d\tau_{t+1}}\frac{d\tau_{t+1}}{db_t}, \qquad (9.31)$$

$$b_s\frac{dN_s}{d\tau_{s+1}}\frac{d\tau_{s+1}}{db_t} = -\frac{d\tau_s}{db_t}N_{s-1} + \frac{b_sN_s}{N_{s-1}}\frac{dN_{s-1}}{d\tau_s}\frac{d\tau_s}{db_t} \quad \forall\, s \geq t+2. \qquad (9.32)$$

Conditions (9.29)–(9.32) indicate that the neutrality thesis does not hold in general. (See Section 9.4.2 for a proof of Propositions 9.2 and 9.3.)

Proposition 9.2. *Local public debt is not neutral in general, even if $\delta = 1$. Not every debt path b_s ($s \geq 1$) constitutes a Nash equilibrium, and there exist Nash equilibria that distort locational choices of households.*

The potentially distortive nature of local debt finance was stressed by Gordon (1991), Homburg and Richter (1993), and Wildasin (1994b). It was not emphasized by Daly (1969) and Oates (1972), who concentrated on wealth effects. Analysis has shown that both effects are intertwined. Contrary to Daly's (1969, p. 48) claim, local public debt policies generate net wealth effects if the debt has to be serviced by residence-based local taxes that distort locational choices of households.

The next proposition states that local debt finance is neutral if there is no debt to be serviced.

Proposition 9.3. *If $\delta = 1$ then, for all s, $b_s = 0$ is an undistortive intergenerational Nash equilibrium.*

However, the proof of Proposition 9.3 (see Section 9.4.2) also indicates that, even at a debt path $b_s = 0$ for all s, a marginal increase of local public debt creates a positive wealth effect if there are nonresident owners of local property, $\delta < 1$. Proposition 9.3 can be interpreted as saying that local public debt is neutral under the stated conditions. An alternative way to express this is as follows:

if no subsequent government issues debt that has to be serviced by distortionary taxes, then current decision makers have no incentive to issue debt and to postpone residence-based taxes. Unfortunately, as Proposition 9.2 explains, this condition of avoiding public debt finance is not satisfied in an overlapping generations framework. The point is that governments cannot avoid the distortions caused by their successors.

The analysis in this section contributes to the discussion of harmonizing public debt policies in the EU. The potentially distorting nature of local public debt has been emphasized by several authors. However, a case for harmonization can be derived only if it can be shown that regions indeed issue public debt and therefore engage in intergenerational redistribution. At first sight, this criterion may seem ambiguous because all kinds of residence-based taxation of households are potentially distorting, and we derived in Chapter 3 that small regions abstain from taxing mobile households for redistributive purposes. In other words, they avoid migration distortions in their own interest. This result does not, however, apply to intergenerational redistribution. Hence, even under ideal conditions of perfect interregional competition, regions generally engage in intergenerational redistribution – although they take the interests of future generations into account. This conclusion can be seen as an efficiency base for a harmonization of public debt policies in the EU.

9.4   Appendix

9.4.1   Decentralized Environmental Policy

The basic purpose of this section is to prove Proposition 9.1 and to derive the first-order condition (9.20). Let us first show that the first-order conditions (9.8) and (9.9) are always satisfied. Since all regions face the same interregional interest rate, an efficient intertemporal consumption pattern (9.8) is ensured by the households' optimal intertemporal consumption profile (9.13). Locational efficiency (9.9) is guaranteed by the household constraint (9.12) and by the land owners' necessary condition of an optimal labor employment (9.16). Inserting (9.16) into (9.12) and using (9.13) yields

$$F_N^t - x_t - \frac{U_y^t}{U_x^t} y_{t+1} = 0 \quad \text{for all regions.} \tag{A.9.1}$$

Consumption and locational efficiency do not rely on conditions (i) and (ii) set out in Proposition 9.1. However, these conditions are crucial for an efficient environmental policy, which we consider next.

To prove that local environmental policy internalizes all intergenerational externalities if (i) or (ii) are satisfied, it is necessary to compare the first-order condition of an optimal environmental policy with the efficiency condition

(9.10). According to (9.19), the first-order condition of an optimal environmental policy is

$$0 = \frac{dU^{t-1}}{de_t} = U_y^{t-1}\frac{\partial y_t}{\partial e_t} + U_1^{t-1}\frac{da_t}{de_t}. \tag{A.9.2}$$

By (9.1), $da_t/de_t = 1$. Using (9.15)–(9.18) to substitute for $\partial y_t/\partial e_t$ and rearranging terms yields

$$-N_{t-1}\frac{U_1^{t-1}}{U_y^{t-1}} = \delta\left(F_e^t - N_t\frac{dw_t}{de_t} + \frac{dq_t}{de_t}\right). \tag{A.9.3}$$

It is necessary to compare (A.9.3) with (9.10). For this purpose, dw_t/de_t and dq_t/de_t must be expressed in terms of marginal benefits and products. Total differentiation of (9.14) with respect to e_t yields

$$V_w^s\frac{dw_s}{de_t} + V_0^s\frac{da_s}{de_t} + V_1^s\frac{da_{s+1}}{de_t} = 0 \quad \text{for } s \geq t. \tag{A.9.4}$$

By (9.1), $da_s/de_t = (1-\alpha)^{(s-t)}$. Inserting this and making use of the properties of the indirect utility function, it follows that

$$\frac{dw_s}{de_t} = -(1-\alpha)^{(s-t)}\frac{[U_0^s + (1-\alpha)U_1^s]}{U_x^s}. \tag{A.9.5}$$

Two immediate implications are

$$\frac{dw_t}{de_t} = -\frac{[U_0^t + (1-\alpha)U_1^t]}{U_x^t}, \tag{A.9.6}$$

$$\frac{dw_s}{de_{t+1}}(1-\alpha) = \frac{dw_s}{de_t} \quad \text{for } s \geq t+1. \tag{A.9.7}$$

By (9.17) and (A.9.7), it follows that

$$\begin{aligned}
\frac{dq_t}{de_t} &= \sum_{s>t}\frac{1}{(1+r)^{s-t}}\frac{dR_s}{de_t} \\
&= -\frac{N_{t+1}}{1+r}\frac{dw_{t+1}}{de_t} - \frac{N_{t+2}}{(1+r)^2}\frac{dw_{t+2}}{de_t} - \cdots \\
&= -\frac{1-\alpha}{1+r}\left[N_{t+1}\frac{dw_{t+1}}{de_{t+1}} + \frac{N_{t+2}}{1+r}\frac{dw_{t+2}}{de_{t+1}} + \cdots\right] \\
&= -\frac{1-\alpha}{1+r}\left[N_{t+1}\frac{dw_{t+1}}{de_{t+1}} - \frac{dq_{t+1}}{de_{t+1}}\right]. \tag{A.9.8}
\end{aligned}$$

Substituting (A.9.3) for period $t + 1$ into (A.9.8) yields

$$\frac{dq_t}{de_t} = -\frac{1-\alpha}{1+r}\left[F_e^{t+1} + \frac{N_t}{\delta}\frac{U_1^t}{U_y^t}\right]. \tag{A.9.9}$$

Inserting (A.9.6) and (A.9.9) into (A.9.3) and making use of (9.13) yields the first-order condition (9.20):

$$-N_{t-1}\frac{U_1^{t-1}}{U_y^{t-1}} = \delta\left(F_e^t + N_t\frac{U_0^t}{U_x^t} - \frac{1-\alpha}{1+r}F_e^{t+1}\right.$$

$$\left. + \frac{\delta-1}{\delta}\frac{1-\alpha}{1+r}N_t\frac{U_1^t}{U_y^t}\right). \tag{A.9.10}$$

Assuming $\delta = 1$ and/or $U_1^{t-1} = U_1^t = 0$, (A.9.10) reduces to (9.10). This proves that decentralized environmental policy is socially efficient if condition (i) or (ii) set out in Proposition 9.1 is satisfied.

9.4.2   *Nonneutrality of Local Public Debt*

The objective of this section is to prove Propositions 9.2 and 9.3. Let us begin with the proof of Proposition 9.2. The first step is to present an example serving to demonstrate that not all debt paths constitute Nash equilibria. Setting $b_s = 0$ for $s > t$ and inserting this into (9.30)–(9.32) yields, by backward solution,

$$\frac{d\tau_s}{db_t} = 0 \quad \text{for } s \geq t+2, \qquad \frac{d\tau_{t+1}}{db_t} = 1+r, \tag{A.9.11}$$

$$\frac{d\tau_t}{db_t} = -\frac{N_t}{N_{t-1}} - b_t\frac{dN_t}{d\tau_{t+1}}\frac{1+r}{N_{t-1}}. \tag{A.9.12}$$

Inserting these expressions into (9.29) and taking (9.28) into account reveals that

$$0 = \frac{dy_t}{db_t} \text{ is obtained for } \delta = 1 \quad \text{only if } \frac{b_t}{F_{NN}^t N_{t-1}} = 0. \tag{A.9.13}$$

Since $F_{NN}^t N_{t-1} < 0$, it follows that $b_t = 0$ must hold if $b_s = 0$ ($s > t$) is to be part of a Nash equilibrium. This proves the first part of Proposition 9.2 – namely, that the debt path $b_t \neq 0$ and $b_s = 0$ (for all $s > t$) does not constitute an intergenerational Nash equilibrium.

The second part of Proposition 9.2 is likewise shown by an example. Consider a stationary equilibrium characterized by $\delta = 1$, $N_t = N$, and $b_t = b > 0$ for all t, with $\tau = rb > 0$. This constellation produces a Nash equilibrium. For a proof, set

$$g \equiv \left(\frac{b_t}{N_t} \frac{dN_t}{d\tau_{t+1}} \right)^{-1} = \frac{N(1+r)F_{NN}}{b} \tag{A.9.14}$$

and verify that

$$\frac{d\tau_t}{db_t} = 0, \qquad \frac{d\tau_{t+1}}{db_t} = -g,$$

$$\frac{d\tau_{t+2+s}}{db_t} = (1-g)^s g(g+r) \quad \text{for } s \geq 0 \tag{A.9.15}$$

satisfy (9.29)–(9.32). If regions are not symmetric, they choose different per-capita public debt levels b^i. When these b^i differ, $\tau^i = rb^i$ fails to be constant across regions, which leads to migration distortions. However, location efficiency requires

$$F_N^t - x_t - \frac{U_y^t}{U_x^t} y_{t+1} = w_t - x_t - \frac{y_{t+1}}{1+r} = \frac{\tau_{t+1}}{1+r} \tag{A.9.16}$$

to be constant across regions.

We now turn to the proof of Proposition 9.3. Inserting $b_s = 0$ for all s into (9.30)–(9.32) yields

$$\frac{d\tau_t}{db_t} = -\frac{N_t}{N_{t-1}}, \qquad \frac{d\tau_{t+1}}{db_t} = 1 + r,$$

$$\frac{d\tau_s}{db_t} = 0 \quad \text{for all } s \geq t + 2. \tag{A.9.17}$$

Inserting these expressions and $b_t = 0$ into (9.29) gives

$$\frac{dy_t}{db_t} = -\frac{\delta}{N_{t-1}} \frac{N_t}{1+r} \frac{d\tau_{t+1}}{db_t} - \frac{d\tau_t}{db_t} = \frac{N_t}{N_{t-1}}(1-\delta), \tag{A.9.18}$$

from which Proposition 9.3 follows.

CHAPTER 10

Informational Asymmetry between the
Regions and the Center

In order to derive an intervention scheme that induces regions to choose an efficient allocation or an optimal income distribution when regional decisions fail to do so, we have assumed in preceding chapters that the central government has all necessary information. However, as explained in Section 1.3, there is a widespread belief that regional governments are better informed about those basic economic variables that determine the optimal provision of local public goods and the optimal income redistribution: the tastes and income levels of their constituents. In addition, the central government cannot directly observe the efforts of regional governments to achieve a certain regional income level or a certain amount of regional tax revenues. This chapter therefore takes a closer look at the consequences of asymmetric information between the regions and the center.

Within this environment, two problems arise. The first is the problem of *adverse selection*. Regions may hide data that is necessary for the optimal central government intervention, so the center must design its intervention scheme such that it pays for the regions to self-select. The second problem is the issue of *moral hazard*. Regions may influence by their own efforts – public infrastructure investments, bureaucratic efforts, or tax enforcement – economic variables that the center can observe. Regions thereby try to avoid becoming a net contributor to the central government budget. To capture both phenomena, this chapter builds on contributions to the literature on adverse selection and efficient taxation – most notably, on Stiglitz (1982) – and on the literature on incentive problems, as in Laffont and Tirole (1993).

To be more precise, we concentrate on a particular high-priority problem in the EU and also in other federal states such as Canada. As labor markets become more and more integrated, the central government may be interested in two kinds of redistribution. First, as regional income levels differ, it faces incentives to smooth any (per-capita) income disparities among regions by an interregional transfer program, exemplified by the European Regional Development Fund or the European Social Fund. Second, as outlined in Chapters 3, 8, and 9,

170

regional governments have little interest in redistributing income among different income groups because they wish to avoid undesirable migration responses, which increase the costs of redistribution. Thus, the central government may provide regions with a grant in order to stimulate interpersonal redistribution. However, in order to perform such policies, the center needs information about regional tastes for redistribution and in particular about per-capita income levels in the regions. Rich regions may not be willing to reveal their information about income levels, and they may even lower own efforts to achieve a certain income level as they become net contributors to the EU-wide grant and transfer program. As a consequence, the center must design its redistribution program such that rich countries face no incentives to hide the necessary information or to avoid own efforts. This results in distortions compared to a social optimum in which the central government has complete information.

To illustrate the basic problems of the optimal central government policy with incomplete information, we first make a simplifying assumption with regard to informational asymmetry. Following Baumann and Wellisch (1998), we assume that the central government cannot observe regional factor prices. This allows us to capture the issue of adverse selection. Having derived the basic structure of the informational problem, we then follow Raff and Wilson (1997) by using more realistic assumptions on informational asymmetry to discuss the case in which both moral hazard and adverse selection problems arise.

Other research analyzing incentive problems of interregional transfers includes the study by Bucovetsky, Marchand, and Pestieau (1998), which can be seen as a natural complement to the analysis in this chapter. Bucovetsky et al. use a model of interregional tax competition for mobile capital (as outlined in Chapter 4) to derive the optimal central government intervention when regions are better informed than the center about tastes of their constituents for local public goods. Hence, whereas the current chapter focuses on private information about regional income levels, the study by Bucovetsky et al. concentrates on asymmetric information about the second important economic variable determining an optimal regional policy – tastes for local public goods.

In contrast to the analysis in this chapter and in Bucovetsky et al. (1998), the following contributions do *not* consider factor mobility. In Cremer, Marchand, and Pestieau (1996), the central government implements a revenue sharing scheme with regional governments in order to finance a national public good. However, the center cannot base this scheme on regional income or preferences for local public goods, since these variables are the private information of regional governments. Gilbert and Picard (1996) analyze the optimal territorial organization in a federal state when regional governments have an informational advantage about production costs of local public goods and when the central government has imperfect information on spillover effects caused by local projects. Finally, Bordignon, Manasse, and Tabellini (1996) analyze redistribution across regions in a model with adverse selection and moral hazard. Here, regional governments have private information about their tax bases and supply unobservable tax enforcement.[1]

In its discussion of the informational problems between different governmental levels, Chapter 10 is divided into four sections. Section 10.1 extends the model of regional distribution policy outlined in Chapter 8 to allow for informational asymmetry. It then derives the social optimum if the center has complete information about all economic variables in each individual region as a reference case. Section 10.2 emphasizes the problem of adverse selection, where regions can hide some information that is necessary to infer the region-specific productivity. It studies how a central government must design a grant scheme aimed at redistributing within and across regions in order to ensure that rich regions are willing to reveal the necessary data. Section 10.3 extends the analysis to the problem of moral hazard. Regional governments can strategically influence regional productivity by investment in local public infrastructure. Thus they can affect the economic variables that determine the amount of the grant they receive. Finally, the appendix in Section 10.4 proves some important results stated in the previous sections.

10.1   Optimal Redistribution with Complete Information

10.1.1   Private Behavior

The framework in this chapter captures the essential features of the model we considered in Chapter 8. However, in contrast to Chapter 8 (but similar to Chapter 3), here the federal state is made up of a large number of small regions, indexed by i. Each region produces a homogeneous output, taken as a numeraire, by using two (types of) inputs. The first input is assumed to be immobile and is called the fixed factor – land, for example. The variable L_i stands for the amount of the fixed factor in region i. We assume that land is owned by a representative immobile resident, indexed by A. The second input is mobile labor, referring to a class of identical workers who are mobile among regions. This group is indexed by B, and each worker is assumed to supply one unit of labor in the region where the worker resides. The variable N_i denotes the size of the mobile labor force in region i. The only difference among regions is represented by their land endowments. Production in region i takes place by the linear homogeneous function $F^i \equiv F(L_i, N_i)$. The different land endowment allows us to capture income disparities among regions.

To make matters simple, let us assume that there are only two types of regions, with respective land endowments of L_1 and L_2. We assume that $L_2 > L_1$

---

[1] Further studies on incentive problems include Boadway, Horiba, and Jha (1994), Laffont (1995), Cornes and Silva (1996), Cremer and Pestieau (1996), and Lockwood (1996).

in the subsequent analysis, and we refer to regions with a land endowment of L_2 as high-productivity regions and to regions with L_1 as low-productivity juris-dictions. The informational asymmetry between regional governments and the central government can now be traced back to the fact that regional govern-ments are aware of their regional land endowment yet this realization of L is not known to the center. The central government knows only that, among the large number of regions, I_1 are of type 1 and I_2 are of type 2, where a type-i region is one with $L = L_i$ for $i = 1, 2$.

We further assume competitive factor markets throughout the economy, so that workers living in region i attain wages w_i equal to their marginal product,

$$F_N(L_i, N_i) = w_i. \tag{10.1}$$

Following (10.1), if wages and labor inputs were observed then a government could infer the regional endowment with land L_i. Informational asymmetry between governmental levels then occurs because regional governments can more easily collect data on wages and factor inputs than their (supra) national counterpart. The assumption that the center is unable to observe both wage and employment figures in the regions is somewhat critical, especially since the means to collect and process data have improved substantially and will con-tinue to do so. However, this approach is taken mainly to illustrate the basic problems involved if there is private information about some region-specific economic variables; it should not be taken too literally. In Section 10.3, we extend the analysis to allow for the more realistic assumption that both employ-ment and wage figures are observable to the central government. We shall see that the basic insights of the analysis remain valid using this extension.

Thus, let us assume for the moment that regional governments observe wages and employment levels and so can compute L_i, while the central government observes only the amount of labor inputs N_i in the regions – not enough to in-fer L_i. According to (10.1), this means that the center does not know regional factor prices. To determine its policy measures, the central government must rely on data supplied by regional governments.

For the subsequent analysis, it is important to note that the different land endowments imply

$$F(L_2, N) > F(L_1, N) \tag{10.2}$$

and

$$F_N(L_2, N) > F_N(L_1, N) \tag{10.3}$$

for any given employment level N. Thus, high-productivity regions have not only higher income but also higher wages for any regional employment level.

In order to sign the direction of the redistributive efforts, we assume that the representative owner of the fixed factor is a high-income individual while work-ers are low-income individuals. The central government is concerned with two objectives. First, we know from the analysis in Chapter 3 that small regions have no incentive to redistribute income from owners of immobile resources to owners of mobile factors like labor, since this would imply an income loss for owners of immobile factors without any change in the net income level of workers (owing to perfect mobility). This is considered as undesirable by the central government, which therefore intends to induce regions to redistribute toward workers by designing an appropriate grant scheme. Second, the central government values interregional equity and hence an equalization of net income levels of immobile households among regions as the net income of workers is equated by migration. This latter objective results in incentive problems, since it may be rational for regional governments to hide information about the land endowment L_i in order to avoid an interregional transfer of resources to low-income regions. We will discuss in the next section how the central government must design its redistribution scheme so that rich regions will not mimic their poor neighbors.

Turning now to regional policies, a government in a low-productivity region may provide a redistributive transfer τ_1^B to mobile workers (induced by an appropriate central government grant) that must be financed by a tax on the fixed factor and a net transfer from the central government. Accordingly, in high-productivity regions, the redistributive transfer τ_2^B and the net contribution to the central government's budget must be financed by a tax on the fixed factor. Let S_1 denote the net transfer payment of the central government to a low-productivity region, and let $-S_2$ be the net contribution of a high-productivity region to the central government budget. Note that, under incomplete information, the grant function offered to regions must be identical across regions; the differentiation between S_1 and S_2 serves only to facilitate the comparison between both types of regions.

The instruments S_1 and S_2 consist of two parts. Since the central government aims to induce interpersonal redistribution activities in small regions, the central government's transfers S_i must have (from the regions' viewpoint) a variable part that depends on the regional choice variable, making regional redistribution less costly. The transfers S_i must also contain a lump-sum part in order to redistribute income interregionally. Since the central government does not provide direct transfers to workers, the net income of a representative mobile worker living in a type-i region is equal to $x_i^B = w_i + \tau_i^B$. Inserting the budget constraint of regional governments into the private budget restriction of the representative owner of the fixed factor in a type-i region gives a net income of $x_i^A = F^i - N_i x_i^B + S_i$. Moreover, net contributions of high-productivity regions are just enough to finance net transfers to low-productivity regions. Thus, the central government budget constraint reads as

$$I_1 S_1 + I_2 S_2 = 0. \tag{10.4}$$

Since all members of the mobile work force are costlessly mobile among regions, a migration equilibrium requires that the net income of mobile workers be identical, regardless of where they live:

$$x_1^B = x_2^B = x^B, \tag{10.5}$$

where x^B denotes the common net income level of mobile workers. Finally, total employment in all regions must be equal to total labor supply:

$$N = I_1 N_1 + I_2 N_2, \tag{10.6}$$

where N is the entire work force in the federal state.

10.1.2 Regional Government Behavior

Let us assume that a regional government maximizes the following additive social welfare function, defined over the net income of its immobile factor owner and the net income of a representative native worker: $W^i(x_i^A, x_i^B) \equiv V(x_i^A) + U^i(x_i^B)$, where the utility functions V and U^i are strictly concave in x_i^A and x_i^B, respectively. Note that V, the part of the welfare function covering the net income of immobile residents, is identical in all regions. This assumption sharpens the results with respect to the desired interregional income distribution. The social marginal rate of substitution in region i is given by $MRS_i \equiv (\partial U^i / \partial x_i^B)/(\partial V / \partial x_i^A)$. Since regions are assumed to be small, each regional government conjectures in choosing its redistributive transfer τ_i^B that it cannot affect the net income level of its mobile resident workers. For a given x^B, this problem is equivalent to

$$\text{maximizing } F(L_i, N_i) - N_i x^B + S_i(N_i) \tag{10.7}$$

by choice of the number of workers N_i. Then condition (10.1) determines the regional wage rate w_i and, via the budget constraint of mobile workers, the optimal τ_i^B. Note again that the central government's transfer depends on the regional choice variable. The first-order condition of this problem is:

$$\tau_i^B = \frac{\partial S_i}{\partial N_i}, \tag{10.8}$$

where we have used condition (10.1) and the budget restriction of mobile workers. Hence, by choice of its marginal grant rate $\partial S_i / \partial N_i$, the central government can determine the redistributive transfers of regions τ_i^B and thus also regional wage rates and the distribution of mobile workers among regions. In addition, by choosing the lump-sum part of its instrument S_i, the central government can also achieve its desired interregional net income distribution for the owners of the fixed factor.

10.1.3   Socially Optimal Allocation

The central government must know the land endowments and hence factor prices in each region in order to design its grant–transfer scheme. Before characterizing the optimal allocation that a central government can achieve if it faces informational constraints, it is instructive to derive the unconstrained optimal allocation for reference purposes. Here, the central government is aware of the land endowments in each individual region and is assumed (as a benevolent government) to maximize the sum of the regional social welfare functions,

$$\sum_{i=1,2}\{I_i V(F[L_i, N_i] + \tilde{S}_i) + I_i U^i(x^B)\},\tag{10.9}$$

where $\tilde{S}_i \equiv S_i - N_i x^B$ denotes the grant provided by the center to type-i regions in excess of net incomes of mobile workers. In doing so, the central government faces its budget constraint (10.4) and the labor market equilibrium condition (10.6) as constraints.

Section 10.4.2 proves the following

Proposition 10.1.   *With complete information, the central government chooses its instruments in such a way that migration distortions are avoided, $w_1 = w_2 = w^*$, immobile households in all regions have the same net income level, $x_1^A = x_2^A = x^{A*}$, and the net income of workers satisfies the Samuelson condition $I_1 MRS_1 + I_2 MRS_2 = N$ of the optimal interpersonal income distribution.*

Thus, if regions cannot hide any information, the central government achieves the first-best allocation with respect to the social welfare function (10.9), as in Chapter 8. The equalization of wage rates across regions has a further important implication that is reminiscent of the results derived in earlier chapters: the central government induces regions to choose identical transfers, $\tau_1^B = \tau_2^B = \tau^{B*}$, by its grant scheme. If the center controls only the grant scheme, it can implement the allocation described in Proposition 10.1 by choosing the following marginal grant rates:

$$\frac{\partial S_i}{\partial N_i} = \tau^{B*}, \quad i = 1, 2.\tag{10.10}$$

Inserting (10.10) into the first-order condition (10.8) of the optimal regional behavior confirms that migration distortions are avoided in a first-best optimum with complete information. Using the lump-sum part of the transfer, the central government can also equate net income levels of immobile residents across regions.[2]

---

[2]   The linear grant schedule $S_i(N_i) = N_i \tau_i^B + \tilde{S}_i$, where $\tilde{S}_i$ is the lump-sum part, satisfies condition (10.10) for $\tau_1^B = \tau_2^B = \tau^{B*}$. It is also appropriate in the case of incomplete information, as discussed in the next section.

But how should the central government design its policy menu, and what is the resulting allocation when high-productivity regions can mimic their low-income neighbors?

10.2 Incomplete Information, Adverse Selection, and Optimal Redistribution

10.2.1 Incentive Compatibility Constraints

If the central government wants to redistribute among regions, it first has to ensure that regions do not face any incentives to hide information about land endowments. Hence, the center must design a grant scheme $S(N)$ such that it pays for regional governments to disclose the correct data – the self-selection or "incentive compatibility" constraint. When revealing all information, social welfare of regions must be at least as high as in the case of mimicking other regions. As the net income level of mobile workers is given from the viewpoint of any single small region, the incentive compatibility constraints can be expressed as

$$F(L_i, N_i) + \tilde{S}_i \geq F(L_i, N_j) + \tilde{S}_j, \quad i, j = 1, 2, \ i \neq j. \quad (10.11)$$

Since the central government can observe regional employment levels, condition (10.11) states that the net income of immobile residents living in regions that use their optimal employment level must be at least as high as in the case of choosing the labor input of the other type of region.

We can depict the indifference curve of each regional government in the $(N, \tilde{S})$ space simply by differentiating the left side of (10.11). Then, the slope of region i's indifference curve is derived as

$$\frac{d\tilde{S}_i}{dN_i} = -\frac{\dfrac{\partial V}{\partial N_i}}{\dfrac{\partial V}{\partial \tilde{S}_i}} = -F_N(L_i, N_i), \quad (10.12)$$

and the second derivative is

$$\frac{d^2\tilde{S}_i}{dN_i^2} = -F_{NN}(L_i, N_i). \quad (10.13)$$

The derivative (10.12) shows that the indifference curves are downward sloping. Condition (10.3) states that $-F_N(L_2, N) < -F_N(L_1, N)$ for any given regional employment level N, implying that a type-2 region's indifference curve is steeper, crossing a type-1 region's indifference curve only once. In Figure 10.1 we depict two representative indifference curves, one for each type of region. The indifference curve of a type-i region is simply labeled W^i.

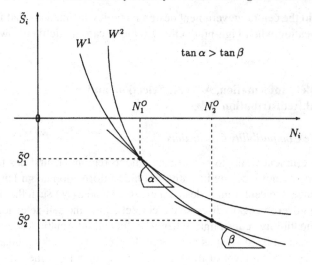

Figure 10.1. Indifference curves of regional governments.

When choosing its optimal policy under conditions of incomplete information, the central government must also take the incentive constraints of both types of regions into account, in principle. However, we shall argue that only the incentive constraint of high-income regions is binding at a second-best optimum. Intuitively, high-income regions become net contributors to the interregional redistribution program and may therefore have incentives to mimic their poor neighbors, whereas poor regions as net beneficiaries have no incentive to hide any information. In order to show that the incentive constraint of high-productivity regions is binding, we rewrite (10.2) as

$$F(L_2, N_1) + \tilde{S}_1 > F(L_1, N_1) + \tilde{S}_1. \tag{10.14}$$

Condition (10.14), together with the incentive constraint of high-productivity regions (10.11), yields

$$x_2^A = F(L_2, N_2) + \tilde{S}_2 > F(L_1, N_1) + \tilde{S}_1 = x_1^A. \tag{10.15}$$

Following (10.15), immobile residents living in high-productivity regions have the higher net income level. With concave utility functions, this implies that they have the lower marginal utility of income at the optimum. A marginal interregional transfer of income toward low-income regions would raise social welfare. Hence, there must exist an offsetting cost at the optimum, and this cost can come only from a binding incentive constraint of type-2 regions.

On the other hand, if the optimal menu of high-income regions $(N_2^O, \tilde{S}_2^O)$ must be located on the same indifference curve W^2 as the optimal menu

$(N_1^O, \tilde{S}_1^O)$ of low-productivity regions (owing to the binding incentive compatibility constraint of rich regions), then $(N_2^O, \tilde{S}_2^O)$ cannot be located on the indifference curve W^1 that indicates the welfare level of the menu $(N_1^O, \tilde{S}_1^O)$. This follows immediately from the single-crossing condition, as illustrated in Figure 10.1. Thus, we can limit our analysis to the case where the incentive constraint of low-productivity regions does not bind.

10.2.2   Central Government Policy

If the central government faces the binding incentive compatibility constraint of high-productivity regions (10.11), its problem is to

$$\text{maximize} \sum_{i=1,2} \{I_i V(F[L_i, N_i] + \tilde{S}_i) + I_i U^i(x^B)\} \qquad (10.16)$$

by choosing x^B and the vectors $(\tilde{S}_i)$ and (N_i) subject to the following constraints:

$$-\sum_{i=1,2} I_i \tilde{S}_i - Nx^B = 0, \qquad (10.17)$$

$$N - \sum_{i=1,2} I_i N_i = 0, \qquad (10.18)$$

$$F(L_2, N_2) + \tilde{S}_2 - F(L_2, N_1) - \tilde{S}_1 = 0. \qquad (10.19)$$

Hence, the central government maximizes social welfare (10.16), defined over the sum of the regional welfare functions, while taking into account the budget balance (10.17), the labor market equilibrium (10.18), and the binding incentive compatibility constraint of high-income regions (10.19).

Section 10.4.3 provides an algebraic solution to the central government's second-best optimum. Here, we can summarize the results in

Proposition 10.2.   *In the case of incomplete information, the central government cannot achieve the first-best allocation. The optimal incentive-compatible intervention scheme results in an allocation with migration distortions. Wages in low-productivity regions exceed wages in high-income regions, $w_1 > w_2$, and the central government does not succeed in equalizing interregional income disparities completely.*

Of course, since the central government does not directly interfere with the interpersonal redistribution process, Proposition 10.2 implies that regions choose different redistributive transfers for mobile workers. More precisely, because wages in high-productivity regions are lower and all workers receive the same net income via migration, low-productivity regions choose lower transfers,

$\tau_1^B < \tau_2^B$. We can use Figure 10.1 to characterize the second-best allocation. Suppose that $(N_1^O, \tilde{S}_1^O)$ is the optimal menu of low-productivity regions. Then, since budget clearing for the central government requires $\tilde{S}_2^O = -I_1\tilde{S}_1^O/I_2 - Nx^B/I_2$, the menu $(N_2^O, \tilde{S}_2^O)$ characterizes the second-best optimum for high-income regions. Thus, employment levels are higher in high-income regions. As Proposition 10.2 states, employment levels in high-productivity regions sufficiently exceed those in low-income regions that wages in the former regions fall short of those in the latter ones, $w_2 < w_1$, and hence $\tan\beta < \tan\alpha$.

Intuitively, the central government can implement some interregional transfer toward low-income regions, as long as it ensures that its grant policy for low-income regions is sufficiently less preferable to high-income regions that the latter do not choose to mimic poor regions. This leads to migration distortions. But why does the center prefer higher redistributive transfers and thus lower wages in high-income regions than in low-productivity regions? This can be explained by the following perturbation argument.

Starting at the central government's optimum, a small relocation of labor from low- to high-productivity regions, $dN_2 = -I_1dN_1/I_2 > 0$, alters the net income of immobile residents by $w_i dN_i$, since w_i is the marginal productivity of labor in region i. In order to hold welfare constant, this requires an accompanying interregional transfer of $d\tilde{S}_i = -w_i dN_i$. However, despite this compensation, the incentive constraint of type-2 regions is affected. To see why, recall that the change in net income of type-2 regions when mimicking type-1 regions is equal to $d\tilde{S}_1 + F_N(L_2, N_1)dN_1 = (F_N[L_2, N_1] - F_N[L_1, N_1])dN_1 < 0$, as condition (10.3) states. If the initial policy is optimal as assumed, then there must be an offsetting cost to this welfare-increasing perturbation. This cost is given by a drop in total production, implying $w_1 - w_2 > 0$ initially. Accordingly, compensating changes in transfers to hold welfare unchanged produce a deficit in the central government's budget, $I_2 d\tilde{S}_2 + I_1 d\tilde{S}_1 = -I_2 w_2 dN_2 - I_1 w_1 dN_1 = I_2(w_1 - w_2)dN_2 > 0$.

A final point of interest concerns the design of the central government's grant policy to achieve the second-best allocation described in Proposition 10.2. Comparing Proposition 10.2 with the first-order condition (10.8) for the optimal regional policy requires the following marginal grant rates:

$$\frac{\partial S_2}{\partial N_2} = \tau_2^B \quad \text{and} \quad \frac{\partial S_1}{\partial N_1} = \tau_1^B < \tau_2^B. \tag{10.20}$$

In summary, redistributive transfers and therefore wages are generally not equalized across regions in a second-best optimum. Under incomplete information, harmonization of redistribution policy is not socially optimal, even if the beneficiaries of such a policy are mobile. Interpersonal transfers are intrinsically intertwined with interregional transfers. If a system of equalizing interregional transfers is to be implemented, net contributors to the system should be treated differently from net recipients with respect to interpersonal redistribution.

10.3 Incomplete Information and Moral Hazard

In the previous section we assumed that regions can hide information and that the central government must therefore implement a grant scheme depending on the observable variable labor input so that regions self-select. This is a typical problem of adverse selection. The other fundamental problem with incomplete information is moral hazard. However, taking a closer look, a moral hazard problem has already been included in the preceding section because regions can manipulate regional employment figures N_i by choosing their transfer levels τ_i^B. Thus, they can affect the amount of the grant they receive by own actions. To make the problem of moral hazard more explicit, we extend the analysis of the last section by assuming that regions additionally provide local public infrastructure to regional firms. Since regions can manipulate all variables observable to the center by choosing local public inputs, they can strategically influence the amount of grants they receive. Hence, regions may have incentives to reduce their efforts in order to drop regional income.

Extending the analysis by introducing local public infrastructure has another advantage with regard to the informational assumption. Section 10.2 set forth a model with asymmetric information about the regional land endowment. Therefore, we had to assume that the center is unable to collect data on regional wage levels. On the verge of the 21st century, in what is supposed to be the "information age," the assumption that regions can hide data on wage figures is critical. Including local public infrastructure into the model avoids this problem. Even if both employment levels and wages are observable to the center, it can assess neither regional land endowments nor (thus) productivity levels.

10.3.1 Private Behavior

In contrast to the analysis in the previous sections, aggregate production in region i is now represented by the function $F^i \equiv F(L_i, N_i, g_i)$, which depends not only on land and labor but also on the level of local public infrastructure g_i. The variable g_i can also be interpreted as bureaucratic efforts or other attempts of regional governments to make regions more productive. As we shall explain further, the inability of the central government to observe this supply (in efficiency units) prevents it from inferring the type of the region. We assume that the marginal product of labor increases with higher levels of public infrastructure, $\partial^2 F^i/(\partial N_i \partial g_i) \equiv F_{Ng}^i > 0$. The costs of supplying the local public factor are given by the region-independent function $H^i \equiv H(g_i)$, expressed in units of the private numeraire good.[3] Again, there are only two different types of

---

[3] Another source of private information on behalf of regions is the cost function for local public factors, which may differ across regions. Including such differences does not change the analysis or the results.

regions, $i = 1, 2$. Differences are expressed in regional land endowments: the endowment with land is higher in a region of type 2 than in a type-1 region.

Let us assume that the land owner runs the regional firms. Firms' profits also include the rent to the local public factor and can be written as

$$F(L_i, N_i, g_i) - w_i N_i. \tag{10.21}$$

Firms choose the number of workers N_i to maximize profits while taking the wage rate w_i as given. This implies

$$F_N(L_i, N_i, g_i) = w_i. \tag{10.22}$$

Condition (10.22) can be used to derive a function relating the public input level to regional employment and wages:

$$g_i = G_i(N_i, w_i), \quad \text{with} \tag{10.23}$$

$$G_{iN} = -\frac{F^i_{NN}}{F^i_{Ng}} > 0 \quad \text{and} \quad G_{iw} = \frac{1}{F^i_{Ng}} > 0.$$

We assume that regional governments can control the level of public infrastructure directly. Although the central government can now observe both regional wages and regional employment levels, this does not mean that the center is able to infer the productivity (land endowment) of a region by looking at (10.22). The reason is that regional governments can achieve all combinations of employment and wage levels by strategically choosing the level of local public inputs, regardless of their land endowment.

For the subsequent analysis, we introduce two important assumptions that drive the basic results. Define

$$R_i(N, w) \equiv F(L_i, N, G_i[N, w]) - H(G_i[N, w])$$

as the regional net production. Then, the assumptions can be expressed as

$$R_2(N, w) > R_1(N, w) \tag{10.24}$$

and

$$R_{2w}(N, w) > R_{1w}(N, w). \tag{10.25}$$

Assumption (10.24) means that regional net production in high-productivity regions exceeds that of low-productivity regions when evaluated at the same amount of labor employed and the same wages. Assumption (10.25) implies that the wage that maximizes $R_2(N, w_2)$ is higher than the wage maximizing $R_1(N, w_1)$ when evaluated at the same employment level. Hence, provided the local public input is chosen so as to maximize regional net production, type-2 regions have the higher labor demand curve at any employment level, $w_2(N) > w_1(N)$.

Turning now to regional policies, a government in a low-productivity region may again provide a redistributive transfer τ_1^B to mobile workers and supplies the local public input g_1, where both are financed by a tax on the fixed factor and a net transfer S_1 from the central government. Accordingly, in high-productivity regions, the redistributive transfer τ_2^B, the provision of local public infrastructure g_2, and the net contribution $-S_2$ to the central government's budget must all be financed by a tax on the fixed factor. The net income of a representative mobile worker living in a type-i region is still represented by $x_i^B = w_i + \tau_i^B$. Inserting the budget constraint of regional governments into the private budget restriction of the representative owner of the fixed factor in a type-i region, we derive a net income of $x_i^A = R_i(N_i, w_i) - N_i x_i^B + S_i$.

10.3.2   Regional Government Behavior

Each regional government takes x^B as given when choosing its redistributive transfer τ_i^B and its local public input g_i. This problem is equivalent to

$$\text{maximizing } R_i(N_i, w_i) - N_i x^B + S_i(N_i, w_i) \tag{10.26}$$

by choice of the number of workers N_i and the regional wage rate w_i. Then, condition (10.23) determines the optimal g_i and the budget constraint of mobile workers determines the optimal τ_i^B for a predetermined x^B. Note that the central government's grant depends on both choice variables and also includes a lump-sum part. The first-order conditions of this problem are

$$\tau_i^B - (F_g^i - H_g^i)G_{iN} = \frac{\partial S_i}{\partial N_i} \tag{10.27}$$

and

$$(F_g^i - H_g^i)G_{iw} = -\frac{\partial S_i}{\partial w_i}, \tag{10.28}$$

where we have substituted the definition of $R_i(N_i, w_i)$. Hence, by choice of its marginal grant rates $\partial S_i/\partial N_i$ and $\partial S_i/\partial w_i$, the central government can determine the redistributive transfers τ_i^B and the levels of public infrastructure g_i in the regions. In addition, it can achieve its desired interregional net income distribution for the owners of the fixed factor by choosing the lump-sum part of its instrument S_i.

10.3.3   Optimal Policy with Incomplete Information

Because the central government cannot infer a region's type, its problem is to design a grant schedule $S(N, w)$, based on the variables it observes, that induces regional governments to provide the desired levels of the local public input and redistributive transfers to workers. In the case of complete information, the optimal allocation is characterized by Proposition 10.1. In addition, local public inputs are provided according to the Samuelson condition $F_g^i = H_g^i$ ($i = 1, 2$). With incomplete information, the center must meet the following incentive compatibility constraints for truth telling:

$$R_i(N_i, w_i) + \tilde{S}_i \geq R_i(N_j, w_j) + \tilde{S}_j, \quad i, j = 1, 2, \ i \neq j, \qquad (10.29)$$

with $\tilde{S}_i$ defined as in Section 10.1. The net income of immobile residents living in regions that choose their optimal wages and employment levels must be at least as high as in the case of realizing the wages and population numbers of the other type of region.

As in Section 10.2, we shall argue that only the constraint of high-productivity regions is binding at a second-best optimum, since these regions become net contributors to the interregional redistribution program. In order to show this, we rewrite the assumption of (10.24) as

$$R_2(N_1, w_1) + \tilde{S}_1 > R_1(N_1, w_1) + \tilde{S}_1. \qquad (10.30)$$

Condition (10.30), together with the incentive constraint of high-income regions (10.29), yields

$$x_2^A = R_2(N_2, w_2) + \tilde{S}_2 > R_1(N_1, w_1) + \tilde{S}_1 = x_1^A. \qquad (10.31)$$

Following (10.31), immobile residents living in high-productivity regions have the higher net income level. Since a marginal interregional transfer of income toward low-income regions would raise social welfare, there must be an offsetting cost at the optimum, and this can only come from a binding incentive constraint of type-2 regions.

If, on the other hand, the incentive compatibility constraint of low-productivity regions is *not* binding,

$$R_1(N_1, w_1) + \tilde{S}_1 > R_1(N_2, w_2) + \tilde{S}_2, \qquad (10.32)$$

and if the incentive constraint of type-2 regions is satisfied with equality, then the nonbinding condition (10.32) becomes

$$R_2(N_2, w_2) - R_2(N_1, w_1) > R_1(N_2, w_2) - R_1(N_1, w_1). \qquad (10.33)$$

Our assumptions ensure that (10.33) must hold if $N_2 \geq N_1$ at the optimum. This condition would seem to be the normal case, given the observation that type-2 regions have the higher labor demand curve. We therefore limit our analysis to the case where (10.33) and thus (10.32) are satisfied.

The problem of the central government becomes to

$$\text{maximize} \sum_{i=1,2} \{I_i V(R_i[N_i, w_i] + \tilde{S}_i) + I_i U^i(x^B)\} \qquad (10.34)$$

by choosing x^B and the vectors $(\tilde{S}_i)$, (N_i), and (w_i) subject to the constraints

$$-\sum_{i=1,2} I_i \tilde{S}_i - Nx^B = 0, \tag{10.35}$$

$$N - \sum_{i=1,2} I_i N_i = 0, \tag{10.36}$$

$$R_2(N_2, w_2) + \tilde{S}_2 - R_2(N_1, w_1) - \tilde{S}_1 = 0. \tag{10.37}$$

Hence, the central government maximizes social welfare (10.34) while taking into account the budget balance (10.35), the labor market equilibrium (10.36), and the binding incentive compatibility constraint of high-income regions (10.37).

Section 10.4.4 provides an algebraic solution to the central government's second-best optimum. Here, we summarize the basic results in

Proposition 10.3. *The optimal incentive-compatible intervention scheme results in an allocation with migration distortions and an underprovision of local public factors (relative to the Samuelson rule) in low-productivity regions:*

(i) $F_g^1 - H_g^1 > F_g^2 - H_g^2 = 0,$

(ii) $\text{sign}(w_1 - w_2)$
$$= \text{sign}\left(\frac{\partial w_1(N_1, G_1[N_1, w_1])}{\partial N_1} - \frac{\partial w_2(N_1, G_2[N_1, w_1])}{\partial N_1} \right).$$

Let us first turn to the incentives provided by the center regarding the supply of local public inputs – part (i) of Proposition 10.3. To see why the provision of local public inputs is inefficiently low relative to the Samuelson rule in low-income regions, let us suppose it actually were efficient. If the center now reduces this level of public infrastructure by decreasing w_1 according to (10.23), the change does not affect the owners of immobile factors in type-1 regions (to a first-order approximation). However, this policy creates a strict inequality in the incentive compatibility constraint of rich regions, as assumption (10.25) makes clear. The informational rent is reduced and welfare can be raised.

The result that the provision of public infrastructure is not distorted in high-productivity regions is reminiscent of the conclusions drawn in the literature on principal–agent problems. It does not pay to distort the behavior of the top agent having the binding constraint. Nothing can be gained by distorting the provision of public infrastructure in high-income regions because the incentive constraint of low-productivity regions is not binding at a second-best optimum. However, since the incentive constraint of high-productivity regions *is* binding, distorting the supply of public factors in low-income regions makes it less preferable to mimic their behavior. This is one method of increasing the transfer from high-income regions to low-productivity regions.

As in Section 10.2, part (ii) of Proposition 10.3 states that there are migration distortions at the second-best optimum. The region in which wages are more responsive to changes in labor supply should provide higher redistributive transfers to workers and thus have lower wages. Once again, we can explain this result by a perturbation argument. Suppose that wages in high-income regions are more responsive to changes in the labor supply. If one starts from a central government's optimum and holds local public input levels and grants fixed, a small relocation of labor from low- to high-income regions alters the net income of immobile residents by $w_i dN_i$. This requires an accompanying change in interregional transfers by $d\tilde{S}_i = -w_i dN_i$ in order to hold welfare unchanged. However, despite this compensation, the incentive constraint of type-2 regions not to mimic type-1 regions is affected. To see why, recall that w_1 must rise in response to a decrease in N_1 in order to hold the provision of the local public input $G_1(N_1, w_1)$ fixed. Given that wages are more responsive in type-2 regions,

$$\frac{\partial w_1(N_1, G_1[N_1, w_1])}{\partial N_1} - \frac{\partial w_2(N_1, G_2[N_1, w_1])}{\partial N_1} > 0,$$

this rise in w_1 is too small to keep $G_2(N_1, w_1)$ constant. Indeed, $G_2(N_1, w_1)$ will fall. This reduces the welfare of type-2 regions when mimicking their poor neighbors if $G_2(N_1, w_1)$ is already inefficiently low from the viewpoint of type-2 regions. To see this, note that part (i) of Proposition 10.3 together with (10.23) implies that w_1 falls short of the efficient wage of type-1 regions, given their employment level N_1. Then, assumption (10.25) states that w_1 must lie below the efficient wage of type-2 regions when choosing the labor input N_1. Hence, a type-2 region mimicking a type-1 region must set its local public input at an inefficiently low level. To sum up, if the initial policy is optimal as assumed then there must be an offsetting cost to this decrease in the information rent, implying that $w_1 - w_2 > 0$ initially.

To draw a parallel to Section 10.2, let us finally characterize the optimality-supporting grant policy by the appropriate marginal grants. Comparing the first-order conditions of the second-best optimum under incomplete information (as set out in Proposition 10.3) with the necessary conditions of an optimal regional behavior (10.27) and (10.28), we obtain

$$\frac{\partial S_2(N_2, w_2)}{\partial N_2} = \tau_2^B \quad \text{and} \quad \frac{\partial S_1(N_1, w_1)}{\partial N_1} < \tau_1^B, \tag{10.38}$$

$$\frac{\partial S_2(N_2, w_2)}{\partial w_2} = 0 \quad \text{and} \quad \frac{\partial S_1(N_1, w_1)}{\partial w_1} < 0. \tag{10.39}$$

In order to induce a type-2 region to supply local public factors optimally, the marginal grant with respect to w_2 must vanish. In contrast to that result, the marginal grant with respect to w_1 must be negative for low-income regions, since it is optimal to have an underprovision of local public inputs and G_{1w} is positive. Inserting these results in the necessary condition (10.27), it is clear that the marginal grant with respect to N_2 for type-2 regions must be precisely equal to the desired redistributive transfer level τ_2^B, while the marginal grant rate with respect to N_1 must fall short of the preferred redistributive transfer τ_1^B.

In summary, although the model in this section provides more realistic assumptions on informational asymmetry and makes the moral hazard problem explicit, it nevertheless confirms the basic conclusions derived in Section 10.2. With incomplete information, the second-best optimum distorts the allocation among and within regions. As Bucovetsky et al. (1998) explain, this is also the basic message when regions have private information with respect to their citizens' preferences for local public (consumption) goods and must cover public expenditures by a tax on mobile capital.

10.4 Appendix

The procedure of this appendix is as follows. In Section 10.4.1 we will solve the central government problem (10.16)–(10.19) set out in Section 10.2. Section 10.4.2 deduces from this system the characteristics of the first-best allocation with complete information, thereby proving Proposition 10.1. The second-best allocation with incomplete information and adverse selection will be derived in Section 10.4.3; this proves Proposition 10.2. Finally, in Section 10.4.4 we turn to the moral hazard problem set out in Section 10.3 and prove Proposition 10.3.

10.4.1 First-Order Conditions of the Central Government Problem

Let λ, γ, and μ denote the Lagrange multipliers of the constraints (10.17), (10.18), and (10.19), respectively. Then, the first-order conditions of solving the problem (10.16)–(10.19) are (with control variables set in parentheses)

$$(x^B): \quad I_1 U^{1\prime}(x^B) + I_2 U^{2\prime}(x^B) - \lambda N = 0, \tag{A.10.1}$$

$$(\tilde{S}_1): \quad I_1 V'(x_1^A) - \lambda I_1 - \mu = 0, \tag{A.10.2}$$

$$(\tilde{S}_2): \quad I_2 V'(x_2^A) - \lambda I_2 + \mu = 0, \tag{A.10.3}$$

$$(N_1): \quad I_1 V'(x_1^A) F_N^{11} - \gamma I_1 - \mu F_N^{21} = 0, \tag{A.10.4}$$

$$(N_2): \quad I_2 V'(x_2^A) F_N^{22} - \gamma I_2 + \mu F_N^{22} = 0, \tag{A.10.5}$$

where we have used the definition $F_N^{ij} \equiv F_N(L_i, N_j)$ $(i, j = 1, 2)$.

10.4.2   First-Best Optimum

To characterize the optimum in the case of complete information, we need only ignore the incentive compatibility constraint (10.19) by setting $\mu = 0$ in the first-order conditions just stated. Then, solving (A.10.2) and (A.10.3) for λ yields

$$V'(x_1^A) = V'(x_2^A) \iff x_1^A = x_2^A = x^{A*} \tag{A.10.6}$$

and thus $\lambda = V'(x^{A*})$. Substituting this expression for λ into (A.10.1) and using the definition $MRS_i \equiv U^{i\prime}/V'$ yields the Samuelson condition

$$I_1 MRS_1 + I_2 MRS_2 = N. \tag{A.10.7}$$

Inserting $V'(x^{A*})$ into (A.10.4) and (A.10.5), solving for γ, and observing that $F_N^{ii} = w_i$, we obtain

$$V'(x^{A*})(w_1 - w_2) = 0 \iff w_1 = w_2 = w^*. \tag{A.10.8}$$

The results stated in (A.10.6)–(A.10.8) prove Proposition 10.1.

10.4.3   Optimum with Incomplete Information and Adverse Selection

For the proof of Proposition 10.2, we insert (A.10.3) for $I_2 V'(x_2^A) + \mu = \lambda I_2$ into (A.10.5) and so derive

$$\lambda F_N^{22} = \gamma. \tag{A.10.9}$$

Moreover, solving (A.10.4) for γ and inserting the resulting expression into (A.10.9) yields

$$\lambda F_N^{22} = V'(x_1^A) F_N^{11} - \frac{\mu F_N^{21}}{I_1}. \tag{A.10.10}$$

From (A.10.2), it follows that $V'(x_1^A) = \lambda + \mu/I_1$. Inserting this expression into (A.10.10) and taking into account that wages are equal to marginal labor productivities, $F_N^{ii} = w_i$, we have

$$\lambda I_1(w_1 - w_2) = \mu(F_N^{21} - F_N^{11}). \tag{A.10.11}$$

Condition (10.3) states that $F_N^{21} > F_N^{11}$. Thus, (A.10.11) proves the basic result set out in Proposition 10.2 – that wages in low-income regions exceed those in rich regions. The other result of Proposition 10.2 (that $x_2^A > x_1^A$) was proved by (10.15).

10.4.4   Optimum with Incomplete Information and Moral Hazard

In order to prove Proposition 10.3, we solve the problem (10.34)–(10.37). Let λ, γ, and μ denote the Lagrange multipliers of the constraints (10.35), (10.36), and (10.37), respectively. Then, the first-order conditions of the optimum with incomplete information are (control variables set in parentheses)

$$(x^B): \quad I_1 U^{1'}(x^B) + I_2 U^{2'}(x^B) - \lambda N = 0, \tag{A.10.12}$$

$$(\tilde{S}_1): \quad I_1 V'(x_1^A) - \lambda I_1 - \mu = 0, \tag{A.10.13}$$

$$(\tilde{S}_2): \quad I_2 V'(x_2^A) - \lambda I_2 + \mu = 0, \tag{A.10.14}$$

$$(N_1): \quad I_1 V'(x_1^A) R_{1N}^1 - \gamma I_1 - \mu R_{2N}^1 = 0, \tag{A.10.15}$$

$$(N_2): \quad I_2 V'(x_2^A) R_{2N}^2 - \gamma I_2 + \mu R_{2N}^2 = 0, \tag{A.10.16}$$

$$(w_1): \quad I_1 V'(x_1^A) R_{1w}^1 - \mu R_{2w}^1 = 0, \tag{A.10.17}$$

$$(w_2): \quad I_2 V'(x_2^A) R_{2w}^2 + \mu R_{2w}^2 = 0, \tag{A.10.18}$$

where we have indicated partial derivatives of $R_i(N_j, w_j)$ by R_{iN}^j and R_{iw}^j ($i, j = 1, 2$). For the subsequent analysis, it is useful to introduce the following definitions: $F^{ij} \equiv F(L_i, N_j, G_i[N_j, w_j])$, $H_g^{ij} \equiv H_g^i(G_i[N_j, w_j])$, and $G_i^j \equiv G_i(N_j, w_j)$.

To start, we rewrite (A.10.17) as

$$[I_1 V'(x_1^A) - \mu] R_{1w}^1 = \mu(R_{2w}^1 - R_{1w}^1). \tag{A.10.19}$$

From (A.10.13), it follows that $I_1 V'(x_1^A) - \mu = \lambda I_1$. Inserting this into (A.10.19) gives

$$\lambda I_1 R_{1w}^1 = \mu(R_{2w}^1 - R_{1w}^1). \tag{A.10.20}$$

Assumption (10.25) implies $R_{2w}^1 > R_{1w}^1$. Thus, $R_{1w}^1 = (F_g^{11} - H_g^{11}) G_{1w}^1 > 0$, implying $(F_g^{11} - H_g^{11}) > 0$ as $G_{1w}^1 > 0$. Since (A.10.18) shows that $R_{2w}^2 = 0$ with or without complete information, we have

$$(F_g^{11} - H_g^{11}) > (F_g^{22} - H_g^{22}) = 0, \tag{A.10.21}$$

that is, part (i) of Proposition 10.3.

Using the definition $R_i(N, w) \equiv F(L_i, N, G_i[N, w]) - H(G_i[N, w])$, conditions (A.10.15) and (A.10.17) can be rewritten as

$$I_1 V'(x_1^A)(F_N^{11} + [F_g^{11} - H_g^{11}] G_{1N}^1)$$
$$- \mu(F_N^{21} + [F_g^{21} - H_g^{21}] G_{2N}^1) = \gamma I_1 \tag{A.10.22}$$

and

$$I_1 V'(x_1^A)[F_g^{11} - H_g^{11}] G_{1w}^1 = \mu[F_g^{21} - H_g^{21}] G_{2w}^1, \tag{A.10.23}$$

respectively. Multiplying (A.10.23) by $-G_{1N}^1 / G_{1w}^1$, adding the resulting expression to (A.10.22), and noting that mimicking the other region requires $F_N^{11} = F_N^{21}$ yields

$$[I_1 V'(x_1^A) - \mu] F_N^{11} - \mu [F_g^{21} - H_g^{21}] G_{2w}^1 \left[\frac{G_{2N}^1}{G_{2w}^1} - \frac{G_{1N}^1}{G_{1w}^1} \right] = \gamma I_1. \quad \text{(A.10.24)}$$

Then, substituting from (A.10.16) for γ and using $F_N^{ii} = w_i$ yields

$$[I_1 V'(x_1^A) - \mu] w_1 - \mu [F_g^{21} - H_g^{21}] G_{2w}^1 \left[\frac{G_{2N}^1}{G_{2w}^1} - \frac{G_{1N}^1}{G_{1w}^1} \right]$$

$$= I_1 \left[V'(x_2^A) + \frac{\mu}{I_2} \right] w_2. \quad \text{(A.10.25)}$$

Finally, substituting from (A.10.13) and (A.10.14), we have

$$I_1 \lambda (w_1 - w_2) = \mu [F_g^{21} - H_g^{21}] G_{2w}^1 \left[\frac{G_{2N}^1}{G_{2w}^1} - \frac{G_{1N}^1}{G_{1w}^1} \right]. \quad \text{(A.10.26)}$$

Assumption (10.25) together with (A.10.21) implies $[F_g^{21} - H_g^{21}] G_{2w}^1 > 0$. Using this in (A.10.26) and taking into account that

$$\frac{G_{jN}^i}{G_{jw}^i} = - \frac{\partial w_j (N_i, G_j [N_i, w_i])}{\partial N_i},$$

holding $G_j (N_i, w_i)$ fixed, yields

$\text{sign}(w_1 - w_2)$

$$= \text{sign} \left(\frac{\partial w_1 (N_1, G_1 [N_1, w_1])}{\partial N_1} - \frac{\partial w_2 (N_1, G_2 [N_1, w_1])}{\partial N_1} \right), \quad \text{(A.10.27)}$$

that is, part (ii) of Proposition 10.3.

CHAPTER 11

Conclusions

The basic objective of this study has been to analyze whether the allocative and the redistributive functions of the government can be assigned to the regions of a federal state. This concluding chapter tries to give a comprehensive answer to that question and intends to derive the most important policy applications of the analysis in this book. Section 11.1 first turns to the allocative branch of the government, Section 11.2 proceeds with its redistributive function, and Section 11.3 finally draws the policy conclusions.

11.1 Efficiency and Decentralization

This section aims to reconsider the conditions ensuring that decentralized government decisions result in an efficient allocation if the individual regions of a federal state are connected by a high degree of interregional mobility. It thereby assumes that governments are not self-serving.

The first important condition is that regions must have a sufficiently flexible instrument set available to achieve an efficient allocation. Mobile firms and households cause crowding costs at their location. Regions must therefore be able to collect direct location-based taxes on mobile firms and households in order to internalize these costs. Without such location-based taxes, it is impossible to ensure the efficient locational pattern across regions, in general. Since, however, marginal crowding costs are generally lower than average costs of providing local public goods and factors, the availability of direct firm and household taxes is not sufficient to finance local public services without distorting locational choices. Regions must have an additional undistortionary revenue source (e.g., a tax on land rents) for balancing their budget – a source that may also help to make an efficient interregional transfer of resources. If this minimum requirement of a complete tax instrument set is not satisfied, then an inefficient allocation must always be expected. This holds even if regions had the correct incentives to choose an efficient allocation.

191

A complete instrument set at the regional level is a *necessary condition* to achieve an efficient allocation. Once this condition is met, the analysis in this book has revealed two incentive conditions which guarantee that regional governments have the correct incentives to choose an efficient allocation in their own interest. The *first incentive condition* is a parallel to the framework of perfect competition among private agents – perfect competition among regions for mobile households, firms, and capital. The single region is small and cannot influence by its own actions the prices of mobile factors, the utility level of mobile households, or the profit level of mobile firms. If regions maximize the entire rent of immobile local factors like land, then conditions of perfect interregional competition provide them with the correct incentives to choose an efficient allocation. However, maximization of the entire local land rent requires that regional governments have jurisdiction over the entire strip of land where their residents live. This condition is identical to claiming that the minimal jurisdiction must be an urban area providing all essential local public services that individuals consume at a certain place. If this requirement is satisfied, regional governments provide local public services in line with the Samuelson condition characterizing the efficient level, and they tax mobile firms and households at marginal crowding costs.

Another advantage to decentralizing the provision of local public goods is that migration responses of mobile households to changes in the supply of local public goods reveal their preferences for these public services. This preference revelation mechanism works even in an intergenerational context. Future generations' willingness to pay for changes in local amenities is correctly revealed by changes in the current value of local property. If regional decision makers take into account these changes in the value of the local property, then they have incentives to internalize the interests of currently living and future generations. The preference revelation mechanism through migration responses described by Tiebout (1956) works in small regions. Regions must take the utility level of mobile individuals as a predetermined variable that cannot be influenced by their own decisions. Such an assumption is only applicable to the local level. Therefore, only preferences for local amenities are correctly disclosed by migration responses. The use of public goods must be restricted to the regional boundaries, and there must be no interregional spillover effects.

However, there exists another mechanism that actually leads regions to internalize these interregional externalities and, as such, provides the *second incentive condition* ensuring that regional decisions do not cause allocative distortions. This mechanism is perfect interregional household mobility. It has not only the advantage of revealing the preferences of mobile households for local public goods; under certain conditions, it also ensures that uncoordinated government decisions in large regions result in an efficient allocation. If all households living in a federal state are identical and perfectly mobile, then regions have no incentive to behave strategically. A beggar-my-neighbor policy does not pay for the individual region, since interregional utility differences are incompatible with free mobility: if regions tried to exploit other regions, they would harm their own residents in the end by induced migration responses. In a noncooperative Nash equilibrium, regions therefore behave as if they acted cooperatively. They even have incentives to internalize public good spillover effects. Hence, under the conditions stated here, there are no efficiency reasons for higher governmental intervention. However, these conditions must be seen as highly idealized, and they must be modified accordingly in order to apply the models to problems in existing federations.

One obvious (but not the only) deviation from this stylized world is the existence of migration costs. If migration costs are not constant and differ among households (because e.g. of psychic ties of individuals to their home region), then the objectives of regional governments are no longer coordinated by taking migration responses into account. In this case, distortions must be expected since strategic behavior of regions could be advantageous. The individual region tries to gain its desired share of the interregional resource distribution. Since the migration equilibrium is characterized by different utility levels, at most one of two regions can attain its preferred position. The other region cannot achieve its desired distribution share and has incentives to distort the allocation by using its policy variables strategically. In general, central government intervention is necessary to ensure an efficient allocation of resources.

11.2   Redistribution and Decentralization

Conditions of perfect interregional competition ensure that small regions choose an efficient allocation in their own interest. However, a consequence of this behavior is that – in order to avoid migration distortions – such regions neither subsidize nor tax mobile individuals for redistributive purposes. For example, regions are aware that the amount of any tax revenues they could attain by taxing mobile residents would be exceeded by the regional income loss caused by tax-driven emigration of workers. Thus, under these conditions, assigning redistributive tasks to small regions does not generate a satisfactory outcome.

If regions are larger, the benefit of taxing or subsidizing mobile workers is sufficiently high for regions that there is some positive degree of income redistribution. However, even in this scenario, decentralized redistributive policies must fail relative to the socially optimal outcome. There are two basic problems involved. Uncoordinated redistribution programs result in different tax–transfer levels across regions, and this leads to migration distortions. Furthermore, since regions neglect the positive externalities of their transfer programs on other regions, the degree of redistribution is not zero (as in small regions) but suboptimally low. When a region increases its transfer payments to low-income households living within its borders, it attracts mobile residents from other regions. However, in choosing the transfer, it neglects to consider that the induced immigration reduces the costs of redistribution for neighboring regions.

The government also engages in a wide variety of intergenerational redistribution measures (see Boadway and Wildasin 1993 for an overview). The most visible forms are the redistribution of resources between generations via public debt policies and via pay-as-you-go pension systems. Redistribution by issuing public debt is especially problematic because currently living generations extend their consumption at the expense of future generations who are not being asked. As discussed previously, small regions (in a static model) have no incentive to tax mobile residents for redistributive purposes. If this analysis were applicable without any qualification, a decentralization of debt policies and old-age security policies would avoid any form of undesired intergenerational redistribution, since mobile households can escape the undue tax burden simply by emigrating. However, our analysis has shown that, unlike redistribution between high- and low-income households of the same generation within a period, it cannot be concluded that small regions completely abstain from causing tax burdens on future mobile residents by issuing debt. It is true that regions take the interest of future generations partly into account by considering the value of local property, and this definitively points in the direction of less intergenerational redistribution. However, even under ideal circumstances of perfect interregional competition for mobile households, this does not necessarily mean that the level of intergenerational redistribution via local public debt or pension policies falls to zero. The problem is that local governments cannot prevent their successors from issuing public debt.

Besides the distribution of income *within* regions, there also exists the redistribution of income *across* regions. Although regions may have some incentives to transfer resources to other regions in order to increase income abroad and thereby restrict undesirable immigration, the voluntary transfers are insufficient to avoid any interregional differences in per-capita incomes if there are some groups of individuals that are relatively immobile. Any further equalization of income disparities across regions requires a central government redistribution scheme – which may, however, result in adverse incentive effects on behalf of regional governments.

11.3   Policy Applications

We are now in a position to discuss conclusions that can be drawn from the analysis for the problem of decentralizing government activities.

11.3.1   Tax Autonomy of Local Governments

Our analysis shows that it is necessary to endow local decision makers with a sufficiently flexible tax instrument set if an efficient allocation is to be achieved. If this requirement is met, and if one takes into account that local governments are more sensitive to the preferences of their voters than the federal government, there is a strong argument to assign the provision of local public goods and factors to the local level.

Against this background, the situation in many EU countries must be seen with reservation, since the necessary condition to equip local governments with a complete tax instrument set is not satisfied. Take, for example, Germany. Here, one major problem is that communities have no authority to tax their residents. The responsibility for collecting direct household taxes is delegated entirely to the federal level. There are also no zoning arrangements that could serve as a substitute for taxes on individuals. Moreover, although communities have a local firm tax (the *Gewerbeertragsteuer*) at their disposal, this tax is not a pure profit tax, and it distorts the use of capital by firms. Finally, it is true that local governments may levy an (almost) undistortionary tax on land, the *Grundsteuer*. However, since its tax base is rather small (partly because it does not reflect current values) and since the tax rates are restricted not to exceed a certain level, it is doubtful that the *Grundsteuer* could generate enough tax revenues to balance the budget when marginal crowding costs are lower than average costs of supplying public services. Therefore, the task of strengthening the tax autonomy of local governments has high priority in Germany and in other EU countries. In this regard, it is important not only that local governments can freely choose the tax base; it is equally important that they are not restricted in setting their desired tax rates once the tax bases are chosen.

11.3.2   Interregional Tax Competition

It is often argued (see e.g. the contributions in Siebert 1990) that the responsibility for levying source-based taxes on mobile capital should be assigned to the central level, since interregional tax competition for mobile capital results in an inefficient allocation. Our analysis shows that this requirement is rather a second-best argument. If benevolent regional governments are endowed with an unconstrained tax instrument set, including taxes on immobile factors like land, then there is no need to harmonize the tax on capital. With an unconstrained tax instrument set, regions that cannot affect the interregional terms of trade do not use capital taxes to finance local public goods.

However, even if regions must rely on capital taxes, interregional tax competition can also serve a valuable purpose. If politicians are not fully benevolent and also follow own objectives, they waste part of the tax revenues. In this case, interregional tax competition for a mobile tax base like capital is a way to limit the taxing power of governments. The analysis reveals that, indeed, interregional tax competition can increase the welfare of citizens as compared to a central provision of local public goods. In contrast to the case of benevolent governments, this benefit of fiscal decentralization can be achieved only if governments have no (unlimited) access to undistortive land taxes. Only if governments must rely on taxes on mobile capital can we speak literally of interregional tax competition. Therefore, the requirement of an unconstrained tax instrument set must be interpreted with some caution. If governments are benevolent, it is a necessary condition to ensure that local governments achieve an efficient allocation. Yet if politicians are partly self-serving, this requirement *prevents* the benefits of fiscal decentralization that would otherwise be possible.

11.3.3   Restructuring of Jurisdictional Boundaries

Although the benefits of some decentralization are obvious, the question arises about the optimal degree of decentralization and thus about the optimal structure of jurisdictions in a federal state. In answering this question, several aspects must be taken into account. One objective is to avoid public good spillover effects and other interregional externalities due to decentralized government behavior. This would require, according to the principle of fiscal equivalence, jurisdictions of different size for each public good. Given this constraint in size, each jurisdiction must, on the other hand, be as small as possible because decentralized governments are more sensitive to the wishes of their citizens.

However, these traditional criteria ignore one severe problem of fiscal decentralization. Regional governments must also be endowed with the correct incentives to choose the efficient allocation in their own interest. With mobile individuals, this implies that the smallest jurisdiction facing such incentives is an area that provides all local public services that are essential in the constituents' preference structure. Any further decentralization would take away the incentives for socially efficient government behavior. Since different local public services have different and overlapping market areas, ranging from suburbs (public schools) to large metropolitan areas (public utilities like electricity), this means that the smallest jurisdiction that fulfils the incentive condition is one over the territory of a large urban area. Following this line of reasoning, the optimal structure of jurisdictions in a federal state must consist of several large metropolitan areas; this would require a substantial restructuring of jurisdictional boundaries in many federal states such as Germany and the United States.

Yet the need of supplying all necessary local public goods via one metropolitan government is only one side of the coin. The other is that such a jurisdiction is likely to be too large to take the utility of mobile residents and other interjurisdictional prices as being unaffected by own measures. It thus has some market power, creating other adverse incentive effects. The lesson to be learned from our analysis of local government incentives is that the optimal structure of jurisdictions must balance the costs of increased fragmentation of urban areas against the benefits of a decrease in market power; determining the optimum must be left to an empirical analysis of the associated costs and benefits.

11.3.4 Degree of Higher Governmental Intervention

For large regions like the member states of the EU, our analysis reveals that an increasing degree of household mobility improves the conditions of efficiency of uncoordinated regional government decisions. If all individuals are mobile and so regions make an interregional transfer of resources in order to restrict immigration, then they have incentives to internalize all external effects on neighboring regions in their self-interest. This result holds even if one realistically abstracts from perfect interregional household mobility and takes migration costs into account. In the case of migration costs, a region will make a transfer if its endowment of immobile factors of production like land exceeds by a sufficient amount the endowment of neighboring regions. Regions that do not voluntarily make an interregional transfer do not achieve their desired interregional income share, so they use their policy instruments strategically in order to increase their income. This strategic behavior results in allocative distortions. However, even such regions as these must take the welfare of nonresidents into account in order to assess their migration responses.

The derived behavior of large regions has important implications for the decentralization of government activities in the EU. Following the subsidiarity principle introduced into the Maastricht Treaty, the EU commission is empowered to take over government functions that cannot satisfactorily be fulfilled by the member states. This can be achieved by an assignment of these activities to the central level or by a central government intervention that corrects regional behavior. Following the present analysis, the EU must first ascertain whether individual member countries make migration-related interregional transfers before it takes over regional activities. Even if it concludes that a region does not make any transfer, the EU must take the interregional mobility of households into account when deciding on its intervention. Hence, the basic insight that can be derived from this analysis is that, compared to the well-known corrective Pigouvian remedies derived in the older literature (e.g. Oates 1972), the EU has to adapt its interventions downward. Regions internalize part of the externalities created by their actions in their own interest.

11.3.5   Redistribution Policy within the Regions of a Federal State

This study has also shown that local decision makers have very limited (if any) incentives to redistribute income among different household types. If the distributional function of the government is left to the individual member states in the EU, then a rising degree of household mobility among the member countries would have an undesirable impact on the level of redistribution between poor and rich individuals. Rich mobile residents are no longer taxed in order to avoid an emigration of this group, while poor mobile workers are no longer recipients of transfer payments since regions fear an uncontrolled influx of low-income workers from neighboring countries, making these programs very costly. There is hence a conflict between efficiency and distributional equity. Whereas efficiency requires equipping regional governments with the widest tax autonomy and giving them access to all tax bases, this implies that the incentives to redistribute income between individuals are rather low.

A resolution to this conflict could be the following. Local governments are free to choose their preferred tax bases, but the central government collects uniform taxes on wealthy mobile households and uses the proceeds to grant subsidies to low-income workers. Alternatively, the center can induce regions to redistribute more heavily by providing matching grants that reduce the costs of redistribution from the regions' viewpoint. Following these policies, the center achieves a fair income distribution without eliminating the incentives of local governments to choose an efficient allocation in their own interest. However, since such policies generally involve some interregional redistribution, other important incentive problems arise, to which we turn next.

11.3.6   Redistribution Policy across the Regions of a Federal State

Even if regions voluntarily make some interregional transfers to restrict immigration, the central government may have a different concept of a "fair" distribution of resources across regions. Hence, the center may wish to redistribute further among regions – but then, severe informational problems may arise. In order to smooth interregional income disparities, the center must know per-capita incomes in the regions and must ensure that regions do not cut back on own efforts to achieve a high income level. However, because regions have the better data basis, the central government is forced to rely on the data that regions collect and process. But how can the center make sure that high-income regions have incentives to reveal the correct data and avoid strategic behavior, especially when this implies that they become net contributors to the interregional redistribution scheme? One way of inducing rich regions not to mimic their poor neighbors is to combine the less favorable interregional transfer scheme with a region-specific corrective grant scheme that cushions some distortions within regions.

One possibility for such a combined scheme is as follows. The center may want to redistribute across regions and within regions, since regional redistribution among individuals is suboptimal due to expected migration responses. The center can differentiate its corrective grant scheme to stimulate interpersonal redistribution within regions, so that it provides higher grants to high-income regions than to low-income regions. If this differentiation is sufficiently pronounced, then it may be better for high-income regions not to mimic poor ones in order to get higher grants, even at the cost of some transfer of resources to poor regions. Of course, in doing so, the central government cannot achieve the income distribution that it would prefer in a world of complete information, but it can improve the allocation that would result without any intervention.

11.3.7 Harmonization of Debt and Pension Policies in the EU

The last point to be raised is of particular political importance in the EU: there is an intensive discussion about whether it is necessary to harmonize public debt policies for the creation of a stable monetary union. Leaving the monetary dimension of the problem aside, the analysis in this book suggests that there might also be efficiency reasons to harmonize regional debt policies. Issuing public debt is accompanied by higher taxes for future residents in order to balance the intertemporal budget restrictions of governments. If these taxes are residence-based, then any uncoordinated regional public debt policy (or old-age pension system on a pay-as-you-go basis) will cause migration distortions. However, before the case for a harmonization of public debt policies can be derived, it is first necessary to study whether regions indeed have incentives to issue public debt if they are connected by mobility of households. If one could conclude that (even under ideal conditions) regions partly finance their expenditures by running budget deficits, then a harmonization can be justified for efficiency reasons. The observed, less-than-ideal conditions in existing federations like the EU make it even more likely that regions issue public debt.

Our analysis shows that decentralization takes away the incentives for excessive intergenerational redistribution, but it does not avoid all incentives to disfavor future generations. This result provides a strong case for a harmonization of such measures. However, since intergenerational redistribution via issuing public debt is seen as undesirable (because future generations must bear the costs of current public expenditures without being asked to do so), any harmonization at too high a level could be disadvantageous. This leads us to the conclusion that harmonization at zero debt levels achieves two objectives: it avoids locational distortions and protects the interests of future generations.

References

Aaron, H. J. (1975). *Who Pays the Property Tax?* Washington, DC: Brookings.

Arnott, R. J. (1979). Optimal city size in a spatial economy. *Journal of Urban Economics* 6: 65–89.

Arnott, R. J., and R. E. Grieson (1981). Optimal fiscal policy for a state or local government. *Journal of Urban Economics* 9: 23–48.

Arnott, R. J., and J. E. Stiglitz (1979). Aggregate land rent, expenditure on public goods, and the optimal city size. *Quarterly Journal of Economics* 93: 471–500.

Atkinson, A. B., and J. E. Stiglitz (1980). *Lectures on Public Economics.* New York: McGraw-Hill.

Bailey, M. J. (1993). Note on Ricardian equivalence. *Journal of Public Economics* 51: 437–46.

Barro, R. J. (1974). Are government bonds net wealth? *Journal of Political Economy* 87: 1095–1118.

Barro, R. J., and X. Sala-i-Martin (1995). *Economic Growth.* New York: McGraw-Hill.

Baumann, E., and D. Wellisch (1998). Verteilung und Migration. In B. Gahlen, H. Hesse, and H. J. Ramser (Eds.), *Verteilungsprobleme der Gegenwart,* pp. 331–48. Tübingen: Mohr.

Berglas, E. (1976). On the theory of clubs. *American Economic Review* 66: 116–21.

(1981). Harmonization of commodity taxes. *Journal of Public Economics* 11: 377–87.

Berglas, E., and D. Pines (1981). Clubs, local public goods, and transportation models. *Journal of Public Economics* 15: 141–62.

Bergstrom, T. C., and R. P. Goodman (1973). Private demands for public goods. *American Economic Review* 63: 280–96.

Bewley, T. F. (1981). A critique of Tiebout's theory of local public expenditures. *Econometrica* 49: 713–40.

Boadway, R. W. (1982). On the method of taxation and the provision of local public goods: Comment. *American Economic Review* 72: 846–51.

Boadway, R. W., and F. Flatters (1982a). Efficiency and equalization payments in a federal system of government: A synthesis and extension of recent results. *Canadian Journal of Economics* 15: 613–33.

(1982b). *Equalization in a Federal State.* Ottawa: Economic Council of Canada.

Boadway, R. W., I. Horiba, and R. Jha (1994). The design of conditional grants as a principal-agent problem. Economics Department, Queen's University, Kingston, Ontario.

Boadway, R. W., and D. E. Wildasin (1984). *Public Sector Economics,* 2nd ed. Boston: Little Brown.

201

(1993). Long term debt strategy: A survey. In H. A. Verbon and F. A. Winden (Eds.), *The Political Economy of Government Debt*, pp. 37–68. Amsterdam: Elsevier.

Borcherding, T. E., and R. T. Deacon (1972). The demand for the services of non-federal governments. *American Economic Review* 62: 891–901.

Bordignon, M., P. Manasse, and G. Tabellini (1996). Optimal regional redistribution under asymmetric information. Center for Economic Policy Research, London.

Boskin, M. J. (1973). Local government tax and product competition and the optimal provision of public goods. *Journal of Political Economy* 81: 203–10.

Bradford, D. F. (1978). Factor prices may be constant but factor returns are not. *Economics Letters* 1: 199–203.

Braid, R. M. (1996). Symmetric tax competition with multiple jurisdictions in each metropolitan area. *American Economic Review* 86: 1279–90.

Break, G. F. (1967). *Intergovernmental Fiscal Relations in the United States.* Washington, DC.: Brookings.

Brennan, G., and J. M. Buchanan (1980). *The Power to Tax: Analytical Foundations of a Fiscal Constitution.* Cambridge University Press.

Brown, C. C., and W. E. Oates (1987). Assistance to the poor in a federal system. *Journal of Public Economics* 32: 307–30.

Brueckner, J. K. (1983). Property value maximization and public sector efficiency. *Journal of Urban Economics* 14: 1–16.

(1997). Fiscal federalism and capital accumulation. College of Commerce and Business Administration, University of Illinois, Champaign–Urbana.

Brueckner, J. K., and M.-S. Yoo (1991). Voting with capitalization. *Regional Science and Urban Economics* 21: 453–67.

Buchanan, J. M. (1965). An economic theory of clubs. *Economica* 32: 1–14.

Buchanan, J. M., and C. J. Goetz (1972). Efficiency limits of fiscal mobility: An assessment of the Tiebout model. *Journal of Public Economics* 1: 25–43.

Bucovetsky, S. (1991). Asymmetric tax competition. *Journal of Urban Economics* 30: 167–81.

(1995). Rent seeking and tax competition. *Journal of Public Economics* 58: 337–63.

Bucovetsky, S., M. Marchand, and P. Pestieau (1998). Tax competition and revelation of preferences for public expenditure. *Journal of Urban Economics* 44: 367–90.

Buiter, W. H. (1989). Debt neutrality, Professor Vickrey and Henry George's "single tax." *Economics Letters* 29: 43–7.

Burbidge, J. B., and G. M. Myers (1994a). Redistribution within and across the regions of a federation. *Canadian Journal of Economics* 27: 620–36.

(1994b). Population mobility and capital tax competition. *Regional Science and Urban Economics* 24: 441–59.

Calvo, G. A., L. J. Kotlikoff, and C. A. Rodriguez (1979). The incidence of a tax on pure rent: A new reason (?) for an old answer. *Journal of Political Economy* 87: 869–74.

Commission of the European Communities (1993). *European Economy,* no. 54. Brussels: EC Commission.

Cornes, R., and E. Silva (1996). Transfers between jurisdictions with private information. The equity–efficiency tradeoff. Department of Economics, Keele University, Staffordshire.

Courant, P. N. (1977). A general equilibrium model of heterogeneous local property taxes. *Journal of Public Economics* 8: 313–27.

Cremer, H., V. Fourgeaud, M. L. Monteiro, M. Marchand, and P. Pestieau (1995). Mobility and redistribution: A survey. Discussion Paper no. 9469, CORE, Louvain-la-Neuve.

Cremer, H., M. Marchand, and P. Pestieau (1996). Interregional redistribution through tax surcharge. *International Tax and Public Finance* 3: 157–73.

Cremer, H., and P. Pestieau (1996). Distributive implications of European integration. *European Economic Review* 40: 747–57.

Crombrugghe, A., and H. Tulkens (1990). On Pareto improving commodity tax changes under fiscal competition. *Journal of Public Economics* 41: 335–50.

Cukierman, A., Z. Hercowitz, and D. Pines (1994). Political economics of migration. Department of Economics, Tel Aviv University.

Daly, G. G. (1969). The burden of the debt and future generations in local finance. *Southern Economic Journal* 36: 44–51.

DePater, J. A., and G. M. Myers (1994). Strategic capital tax competition: A pecuniary externality and a corrective device. *Journal of Urban Economics* 36: 66–78.

Edwards, J., and M. Keen (1996). Tax competition and Leviathan. *European Economic Review* 40: 113–34.

Eichengreen, B. (1993). European monetary unification. *Journal of Economic Literature* 31: 1321–57.

Epple, D., and T. Romer (1991). Mobility and redistribution. *Journal of Political Economy* 99: 828–58.

Eurostat (1991). *Direct Investments in the EC 1984–1989*. Luxembourg: Eurostat.

(1993). *Internationale Wanderungsströme in ausgewählten EG – Ländern 1991* (Schnellberichte: Bevölkerung und soziale Bedingungen, no. 12). Luxembourg: Eurostat.

(1994). *Direct Investments in the EC 1984–1991*. Luxembourg: Eurostat.

(1995a). *Die internationalen Wanderungen in den Ländern der Europäischen Union – 1992* (Statistik kurzgefaßt: Bevölkerung und soziale Bedingungen, no. 3). Luxembourg: Eurostat.

(1995b). *Europa in Zahlen*. Luxembourg: Eurostat.

(1995c). *Eurostat Jahrbuch 1995*. Luxembourg: Eurostat.

(1996). *Eurostat Jahrbuch 1996*. Luxembourg: Eurostat.

(1997a). *Direktinvestitionsströme der Europäischen Union – Erste Resultate* (Statistik kurzgefaßt: Wirtschaft und Finanzen, no. 9). Luxembourg: Eurostat.

(1997b). *Der Sozialschutz in der Europäischen Union* (Statistik kurzgefaßt: Bevölkerung und soziale Bedingungen, no. 3). Luxembourg: Eurostat.

Fane, G. (1984). The incidence of a tax on pure rent: The old reason for the old answer. *Journal of Political Economy* 92: 329–33.

Feldstein, M. S. (1977). The surprising incidence of a tax on pure rent: A new answer to an old question. *Journal of Political Economy* 85: 349–60.

Fischel, W. A. (1975). Fiscal and environmental considerations in the location of firms in suburban communities. In E. S. Mills and W. E. Oates (Eds.), *Fiscal Zoning and Land Use Controls,* pp. 119–73. Lexington: D. C. Heath.

(1992). Property taxation and the Tiebout model: Evidence for the benefit view from zoning and voting. *Journal of Economic Literature* 30: 171–7.

Flatters, F., V. Henderson, and P. Mieszkowski (1974). Public goods, efficiency and regional fiscal equalization. *Journal of Public Economics* 3: 99–112.

Gandenberger, O. (1981). Theorie der öffentlichen Verschuldung. In F. Neumark (Ed.), *Handbuch der Finanzwissenschaft,* Bd. III, pp. 4–49. Tübingen: Mohr.

George, H. (1914). *Progress and Poverty.* New York: Doubleday.

Gilbert, G., and P. Picard (1996). Incentives and optimal size of local jurisdictions. *European Economic Review* 40: 19–41.

Gordon, R. H. (1983). An optimal taxation approach to fiscal federalism. *Quarterly Journal of Economics* 98: 567–86.

(1991). Discussion of Buiter, W. H., and K. M. Kletzer, Reflections on the fiscal implications of a common currency. In A. Giovannini and C. Mayer (Eds.), *European Financial Integration,* pp. 244–51. Cambridge University Press.

Hamilton, B. W. (1975a). Property taxes and the Tiebout hypothesis: Some empirical evidence. In E. S. Mills and W. E. Oates (Eds.), *Fiscal Zoning and Land Use Controls,* pp. 13–29. Lexington: D. C. Heath.

(1975b). Zoning and property taxation in a system of local governments. *Urban Studies* 12: 205–11.

(1976). Capitalization of intrajurisdictional differences in local land prices. *American Economic Review* 66: 743–53.

Haufler, A. (1993). *Commodity Tax Harmonization in the European Community.* Heidelberg: Physika.

Henderson, J. V. (1977a). *Economic Theory and the Cities.* New York: Academic Press.

(1977b). Externalities in a spatial context. *Journal of Public Economics* 7: 89–110.

(1985). The Tiebout model: Bring back the entrepreneurs. *Journal of Political Economy* 93: 248–64.

(1994). Community choice of revenue instruments. *Regional Science and Urban Economics* 24: 159–83.

Hercowitz, Z., and D. Pines (1991). Migration with fiscal externalities. *Journal of Public Economics* 46: 163–80.

Hochman, H. M., and J. D. Rodgers (1969). Pareto optimal redistribution. *American Economic Review* 59: 542–57.

Hochman, O., D. Pines, and J.-F. Thisse (1995). On the optimal structure of local governments. *American Economic Review* 85: 1224–40.

Homburg, S., and W. F. Richter (1993). Harmonizing public debt and public pension schemes in the European Community. In B. Felderer (Ed.), *Public Pension Economics,* pp. 51–63. *Journal of Economics* 7 (suppl.).

Hoyt, W. H. (1991a). Competitive jurisdictions, congestion, and the Henry George Theorem: When should property be taxed instead of land? *Regional Science and Urban Economics* 21: 351–70.

(1991b). Property taxation, Nash equilibrium, and market power. *Journal of Urban Economics* 30: 123–31.

Hülshorst, J., and D. Wellisch (1996). Optimal local environmental and fiscal policy in second-best situations. *Finanzarchiv* 53: 387–410.

Inman, R. P. (1978). Optimal fiscal reform of metropolitan schools. *American Economic Review* 68: 107–22.

Inman, R. P., and D. L. Rubinfeld (1979). The judicial pursuit of local fiscal equity. *Harvard Law Review* 92: 1662–1750.

(1992). Fiscal federalism in Europe. Lessons from the United States experience. *European Economic Review* 36: 654–60.

Keen, M. J. (1983). The welfare economics of tax coordination in the European Community. *Fiscal Studies* 4: 15–36.

(1987). Welfare effects of commodity tax harmonization. *Journal of Public Economics* 33: 107–14.

(1989). Pareto-improving indirect tax harmonization. *European Economic Review* 33: 1–12.

Keen, M. J., and S. Lahiri (1994). The comparison between destination and origin taxation under imperfect competition. Institute for Fiscal Studies 8, London.

Keen, M. J., and S. Smith (1996). The future of the value-added tax in the European Union. *Economic Policy* 23: 373–420.

Kirchgässner, G., and W. W. Pommerehne (1996). Tax harmonization and tax competition in the European Union: Lessons from Switzerland. *Journal of Public Economics* 60: 351–71.

Kotlikoff, L. J. (1984). Taxation and savings: A neoclassical perspective. *Journal of Economic Literature* 22: 1576–1629.

Krelove, R. (1992). Efficient tax exporting. *Canadian Journal of Economics* 25: 145–55.

(1993). The persistence and inefficiency of property tax finance of local public expenditures. *Journal of Public Economics* 51: 415–35.

Krumm, R., and D. Wellisch (1994). On the efficiency of environmental instruments in a spatial economy. *Environmental and Resource Economics* 6: 87–98.

Laffont, J.-J. (1995). Incentives in China's federal tax system. Institut d'Economie Industrielle, Université des Sciences Sociales de Toulouse.

Laffont, J.-J., and J. Tirole (1993). *A Theory of Incentives in Procurement and Regulation.* Cambridge, MA: MIT Press.

LaLonde, R. J., and R. H. Topel (1991). Labor market adjustments to increased immigration. In J. M. Abowd and R. B. Freeman (Eds.), *Immigration, Trade, and the Labor Market,* pp. 167–99. University of Chicago Press.

Lapan, H. E., and W. Enders (1990). Endogenous fertility, Ricardian equivalence, and debt management policy. *Journal of Public Economics* 41: 227–48.

Lejour, A. M. (1995). Integrating or disintegrating welfare states? A qualitative study to the consequences of economic integration on social insurance. Dissertation, Katholieke Universiteit Brabant, Tilburg.

Lockwood, B. (1993). Commodity tax competition under destination and origin principles. *Journal of Public Economics* 52: 141–62.

(1996). Interregional insurance with asymmetric information. Department of Economics, University of Exeter.

Lockwood, B., D. de Meza, and G. Myles (1994a). When are destination and origin regimes equivalent? *International Tax and Public Finance* 1: 5–24.

(1994b). The equivalence between destination and non-reciprocal origin regimes. *Scandinavian Journal of Economics* 96: 311–28.

Mansoorian, A., and G. M. Myers (1993). Attachment to home and efficient purchases of population in a fiscal externality economy. *Journal of Public Economics* 52: 117–32.

(1996). Private sector versus public sector externalities. *Regional Science and Urban Economics* 26: 543–55.

(1997). On the consequences of government objectives for economies with mobile populations. *Journal of Public Economics* 63: 265–81.

McGuire, M. (1974). Group segregation and optimal jurisdictions. *Journal of Political Economy* 82: 112–32.

McLure, C. E., Jr. (1986). Tax competition: Is what's good for the private goose also good for the public gander? *National Tax Journal* 39: 341–8.

Mieszkowski, P. (1972). The property tax. An excise tax or a profits tax? *Journal of Public Economics* 1: 73–96.

(1976). The distributive effects of local taxes: Some extensions. In R. E. Grieson (Ed.), *Public and Urban Economics,* pp. 293–312. Lexington: D. C. Heath.

Mieszkowski, P., and G. R. Zodrow (1989). Taxation and the Tiebout model: The differential effects of head taxes, taxes on land rents, and property taxes. *Journal of Economic Literature* 27: 1098–1146.

Mills, E. S. (1979). Economic analysis of urban land use controls. In P. Mieszkowski and M. Straszheim (Eds.), *Current Issues in Urban Economics,* pp. 511–41. Baltimore: Johns Hopkins University Press.

Mills, E. S., and W. E. Oates (1975). The theory of public services and finance: Its relevance to urban fiscal and zoning behavior. In E. S. Mills and W. E. Oates (Eds.), *Fiscal Zoning and Land Use Controls,* pp. 1–12. Lexington: D. C. Heath.

Mintz, J., and H. Tulkens (1986). Commodity tax competition between member states of a federation: Equilibrium and efficiency. *Journal of Public Economics* 29: 133–72.

Musgrave, R. A. (1959). *The Theory of Public Finance. A Study in Public Economy.* New York: McGraw-Hill.

(1971). Economics of fiscal federalism. *Nebraska Journal of Economics and Business* 10: 3–13.

Myers, G. M. (1990a). Free mobility and the regional authority in a federation. Dissertation, McMaster University, Hamilton, Ontario.

(1990b). Optimality, free mobility, and the regional authority in a federation. *Journal of Public Economics* 43: 107–21.

Myers, G. M., and Y. Y. Papageorgiou (1993). Fiscal equivalence, incentive equivalence and Pareto efficiency in a decentralized urban context. *Journal of Urban Economics* 34: 29–47.

(1996). Towards a better system for immigration control. Department of Economics, McMaster University, Hamilton, Ontario.

(1997a). Efficient Nash equilibria in a federal economy with migration costs. *Regional Science and Urban Economics* 27: 345–71.

(1997b). Immigration control and the welfare state. Department of Economics, McMaster University, Hamilton, Ontario.

Myles, G. D. (1995). *Public Economics.* Cambridge University Press.

Nerlove, M., A. Razin, and E. Sadka (1985). Population size: Individual choice and social optima. *Quarterly Journal of Economics* 100: 321–34.

Netzer, D. (1966). *Economics of the Property Tax.* Washington, DC: Brookings Institution.

Niskanen, W. A., Jr. (1971). *Bureaucracy and Representative Government.* Chicago: Aldine, Atherton.

Oates, W. E. (1969). The effects of property taxes and local public spending on property values: An empirical study of tax capitalization and the Tiebout hypothesis. *Journal of Political Economy* 77: 957–71.

(1972). *Fiscal Federalism.* New York: Harcourt Brace Jovanovich.

(1977). An economist's perspective on fiscal federalism. In W. E. Oates (Ed.), *The Political Economy of Fiscal Federalism,* pp. 3–20. Lexington: Lexington Books.

(1985). Searching for Leviathan: An empirical study. *American Economic Review* 75: 748–57.

Oates, W. E., and R. M. Schwab (1996). The theory of regulatory federalism: The case of environmental management. Department of Economics, University of Maryland, College Park.

OECD (1992a). *Taxing Profits in a Global Economy.* Paris: OECD.

(1992b). *Taxation in OECD Countries.* Paris: OECD.

Olson, M. (1969). The principle of "fiscal equivalence": The division of responsibilities among different levels of government. *American Economic Review* 59: 479–87.

Orr, L. L. (1976). Income transfers as a public good – An application to AFDC. *American Economic Review* 66: 359–71.

Owens, J. (1993). Globalization: The implications for tax policies. *Fiscal Studies* 14: 21–44.

Padoa-Schioppa, T. (1987). *Efficiency, Stability, and Equity.* Oxford University Press.

Pauly, M. V. (1970). Optimality, public goods, and the local governments: A general theoretical analysis. *Journal of Political Economy* 78: 572–84.

(1973). Income redistribution as a local public good. *Journal of Public Economics* 2: 35–58.

Raff, H., and J. D. Wilson (1997). Income redistribution with well-informed local governments. *International Tax and Public Finance* 4: 407–27.

Ramsey, F. P. (1927). A contribution to the theory of taxation. *Economic Journal* 37: 47–61.

Ricardo, D. (1817). *The Principles of Political Economy and Taxation.* London: Bells (reprint).

Richter, W. F. (1994). The efficient allocation of local public factors in Tiebout's tradition. *Regional Science and Urban Economics* 24: 323–40.

(1999). An efficiency analysis of consumption and production taxation with an application to value-added taxation. *International Tax and Public Finance.*

Richter, W. F., and D. Wellisch (1993). Allokative Theorie eines interregionalen Finanzausgleichs bei unvollständiger Landrentenabsorption. *Finanzarchiv* 50: 433–57.

(1994). Internalisierung intergenerationeller Externalitäten durch Regionalisierung. In B. Gahlen, H. Hesse, and H. J. Ramser (Eds.), *Europäische Integrationsprobleme aus wirtschaftswissenschaftlicher Sicht,* pp. 101–20. Tübingen: Mohr.

(1996). The provision of local public goods and factors in the presence of firm and household mobility. *Journal of Public Economics* 60: 73–93.

Richter, W. F., and W. Wiegard (1993). Zwanzig Jahre Neue Finanzwissenschaft. *Zeitschrift für Wirtschafts- und Sozialwissenschaften* 113: 169–224, 337–400.

Rosen, H. S. (1995). *Public Finance,* 4th ed. Chicago: Irwin.

Rubinfeld, D. L. (1979). Judicial approaches to local public sector equity. In P. Mieszkowski and M. Straszheim (Eds.), *Current Issues in Urban Economics,* pp. 542–76. Baltimore: Johns Hopkins University Press.

(1987). The economics of the local public sector. In A. Auerbach and M. Feldstein (Eds.), *Handbook of Public Economics,* vol. II, pp. 571–645. Amsterdam: North-Holland.

Schneider, K., and D. Wellisch (1997). Eco-dumping, capital mobility, and international trade. *Environmental and Resource Economics* 10: 387–404.

Schweizer, U. (1996). Endogenous fertility and the Henry George Theorem. *Journal of Public Economics* 61: 209–28.

Scotchmer, S. (1994). Public goods and the invisible hand. In J. Quigley and E. Smolensky (Eds.), *Modern Public Finance,* pp. 93–125. Cambridge, MA: Harvard University Press.

Scotchmer, S., and M. Wooders (1987). Competitive equilibrium and the core in club economies with anonymous crowding. *Journal of Public Economics* 34: 159–74.

208   References

Siebert, H. (1990). *Reforming Capital Income Taxation.* Tübingen: Mohr.

(1991). Europe 92. Decentralizing environmental policy in the single market. *Environmental and Resource Economics* 1: 271–87.

Simon, H. A. (1943). The incidence of a tax on urban real property. *Quarterly Journal of Economics* 59: 398–420.

Sinn, G., and H.-W. Sinn (1992). *Jumpstart: The Economic Unification of Germany.* Cambridge, MA: MIT Press.

Sinn, H.-W. (1987). *Capital Taxation and Resource Allocation.* Amsterdam: Elsevier.

(1990). Tax harmonization and tax competition in Europe. *European Economic Review* 34: 489–504.

(1994). How much Europe? Subsidiarity, centralization and fiscal competition. *Scottish Journal of Political Economy* 41: 85–107.

(1997). The selection principle and market failure in systems competition. *Journal of Public Economics* 66: 247–74.

Smith, S. (1993). Subsidiarity and the coordination of indirect taxes in the European Community. *Oxford Review of Economic Policy* 9: 67–94.

Stahl, K., and P. Varaiya (1983). Local collective goods: A critical re-examination of the Tiebout model. In J.-F. Thisse and H. G. Zoller (Eds.), *Locational Analysis of Public Facilities,* pp. 43–53. Amsterdam: North-Holland.

Starrett, D. A. (1988). *Foundations of Public Economics.* Cambridge University Press.

Statistisches Bundesamt (1994). *Statistisches Jahrbuch 1994 für das Ausland.* Stuttgart: Metzler-Poeschel.

(1996). *Statistisches Jahrbuch 1996 für das Ausland.* Stuttgart: Metzler-Poeschel.

Stigler, G. J. (1957). The tenable range of functions of local government. In Joint Economic Committee, *Federal Expenditure Policy for Economic Growth and Stability,* pp. 213–19. Washington, DC.: U.S. Government Printing Office.

Stiglitz, J. E. (1977). The theory of local public goods. In M. Feldstein and R. P. Inman (Eds.), *The Economics of Public Services,* pp. 274–333. London: Macmillan.

(1982). Self selection and Pareto-efficient taxation. *Journal of Public Economics* 17: 213–40.

(1986). *Economics of the Public Sector.* New York: Norton.

Straubhaar, T., and K. F. Zimmermann (1993). Towards a European migration policy. *Population Research and Policy Review* 12: 225–41.

Tiebout, C. M. (1956). A pure theory of local expenditures. *Journal of Political Economy* 64: 416–24.

Topel, R. H. (1986). Local labor markets. *Journal of Political Economy* 94 (pt. 2): 111–76.

Tresch, R. W. (1981). *Public Finance: A Normative Theory.* Plano, TX: Business Publications.

United Nations (1976). *Statistical Yearbook 1975,* 27th issue. New York: United Nations.

(1995). *Statistical Yearbook 1993,* 40th issue. New York: United Nations.

U.K. Treasury (1988). *Taxation in the Single Market: A Market-Based Approach.* London: U.K. Treasury Press Office.

U.S. Bureau of the Census (1995). Annual geographical mobility rates, by the type of movement: 1947–1994. http://www.census.gov/population/socdemo/migration/tab-a-1.txt, 05/12/97. Washington DC: Bureau of the Census.

von Hagen, J. (1992). Fiscal arrangements in a monetary union: Evidence from the U.S. In D. E. Fair and C. de Boissieu (Eds.), *Fiscal Policy, Taxation and the Financial System in an Increasingly Integrated Europe,* pp. 337–60. Dordrecht: Kluwer.

Wellisch, D. (1993). On the decentralized provision of public goods with spillovers in the presence of interregional migration. *Regional Science and Urban Economics* 25: 667–79.

(1994). Interregional spillovers in the presence of perfect and imperfect household mobility. *Journal of Public Economics* 55: 167–84.

(1995a). *Dezentrale Finanzpolitik bei hoher Mobilität.* Tübingen: Mohr.

(1995b). Locational choices of firms and decentralized environmental policy with various instruments. *Journal of Urban Economics* 37: 290–310.

(1995c). Can household mobility solve basic environmental problems? *International Tax and Public Finance* 2: 245–60.

(1996). Decentralized fiscal policy with high mobility reconsidered. Reasons for inefficiency and an optimal intervention scheme. *European Journal of Political Economy* 12: 91–111.

Wellisch, D., and J. Hülshorst (1999). A second-best theory of local government policy. *International Tax and Public Finance.*

Wellisch, D., and W. F. Richter (1995). Internalizing intergenerational externalities by regionalization. *Regional Science and Urban Economics* 25: 685–704.

Wellisch, D., and U. Walz (1998). Why do rich countries prefer free trade over free migration? The role of the modern welfare state. *European Economic Review* 42: 1595–1612.

Wellisch, D., and D. E. Wildasin (1995). Uncoordinated regional immigration and redistribution policy: A two-stage analysis. Department of Business Administration and Economics, Dresden University of Technology.

(1996a). Decentralized income redistribution and immigration. *European Economic Review* 40: 187–217.

(1996b). Dezentrale Umverteilung und Einwanderung. *Ifo-Konjunkturhefte* 42: 101–33.

Wheaton, W. C. (1975). Consumer mobility and commodity tax bases: The financing of local public goods. *Journal of Public Economics* 4: 377–84.

White, M. J. (1975a). Fiscal zoning in fragmented metropolitan areas. In E. S. Mills and W. E. Oates (Eds.), *Fiscal Zoning and Land Use Controls,* pp. 31–100. Lexington: D. C. Heath.

(1975b). Firm location in a zoned metropolitan area. In E. S. Mills and W. E. Oates (Eds.), *Fiscal Zoning and Land Use Controls,* pp. 175–202. Lexington: D. C. Heath.

Wiegard, W. (1980). Distortionary taxation in a federal economy. *Zeitschrift für Nationalökonomie* 40: 183–206.

Wildasin, D. E. (1982). More on the neutrality of land taxation. *National Tax Journal* 35: 105–15.

(1986). *Urban Public Finance.* New York: Harwood.

(1987). Theoretical analysis of local public economics. In E. S. Mills (Ed.), *Handbook of Regional and Urban Economics,* vol. II, pp. 1131–78. Amsterdam: North-Holland.

(1988). Nash equilibrium in models of fiscal competition. *Journal of Public Economics* 35: 229–40.

(1989). Interjurisdictional capital mobility: Fiscal externality and a corrective subsidy. *Journal of Urban Economics* 25: 193–212.

(1990). Non-neutrality of debt with endogenous fertility. *Oxford Economic Papers* 42: 414–28.

(1991). Income redistribution in a common labor market. *American Economic Review* 81: 757–74.

(1992). Relaxation of barriers to factor mobility and income redistribution. In P. Pestieau (Ed.), *Public Finance in a World of Transition*, pp. 216–30. *Public Finance* 47 (suppl.).

(1994a). Income redistribution and migration. *Canadian Journal of Economics* 27: 637–56.

(1994b). Public pensions in the EU: Migration incentives and impacts. Department of Economics, Vanderbilt University, Nashville, TN.

Wildasin, D. E., and J. D. Wilson (1996). Imperfect mobility and local government behavior in an overlapping-generations model. *Journal of Public Economics* 60: 177–98.

Wilson, J. D. (1986). A theory of interregional tax competition. *Journal of Urban Economics* 19: 296–315.

(1987a). Trade in a Tiebout model. *American Economic Review* 77: 431–41.

(1987b). Trade, capital mobility, and tax competition. *Journal of Political Economy* 95: 835–56.

(1991). Tax competition with interregional differences in factor endowments. *Regional Science and Urban Economics* 21: 423–51.

(1995). Mobile labor, multiple tax instruments, and tax competition. *Journal of Urban Economics* 38: 333–56.

(1997). Property taxation, congestion, and local public goods. *Journal of Public Economics* 64: 207–17.

World Bank (1994). *World Data 1994*. New York: World Bank.

Zimmermann, K. F. (1995). Tackling the European migration problem. *Journal of Economic Perspectives* 9: 45–62.

Zodrow, G. R., and P. Mieszkowski (1986a). Pigou, Tiebout, property taxation, and the underprovision of local public goods. *Journal of Urban Economics* 19: 356–70.

(1986b). The new view of the property tax: A reformulation. *Regional Science and Urban Economics* 16: 309–27.

Index

211